LONDON CALLING

LONDON CALLING

V. S. Naipaul, Postcolonial Mandarin

ROB NIXON

New York   Oxford
OXFORD UNIVERSITY PRESS
1992

For Andy, and for Anne

Oxford University Press

Oxford   New York   Toronto
Delhi   Bombay   Calcutta   Madras   Karachi
Petaling Jaya   Singapore   Hong Kong   Tokyo
Nairobi   Dar es Salaam   Cape Town
Melbourne   Auckland

and associated companies in
Berlin   Ibadan

Published by Oxford University Press, Inc.,
200 Madison Avenue, New York, New York 10016

Oxford is a registered trademark of Oxford University Press

Library of Congress Cataloging-in-Publication Data
Nixon, Rob, 1954–
London calling: V.S. Naipaul, postcolonial Mandarin / Rob Nixon.
p. cm.   Includes bibliographical references and index.
ISBN 0-19-506717-7
1. Naipaul, V. S. (Vidiadhar Surajprasad), 1932–   —Criticism and interpretation.
2. Naipaul, V. S. (Vidiadhar Surajprasad), 1932–   —Journeys.
3. Authors, Trinidadian—Biography—History and criticism.
4. Intercultural communication in literature.   5. Culture conflict in literature.
6. London (England) in literature.   7. Travel in literature.
8. Autobiography. I. Title.
PR9272.9.N32Z795   1992
823'.914—dc20   91-16697

1 3 5 7 9 8 6 4 2

Printed in the United States of America
on acid-free paper

ACKNOWLEDGMENTS

I would like to thank Edward Said, in particular, for his personal and intellectual companionship. As he observed in 1978, "The literary-cultural establishment as a whole has declared the serious study of imperialism and culture off limits." With all those who have since sought to redress these circumstances, I share a debt to Edward for his unequaled role in bringing the cultural dimensions of imperialism and decolonization within the orbit of serious discussion.

I wish to extend my appreciation toward the friends and colleagues who have read portions of this book or given of their time to discuss the issues at stake. Here I think especially of Jonathan Arac, Homi Bhabha, Hazel Carby, Jean Franco, Andreas Huyssen, Qadri Ismail, Karl Kroeber, Neil Lazarus, Steven Marcus, Aamir Mufti, and Gauri Viswanathan. Arnold Rampersad's timely and incisive reading provided me with precisely the blend of encouragement and suggestive critique that every author yearns for.

Thanks go to Joy Hayton for her many-faceted support and her gift for friendship. Also, to Evelyn Garcia and Richard Moi, who sought to transmit a fraction of their computer wizardry to someone with a quite mortal grasp on technology.

Part of this project was aided by generous funding from The Institute of International Education. Their support is much appreciated.

Chapter 1 appeared in *South Atlantic Quarterly* in 1988 and the conclusion in *Transition,* 1991. A portion of chapter 4 was published in *Research in African Literatures,* 1991. I am grateful to the editors and publishers of these journals for permission to reprint these materials.

I would also like to acknowledge permission to include two passages excerpted from *The Fortunate Traveller,* copyright © 1980, 1981 by Derek Walcott. Reprinted by permission of Farrar, Straus and Giroux, Inc.

My greatest debt, an infinitely varied and inexpressible one, is to Anne.

Contents

Naipaul's Chronology

1957   The Mystic Masseur
1958   The Suffrage of Elvira
1959   Miguel Street
1961   A House for Mr. Biswas
1962   *The Middle Passage*
1963   Mr. Stone and the Knights Companion
1964   *An Area of Darkness*
1967   The Mimic Men
1967   A Flag on the Island
1969   *The Loss of El Dorado*
1971   *In a Free State*
1972   *The Overcrowded Barracoon*
1975   Guerillas
1977   *India: A Wounded Civilization*
1979   A Bend in the River
1980   *The Return of Eva Peron, with The Killings in Trinidad*
1980   *A Congo Diary*
1981   *Among the Believers*
1984   *Finding the Center: Two Narratives*
1987   *The Enigma of Arrival*
1989   *A Turn in the South*
1990   *India: A Million Mutinies Now*

NOTE: The titles of Naipaul's nonfictional writings, as well the titles of works that include both nonfiction and fiction, have been italicized.

LONDON CALLING

Like lice, like lice, the hungry of this earth
swarm to the tree of life. If those who starve
like these rain-flies who shed glazed wings in lights
grew from sharp shoulder blades their battle vans
and soared toward that tree, how it would seethe—
ah, Justice! But fires
drench them like vermin, quotas
prevent them, and they remain
compassionate fodder for the travel book,
its paragraphs like windows from a train,
for everywhere that earth shows its rib cage
and the moon goggles with the eyes of children,
we turn away to read.

DEREK WALCOTT, "The Fortunate Traveller"

You know it's funny. You come some place new and everything
looks just the same.

Eddie, in JIM JARMUSCH, Stranger Than Paradise

Introduction

All my life I have expected some recognition of my difference.
V. S. NAIPAUL

This is part of the price one pays for being different.
JOSEPH EPSTEIN ON NAIPAUL

Despite V. S. Naipaul's gift for provoking extreme admiration or equally pronounced indignation, there remain, among readers of his work, a few outposts of broad agreement. Chief among them is the recognition that at his finest, in books as varied as *A House for Mr. Biswas, The Loss of El Dorado,* and *The Enigma of Arrival,* Naipaul commands an unimpeachable style. Even Derek Walcott, a frequent critic of his ideas, hails him as "our finest writer of the English sentence."[1] Nor can one fail to admire Naipaul's faithfulness to exacting standards of productivity: since his first novel, *The Mystic Masseur,* appeared in 1957, he has held to an average of a book every eighteen months. Many readers would concur that *Biswas,* a tragicomic novel of epic scope delivered at age twenty-nine, remains his most remarkable work. Nothing since has equaled the inventiveness and emotional generosity of that homage to his father's misfortunes in the straitened circumstances of colonial Trinidad.

For the rest, it can only be agreed that Naipaul's work stimulates disagreement. What sets him apart from other controversial writers, however, are the lines of dissent. A clear rift separates his reputation in the United States and Britain, on the one side, from his standing in what I shall provisionally call (with all the customary reservations) the Third World, on the other.[2] The former constituency has heaped distinctions upon him, among them the Booker Prize, the W. H. Smith Prize, the Hawthornden Prize, the Bennett Prize, and the T. S. Eliot Award, this last honoring authors "of abiding importance whose works affirm the moral principles of Western Civilization."[3] In 1990, the queen awarded him a knighthood—the crowning accolade from these quarters.

3

British and American commentators are liable to single Naipaul out as "unarguably the most brilliant interpreter in English (perhaps in any language) of the maelstrom of the Third World," as "far and away the most talented, the most truthful, the most honorable writer of his generation," as "our scourge for truth, a Solzhenitsyn of the third world." Naipaul is, one such critic avers, a veritable "Delphic oracle."[4]

The viewpoints of Caribbeans, South Asians, Arabs, Africans, and Latin Americans offer, on the whole, quite contrary testimony. They are more likely to portray him as "a despicable lackey of neo-colonialism," "a cold and sneering prophet," "a smart restorer of the comforting myths of the white race," or, for that matter, a "Gunga Din" who performs "while the cold smiles of the Pukka Sahibs applaud his antic agility."[5] "He travels to confirm his Eurocentric prejudices," opines one Indian writer, while another perceives his knighthood as perfectly intelligible, given that "he is England's favorite 19th-century Englishman."[6] A Caribbean author is even more forthright: "Ask him why he hates the color of his skin so much."[7] So on the subject of Naipaul's stance toward Third World societies passions run high: one participant at a West Indian literary conference stood up and volunteered to shoot him.[8]

In reflecting on this gulf between his reputations, we should avoid the error of viewing Naipaul simply as a writer. His prestige as a novelist has surely assisted him in sustaining his high profile as an interpreter of the postcolonial world. However, by venturing into travel writing and journalism he has garnered a reputation of a different order, one that goes beyond the conventionally literary to the point where—in those border regions where British and American belles-lettres meet popularized political thought—he is treated as a mandarin possessing a penetrating, analytic understanding of Third World societies. In short, he has grown into an "expert."

Thus a British reviewer of one of Naipaul's Indian travel books can credit him with defining "problems quicker and more effectively than a team of economists and other experts from the World Bank."[9] In the wake of the Iran hostage crisis, Naipaul found his way on to the cover of *Newsweek,* whence he was summoned largely as an expert on Islam.[10] During the 1990 Gulf Crisis, he reappeared on the Op-ed page of *The New York Times* in an almost identical role.[11] And at a *Salmagundi* forum, "The Intellectual in the Post-Colonial World," where Naipaul quickly became the obsessive topic, the impassioned exchanges centered on his political authority rather than on the merits of his fiction.[12] So, too, when David Hare staged a theatrical debate on the politics of poverty between a reactionary Indian mandarin and a young, idealistic

Britisher, Naipaul served as a direct model for the intellectual style of the play's conservative character.[13]

Manifestly, Naipaul's prestige as a novelist has assisted him in sustaining his high profile as an interpreter of postcolonial societies. However, by diversifying into nonfiction he has achieved a reputation of a quite different order, not merely as a powerful imaginative writer, but as a mandarin and an institution.

By now, travel books and journalism comprise the larger portion of Naipaul's oeuvre. His own estimate of his documentary writing has always been high. In this, he is like George Orwell, whom he once hailed as the most versatile and daring of English writers.[14] Certainly, Naipaul does not endorse the pervasive attitude that favors the "literariness" of the novel over "unimaginative" species of nonfictional prose, an attitude that often leaves the latter critically remaindered. Naipaul, like Orwell, refuses to downgrade his essays, journalism, and travel writing by presenting them—in John Updike's phrase—as ways of "hugging the shore," of retreating, in timidity, from the squally waters of the imagination.[15]

Naipaul took up nonfiction in an effort to remedy what he saw as the novel's foreshortened possibilities in the present age. While his comment that "the novel as a form no longer carries conviction" has an overly familiar ring to it, his response to the novel's waning authority has been unorthodox.[16] Instead of overhauling the genre to make it more congruent with the times, he has remained by and large a formally unadventurous novelist while pursuing complementary effects through nonfiction. He found himself unable to be

> a professional novelist in the old sense. I realised then that my response to the world could be expressed equally imaginatively in nonfiction, in journalism; and I take my journalism extremely seriously because I think it's a very fair response to my world. It's something that can't be converted into fiction.[17]

Such writing, Naipaul argues, should not be viewed as ephemeral or occasional, but as work that will survive as literature and help secure his reputation.

At times, Naipaul's investment in his nonfiction is marked by hubris, as when he declines to treat his journalistic travels to the Third World as assignments, insisting instead that they be afforded their proper status as "missions."[18] The choice of idiom here tells of his sense of high purpose, his conviction that such writing serves as a vocation, not just as doodling for his left hand. But to speak of "missions" to the former colonies is to

rouse other, more insidious echoes of preaching and saving, echoes that
connect Naipaul to a colonial tradition of interfering zealotry.[19]

It is my ambition to account for and contest Naipaul's distinctive
authority by exploring the rhetorical character and political circumstances of his nonfiction. The two dimensions to this project are directly
linked: I assume throughout what follows that an understanding of his
almost programmatically negative representation of formerly colonized
societies is inseparable from the question—at once institutional and
textual—of how he has secured a reputation in Britain and the United
States as the foremost literary commentator on the so-called Third
World.

One can best address the political circumstances and implications of his
rhetoric by posing two interdependent questions. First, given his standard
evocations of the former colonies as "barbarous," "primitive," "tribal,"
"simple," "irrational," "static," "without history," "futureless," "bush,"
"philistine," "sentimental," "parasitic," and "mimic," how does his
choice of idiom make his readings of such societies easily assimilable to
imperialist discursive traditions that run deep in Britain and the United
States? Second, how has he managed to reproduce the most standard
racial and colonial positions while simultaneously presenting himself as a
risk taker, someone who swims against the prevailing ideological currents
out of fidelity to difficult and unpopular truths? In other words, how has
Naipaul acquired a reputation as an unconventional, extratraditional
writer while producing an oeuvre suffused with received notions about
the barbarism and dishonesty of Islam, cannibalism in Africa, the simple-
minded irrationality of Indians, the self-destructiveness of Black Power,
and the inability of the Caribbean and India to generate real history?

It is important to pose such questions because they can serve to tease
out the deeply conventional dimensions of his rhetoric in a manner that
challenges the view, commonly held by British and American critics, of
Naipaul as an oddity who writes at a tangent to the dominant traditions
of Anglo-American letters. To contest this view is to recognize that his
ethnic marginality has been used, by Naipaul and his influential supporters, to deflect attention away from the traditional affiliations that permeate his idiom.

In exploring Naipaul's intellectual authority, I have chosen to focus on
his nonfiction for several reasons. For one, it is there that we encounter
his most direct, obsessive, elaborate, and politically charged accounts of
his understanding of the postcolonial world. Furthermore, because of
their frequently inflamed polemics, Naipaul's travel writings and essays
have met with a more acutely divided reception along First World–Third

World lines than has his fiction. Thus, an examination of his nonfiction is fundamental to any attempt to explain how he has accrued a pitch of authority in Britian and the United States that he has never achieved in the former colonies. An ancillary reason for concentrating on his nonfiction stems from my desire to redress the discrepancy between the unusual reach of that work and the shallowness of its academic treatment. His documentary prose has been empowered by its publication in prominent magazines before appearing in book form: essays and excerpts have surfaced in *The New Yorker, Atlantic Monthly, New York Review of Books, Harpers, The Sunday Times Magazine* (London), and *The Daily Telegraph Magazine,* as well as in the *Times Literary Supplement, The Listener, The Spectator, The Encounter,* and the *New Statesman.*[20] In short, his nonfiction has often achieved, through its double distribution in magazine and book form, a wider circulation than his novels. Despite this, literary scholars have been hesitant to attend to it in any depth.

Father and Son

To understand how Naipaul came to exercise an authority that reaches beyond the municipality of the narrowly literary, one has, however, first to consider his youthful romance with the idea of becoming a writer. Naipaul has cultivated complex affiliations with Conrad and shared many literary preoccupations and political stances with his younger brother Shiva. Yet, to judge from Naipaul's autobiographical essays, the most enabling presence behind his emergence as a writer was the less conspicuous, late-flowering figure of his father. Seepersad Naipaul proved an ambiguous inspiration: he came to embody writing as a desirable vocation, and yet, because the unpropitious circumstances of colonial Trinidad stalled his promise, he stood, too, as a chastening example of the lonely destitution that could accompany literary ambition.

V. S.'s grandfather had been brought to Trinidad from Uttar Pradesh in the 1880s under the system of indentured labor.[21] Of Brahman stock, he trained as a pundit, married, and had three children. One of these, Seepersad, was in turn schooled to become a pundit but failed to do so, instead working his way through a maze of jobs (many of them imaginatively chronicled in *A House for Mr. Biswas*). Vidia's huge regard for his father derives principally from the improbable, tragic tenacity of Seepersad's literary commitments. Deprived of forerunners and, until too late, of recognition, he nonetheless wrote from the age of fourteen.

Naipaul has speculated that a Brahman regard for the word may have first sparked this ambition in his father, who had been denied any formal education beyond elementary school.[22] Yet, in anticipation of aspects of V. S.'s own development, the Indian caste legacy and Trinidadian experience required a third element: institutional support from Britain, where the writing profession was more securely established. For Seepersad, the British encouragement took two forms: Fleet Street and the BBC.

In 1929 Gault MacGowan, who had trained at the *Times,* traveled to Port of Spain, where he reanimated the moribund *Trinidad Guardian,* employing and schooling, in the process, Seepersad as a freelance contributor. Fourteen years later, Seepersad Naipaul finally published *Gurudeva and Other Indian Tales,* a book whose more moderate local success in monetary terms had helped Trinidadian writers slough off the stigma of amateurism and perceive writing as a legitimate career. That same year, 1943, V. S., now aged eleven, determined to become a writer.[23]

During the three or four years prior to Seepersad's death in 1953, he and his son glimpsed what might have been. Henry Swanzy, editor of *Caribbean Voices* for the BBC Caribbean Service, discerned Seepersad's ability and frequently ran his stories on the program. This relationship furnished the ailing, debt-ridden man with an imaginary audience and replenished his income. But the belatedness of this recognition restricted Seepersad's assessment of his prospects to a wistful " 'I am beginning to feel I *could* have been a writer.' "[24] Not until 1976, when V. S. brought together a posthumous selection of the stories, did Seepersad realize his goal of issuing a "real" book, that is, in his terms, one published abroad. "The writer begins with his talent," V. S. observes of his father, "finds confidence in his talent, but then discovers that it isn't enough, that, in a society as deformed as ours, by the exercise of his talent he has set himself adrift."[25]

In important aspects, the son's circumstances departed substantially from those of his father. V. S. suffered nothing as extreme as Seepersad's isolation, for he fled the West Indies along with a whole generation of would-be writers lured to England by literary prospects. He first experienced a full colonial education at Queen's Royal College, then bolted down one of the three traditional escape hatches for young men from the Islands: education, cricket, and music. A Trinidadian government scholarship took him to Oxford in 1950. On completing a literary degree in 1954, he moved to London, where, appositely enough, he joined the BBC as an editor of "Caribbean Voices."

Seepersad had written about rural peasant Trinidad, recording the breakup during the first half of the twentieth century of the self-enclosed village societies whose rites and values had been ferried across from the subcontinent. V. S., by contrast, although born in rural, Hindu Chaguanas, spent most of his childhood and adolescence in the capital, Port of Spain, ethnically and culturally a diverse place, with pockets of Indians and whites (most strikingly, in the early forties, the American soldiers stationed there) amid a strong black majority.[26]

Yet one mentions such generational differences between father and son principally to give focus to the psychological legacy that has traveled with V. S.—as inspiration and as wound. It is a legacy that mixes reverence for his father's unorthodox desires with a son's anger at their frustration. V. S.'s recent travel book *A Turn in the South* is dedicated to Seepersad "in ever renewed homage," a sentiment that, Naipaul insists, sustains his work in general.[27]

One detects, then, a strong impulse in the son to compensate for Seepersad's blighted opportunities by carrying forward his father's sensibility and devotion to what V. S. habitually calls the nobility of the profession. Not only does his finest book, *Biswas,* reconceive his father's quest for security, but, in V. S.'s own phrase, he "cannibalized" a Seepersad story, "They Named Him Biswas," for the opening of that novel.[28]

In an important essay fortified by memories of his own Trinidadian childhood, Arnold Rampersad has proposed that, in moving from the Indian countryside to the city, the young Naipaul must have been bruised by the pervasive hostility of Afro-Trinidadians toward Indians, and that such experiences of racial bigotry crucially underlie his angry rejection of his homeland.[29] While Rampersad's proposal is too persuasive to be discounted, Naipaul's own utterances on this score remain ambivalent and contradictory. He recalls, for instance, that during his childhood there were "considerable prejudices against Indians, but I wasn't aware of it."[30] Yet elsewhere he links his lifelong fear of engulfment to the island's polarized ethnic tensions: "Their racial obsessions, which once could tug at my heart, made them simple people. Part of the fear of extinction which I had developed as a child had partly to do with this: the fear of being swallowed up or extinguished by the simplicity of one side or the other, my side or the side that wasn't mine."[31]

What does seem clearcut, however, is that Naipaul's salvaging of his father's profession took on a retributive aspect against all those forces that had threatened to engulf him: employers, the extended family, community orthodoxies, racial tension, and "colonial" society. Looking back on it, Naipaul interpreted his own wish to be a writer less as a consequence of a desire to write than as "something that lay ahead and outside the life I knew—far from family and clan, colony, *Trinidad Guardian,* negroes."[32] He reflects, with astonishment, on how his father simultaneously transmitted to him a vocation and a hysterical fear of engulfment that the pursuit of his calling alone could exorcise.[33]

During Naipaul's childhood, the threatening forces of engulfment took predominantly female and communal forms. He witnessed his mother's immense, powerful, and relatively wealthy family overwhelm Seepersad, whose marginality and destitution were exacerbated by his eccentric devotion to writing. Not only did Naipaul view the women as overbearing, but, like his father, he revolted against the tendency, so marked in his mother, to experience emotion through ritual, communal moments, rather than as an individual.[34] In his negative construal of his woman-dominated family, Naipaul represents the family as an autocratic political institution: in one version it is a "totalitarian organization"; in another, a "microcosm of the authoritarian state."[35] One finds in these metaphors, symptomatically collapsed, his tenacious disdain for collective values of any ilk, community feeling, political institutions, and women.

Because of his background, Naipaul has had lodged in him since childhood the attitude that individuality, not community, is the difficult, improbable attainment. This has left him with a rarified conception of the writer as a pure individual who has transcended all commitments other than to the craft. Permeating Naipaul's autobiographical comments and implicit in the author's note that recurs in his books ("He has followed no other profession") is a conception of himself as a figure existing in a free state, untrammeled by ideologies and beholden to nobody. This jealousy of his autonomy—initially, a mark of the rare willpower required for him to become a writer—has evolved into a form of arrogance and bigotry. Even early on, one sensed that his determination was mingled with revenge, as he nursed an unrequited and ultimately disfiguring anger against the place that had shamed the nobility of his father's ambitions.

Naipaul's Literary Beginnings and the Turn to Nonfiction

Any assessment of Naipaul's literary and intellectual authority in the English-speaking West must take into account the fact that he began as a novelist, writing five volumes of fiction before experimenting with documentary prose. How, then, did he arrive at his elevated conception of his travel writing and journalism, the belief that it was indispensable to his reputation and would allow him to articulate ideas about postcolonial societies in a manner that the novel could not accommodate?

His deferred entry into nonfiction can be partly ascribed to the status of fiction as a more obvious choice for an aspirant writer. But there is a further, more resonant explanation for the delay. From the outset, his colonial education had oriented him toward England, encouraging him to dismiss his indigenous environment. He was schooled to perceive the immediate world of Trinidad as paradoxically remote and insubstantial, as exiled to the margins of an English-centered reality. With this in mind, one can sense a congruence between Naipaul's lasting habits of condescension toward the former colonies and his youthful conception of writers as transcendent, as possessing the power to escape claustral realities by "making things up." Yet ironically, the same colonial frame of mind that encouraged him to disparage his non-Western, Trinidadian circumstances prompted him initially to dismiss the documentary genres that were later to carry his most direct and impassioned critiques of the so-called Third World.

In the fifties and early sixties, Naipaul interpreted the unreality that he read into his surroundings as a symptom of the shallowness of Trinidad's literary tradition: "If landscapes do not start to be real until they have been interpreted by an artist, so, until they have been written about, societies appear to be without shape and *embarrassing.*"[36] He saw himself as having to coax literature out of an environment that, to adapt Salman Rushdie's phrase, seemed "insufficiently imagined."[37] Naipaul recalls how, as a consequence, he lacked "the courage to do a simple thing like mentioning the name of a Port of Spain street."[38]

As the author of twenty-two books, more than half of them nonfictional, Naipaul has clearly overcome his timidity towards realities that have not been braced by secure literary traditions.[39] He has simultaneously surmounted the narrow conception of literary originality that had caused him to shun documentary prose, rife as the form is with mimetic ambitions and empirical constraints. From the vantage point of the mid-eighties, he would look back remorsefully at how he had arrived in England in 1950 with such an ingrained notion of the writer as someone "possessed of sensibility" that he had felt compelled to falsify himself and his material, inflicting, in the process, considerable damage on both.[40]

The crucial shift in his attitude to nonfiction began in 1960 when, after a decade-long absence from the West Indies, he was invited by the Trinidadian premier, Eric Williams, to write a documentary account of the region. Naipaul took up the offer and two years later published *The Middle Passage,* his first book-length work of nonfiction.[41] From that moment on, Naipaul began, accumulatively, to invoke a different style of authority as an "expert" on the Third World.[42] The volume, a record of a journey through the Caribbean, is of further import because it stages, for the first time in an explicit and concentrated manner, what were to become his *idées fixes.*

Naipaul's response to the challenge of diversifying into travel writing was understandably anxious. Even after a decade of moderate success in England, he had apparently not lost his fear of Trinidad as the place where writers, like his father, disappeared into the quicksands of oblivion. Moreover, by earning even minor recognition as a professional novelist in England, V. S. had outstripped the achievements of his father, whose imagination had drowned in newspaper ink; in that context, we may surmise, to return to Trinidad as a journalist must have seemed a perilous form of relapse. This helps account for the fierceness of *The Middle Passage,* which broke with the bounteous comedy of the early fiction and set the tone—wounded, supercilious, and choleric—for much of the nonfiction that would follow.

The foreword to the book suggests a further reason for Naipaul's initial guardedness towards venturing into documentary prose. It voices his fear that undertaking a more analytical, deliberate style of writing might damage his potential as a novelist, which at that stage he still regarded as his unequivocal calling:

> While I was in Trinidad [in 1960], the Premier, Dr. Eric Williams, suggested that I should write a nonfiction book about the West Indies. The publication of the book would be supported by the Trinidad Government; I could write about any aspect of the region and visit whatever territories I wished. . . . But I hesitated. The novelist works towards conclusions of which he is often unaware; and it is better that he should. To analyse and decide before writing would rob the writer of the excitement which supports him during his solitude, and would be the opposite of my method as a novelist. I also felt it as a danger that, having factually analysed the society as far as I was able, I would be unable afterwards to think of it in terms of fiction and that in anything I might write I would be concerned only to prove a point. However, I decided to take the risk.[43]

Naipaul's apprehensiveness before this project was clearly sharpened by the fact that Williams's commission entailed bringing the analytical methods of nonfiction to bear on Trinidad, the land that had served, to date, as his sole fictional preserve.

Ironically, instead of closing down his options, the voyage that pro-

duced *The Middle Passage* broadened his range; from then on he became habituated to travel and drew new settings from it, for his novels as
for his documentary prose. A quarter of a century after accepting Williams's invitation, he was to speak aphoristically of that return voyage to
the West Indies as if it were one term in an almost dialectical personal
development: "Colonial Trinidad had sent me to Oxford in 1950, and I
had made myself a writer. Self-governing Trinidad sent me on a colonial
tour in 1960, and by this accident I became a traveller."[44]

But the voyage of 1960 heralded more than the genesis of a traveler
and his initiation into nonfiction. For in documenting the journey
Naipaul also crossed a historical Rubicon: where previously he had written about a colonized land, from *The Middle Passage* onward he became
what he is now best known as—the author who characterizes most defini-
tively for British and American readers the dashed expectations, traumas, hubris, misplaced idealism, self-deceits, and self-violations that he
discerns in those at least nominally independent societies commonly
assembled under the term *Third World*. Thus, with *The Middle Passage*
Naipaul made a significant advance toward defining his literary terrain:
historically, as the postcolonial era; geographically, as societies formerly
under British, and to a lesser extent French and Dutch, imperial sway;
and generically, so as to include travel writing.

Naipaul's reputation as a buff on postcolonial politics, which began
with *The Middle Passage,* continued to swell over the next twenty years.
During the 1960s, while remaining committed to the novel, he produced
two further books of nonfiction: *An Area of Darkness* (1964), which
recounts the first of his several ventures to India, and *The Loss of El
Dorado* (1969), an autobiographically framed inquiry into Trinidad's
colonial history. Over the next eleven, intense years, Naipaul published
three titles of fiction (*In a Free State, Guerillas,* and *A Bend in the River*)
and five of nonfiction. *The Overcrowded Barracoon* (1972), his most
eclectic volume, gathers together travel essays, principally on India, but
including pieces about Mauritius, St. Kitts, Trinidad, Anguilla, British
Honduras, *Robinson Crusoe,* and Norman Mailer, as well as some autobiographical reflections. *India: A Wounded Civilization* (1977) is the
record of Naipaul's journey through India at the time of Indira Gandhi's
State of Emergency.

Naipaul's authority as a Third World expert crested in the early 1980s.
Following the considerable success of *A Bend in the River* (1979), three
volumes of nonfiction appeared in swift succession: *The Return of Eva
Peron, with The Killings in Trinidad* (1980), an anthology of essays on
Argentina, Uruguay, Zaire, Joseph Conrad, and Trinidadian Black

Power; *A Congo Diary* (1980); and *Among the Believers: An Islamic Journey* (1981). This last, the record of a journey through four Islamic societies (Iran, Pakistan, Malaysia, and Indonesia), brought Naipaul unprecedented exposure in the American media, appearing as it did in the strained atmosphere of the Iran hostage crisis.

Increasingly, Naipaul has shown a declining commitment to writing novels; nonfiction now absorbs most of his literary energies. Since his Islamic book, he has produced four titles. *Finding the Centre: Two Narratives* (1984) falls into two parts: an autobiographical memoire on his beginnings as a writer and a travel account of a journey to Houphouet-Boigny's Ivory Coast. Naipaul then turned, for the first time, to writing extensively about his relationship to England in *The Enigma of Arrival* (1987). The personal tone of that book—half autobiography, half fiction—carried over into his first American travelogue, *A Turn in the South* (1989). Some eighteen months later, Naipaul produced his third full book on India, *India: A Million Mutinies Now* (1990), his longest and in many ways most ambitious work.

The vigor of the debates sparked by Naipaul's work, the tendency of his polemical style to restoke those debates, together with his eminent position as a literary influence on British and American understanding of the postcolonial era, have ensured that he is no longer simply viewed as a writer, but as embodying a set of politically charged ideas about Third World–First World relations. For this reason, and because Naipaul's obsessive concerns repeat themselves across the decades and across the globe, I have not followed, in this book, a conventional development-of-the-author approach. Instead, I have designed my analysis around a series of Naipaul's recurrent fixations.

My first chapter details Naipaul's success in popularizing an image of himself as a "homeless" writer, a permanent exile who has been abandoned by tradition. How has he managed to draw rhetorical advantage from the welter of terms—exile, emigrant, émigré, expatriate, refugee—applied to displaced writers who have accumulated multiple affiliations? How has his reputation as a marginalized figure stripped of affiliations braced the myth of his detachment? I contend that Naipaul has enlisted the idiom of displacement to exaggerate his distance from mainstream Anglo-American traditions, literary and political alike.

The link between the rhetorical traditionalism of Naipaul's travel writing and his political constituency becomes particularly explicit in his appropriation of travel literature as a genre. As I argue in my second chapter, his response to questions of race and empire is congruent with his affection for and simulation of British travel writers from the Victorian era. Even as he adapts the travel genre to the circumstances of a touristic, postcolonial world, he tends to carry forward elements of a suspect generic legacy.

Given that Naipaul travels from a Western metropolis toward societies that have routinely been the objects of ethnographic study, to what extent does he participate in the traditions of looking down at and writing up non-Western cultures? In my third chapter I respond to this question by demonstrating how travel literature, as a hybrid genre, places two quite different styles of authority at Naipaul's disposal: a semiethnographic, distanced, analytic mode and an autobiographical, subjective, emotionally entangled mode. Naipaul maximizes his discursive power by alternating between these forms of authority in a manner that is made to seem expressive of a quasi-global identity that contains both First and Third worlds. By examining the ethnographic dimensions to his travel writings as well as the autobiographical persona that he fashions, I analyze the rhetorical advantage Naipaul draws from the apparent correspondence between the dual modes of the genre and the division in his own identity.

Joseph Conrad emerges as one of Naipaul's most decisive literary forebears. As an émigré, an assimilated Englishman, and a writer obsessed with colonial decrepitude, Conrad has been perceived by Naipaul as a writer "who had been everywhere before me."[45] My fourth chapter explores the political ramifications of this affiliation by situating Naipaul in the durable *Heart of Darkness* tradition of figuring African societies.

The two succeeding chapters focus on the cluster of terms that Naipaul forefronts in his polemics against the postcolonial societies he visits. Over the course of his oeuvre one comes to recognize how he invests terms like *primitive, simple society, colonial, mimicry,* and *parasitism* with a great deal of explanatory power. What lines of thought do these terms connect him with? I analyze here his efforts to reanimate the notion of the 'primitive' in contradistinction to the 'world civilization' and his reliance on the idea of the 'simple society' in order to remove certain cultures from the realm of history. The sixth chapter considers the protean manifestations and rhetorical effects of 'mimicry', one of the great staples in the commerce of his rhetoric, as well as the related notion of 'parasitism', the decisive concept in his Islamic writings. This entails comparing Naipaul's views on cross-cultural mimicry with other theoretical speculations about dependency and resistance in both their psychological and economic aspects.

The book concludes with an analysis of the shifts in locale, temper, and form evident in Naipaul's three most recent works. *The Enigma of Arrival* and *A Turn in the South* represent a major departure from his prior travel writing in that, for the first time, he writes at length about England and the United States, the countries that have furnished him with the bulk of his audience. How much does this correspondence between audience and subject matter alter the mood and methods of the writing? And to what extent do these changes persist when he returns to more customary haunts in *India: A Million Mutinies Now,* his most ambitious travel book yet?

1

The License of Exile

There is no success like exile.

GUILLERMO CABRERA INFANTE

Naipaul's familial and personal displacements figure so boldly in both his work and its critical reception that he has come to be celebrated as the ultimate literary apatride, the most comprehensively uprooted of twentieth-century writers and the most bereft of national affiliations. His admirers—encouraged in this attitude by Naipaul's own reading of his life—portray him as laboring under a burden of insurmountable estrangement; the remark that "Naipaul is, of all the great writers of exile, the most rootless, the least fortified by the tradition in which he writes" expresses, synoptically, the assumption that underlies the dominant approach to his work.[1] Certainly in Britain and the United States, where his influence has been strongest, critics commonly focus on the pathos of his circumstances and embrace him as simultaneously coming from nowhere and everywhere, as so unplaceable that, in the words of one commentator, " 'home' can never ultimately be more than the books he writes or, perhaps more precisely, the action of writing them."[2] Such depictions of Naipaul as an extravagantly, even uniquely displaced literary figure uphold the image of him as embodying a melancholy modernity that can be readily generalized as "alienated": haunted by a global homelessness that is inseparably geographical, existential, and literary.

I probe, in this chapter, Naipaul's success in fashioning and sustaining an autobiographical persona who is accepted at face value as a permanent exile, a refugee, a homeless citizen of the world, and an extranational writer, to invoke some of the assorted terms that are used to articulate the dominant perception of him. In demonstrating how Anglo-American critics have repeatedly ceded authority to this persona, one observes how Naipaul's style of narrating his geographical movements has provided the rationale for ignoring the shape of his commitments. His biography has, I believe, a reversible lining. It is quite possible to turn the conventional account of his life inside out and discover, not Vidia the exiled victim of historical mischance, but Vidia the beneficiary of a narrative of dislocation that ultimately bolsters the myth of his detachment.

Because he derives from the so-called Third World, Naipaul can be invoked, with the help of bold generalizations, as someone with a personal knowledge of "those kinds" of places and peoples, a knowledge that only an insider could hope to command; at other times, the appeal to his authority focuses on his apparent ability to be an uninvolved outsider everywhere. Naipaul's geographical removals and their psychological trappings—the theme and allure of so much of his writing—have come to enhance his standing most subtly by seeming to legitimize his reputation as an objective and disinterested observer. The empirical and even moral authority of his travel writing has been tied to an interpretation of Naipaul as truly uncompromised by national and political attachments. According to this reading, he possesses a singular capacity to marry the roles of insider and outsider, thereby ostensibly achieving an impartial style of apprehension. This line of argument is flawed, however, by crucial slippages that derive from a confusion of dislocation with detachment and from a failure to examine the precise character of Naipaul's displacement to England.

To gauge its full impact on Naipaul's work and his high standing in Britain and the United States, the pattern of his displacements must be retraced and situated in several ways. First, it is necessary to convey a sense of the persona of Naipaul the detached exile as it takes shape through the many autobiographical reflections in his nonfiction and interviews. Second, the medley of terms—*exile, emigrant, émigré, expatriate, refugee,* and *homeless individual*—applied to writers who undergo geographical, cultural, and national displacement should be analyzed in terms of the rhetorical advantage Naipaul draws from them. Finally, it is instructive to examine the importance of Naipaul's dislocation for his reputation as a disinterested observer working in a genre for which the issue of empirical authority is central. This entails assessing how, as the most autobiographical of contemporary travel writers, Naipaul has used his peripatetic history not only as material for his writing, but also to orient his preoccupation with travel and, most importantly, to give legitimacy to an undeclared set of ideological interests. Such an examination discloses the diverse yet interconnected functions of the term *detachment:* geographical, as an expression of his distance from any clearcut national identity or notion of home; empirical, as a mode of vision; and political, as a measure of his freedom from ideology. My central concern in working through the consequences of the rhetorical ambience of exile and detachment that surrounds Naipaul's nonfictional persona is to trace the logical moves whereby a writer who exercises an unusual sway over Anglo-American thinking about postcolonialism has accrued and sustained a strong following persuaded of his nonalignment, despite the evidence of his primary affiliations to metropolitan culture on the London–New York axis.

Naipaul and Caribbean Deracination

The twentieth-century displacement of persons has proved in scale, in frequency, and in the range of origins and destinations quite without equal in human history. Whether fleeing totalitarianism, international conflicts, ethnic feuds, or natural disasters, or simply gravitating toward the seeming promise of proliferating metropolises, more people in this century than any other are intimate with the traumas and possibilities accompanying the species' expanded mobility. Any map that sought to register no more than the major upheavals would still be dense with crosshatching. Accordingly, Naipaul is far from alone among the century's writers when he speaks of exile and the absence of community as "one of the great strands" in his work.[3] Yet at least among writers in English, no one has gone to Naipaul's lengths to cultivate such an emphatic link between the literary theme of exile and his personal history, nor has anyone so consistently played off that connection in the body of his or her work. He stands out, then, as the English-speaking writer who talks most about being afflicted—in John King's keen phrase—by "an almost genetic sense of rootlessness, shipwreck as an ontological condition."[4]

One can flesh out the notion of Naipaul's "almost genetic" uprootedness by arguing that, as almost all the indigenous peoples of the Caribbean were exterminated by European colonists and as contemporary Caribbeans are therefore descended from introduced populations, the inhabitants of the region are *deracinés pur sang*. In these terms, the displacement of Naipaul and other Antillean writers to England (most concentratedly in the 1950s), can be read as a response, several generations later, to the extraordinary violence of that ancestral exile that entailed suffering the middle passage or, in the case of Naipaul's forebears, crossing the *kala pani* (black water) as they were shipped out from India to Trinidad as indentured laborers. So, by leaving for England, West Indian writers effectively retraced the second leg of the Triangular trade, underscoring the geometry of their historical abuse. The standpoint of the displaced Caribbean writers is the reverse of that of the English exiles once admonished thus by Evelyn Waugh:

> It seems to me that there is this fatal deficiency about all those exiles, of infinitely admirable capabilities, who, through preference or by force of untoward circumstance, have made their home outside the country of their birth; it is the same deficiency one finds in those who indulge their consciences with sectarian religious beliefs, or adopt eccentrically hygenic habits of life, or practice curious, newly-classified vices; a deficiency in that whole cycle of rich experience which lies outside personal peculiarities and individual emotion.[5]

Unlike these English writers, reproved by Waugh for flouting tradition by fleeing it, Naipaul and other Caribbeans abandoned the islands in quest of tradition, specifically a heritage of literacy that might provide them with the audience they could never hope to secure at home.

Even writers less dismissive of the Caribbean—Derek Walcott and George Lamming, for instance—have considered displacement to the metropolitan West (at least for the generation who left in the late 1940s and 1950s) the legitimate, even inevitable direction in which an aspirant author would move. Walcott has spoken of "the pardonable desertion of West Indian writers" as a response to "the amnesia [that] is the true history of the New World."[6] And although Lamming has referred knowingly to "the migration of the writer from the Caribbean to the dubious refuge of a metropolitan culture," he has also recognized that the fear of "eternal dispossession" was sufficiently overwhelming to leave prospective writers of his generation little choice.[7]

Most of the West Indian authors who fetched up in England have written in one form or another about a double sense of displacement—a sense of their removal from Trinidad, Barbados, Guyana, or Jamaica as superimposed on the earlier uprooting of their captive forebears. The writers' alertness to their personal upheavals as symbolically connected to ancestral movements is often accompanied by a sense of triregional affiliations: to the West Indies, England, and either Africa or India. Naipaul's high profile in Britain and the United States, his self-intoxication, and his talent for promoting his "homelessness" have allowed him something of a literary monopoly over the theme of triple affiliations, although other Caribbean-born figures—C. L. R. James, Lamming, Walcott, and Edward Kamu Braithwaite among them—have endured related predicaments, living in three or four continents over time and working through their cultural attachments to each. To a degree, Naipaul's version of this general experience has been patterned differently because his grandparents were transplanted to Trinidad in the 1880s: he is only two generations distant from India, whereas Caribbean writers with African roots, regardless of the depth of their partial identification with that continent, work back toward it from a greater historical remove. Without acceding to Naipaul's extravagant account of his homelessness as unique in intensity and pathos, one should remark on a further difference from the more pervasive pattern: for Lamming and the other black writers, London was their first exposure to life as a member of a minority group, whereas when Naipaul arrived there in 1950, he had already experienced minority status as an Indian in Trinidad. But his pundit origins, the hermetic world of his extended family, and their middle-class standing, kept him aloof in his difference rather than rendering him one of an underprivileged minority.[8] In sum, we should make neither the mistake of assuming that Naipaul's anxieties about roots are purely a professional affectation nor the opposite error of assuming that he is distinctively homeless rather than someone who shares, with most people whose ancestors where shipped off to the colonies, a certain curiosity and insecurity toward the family past.

The Rhetoric of Displacement

In forging a sturdy link between exile as a literary theme and his personal history, Naipaul is adamant that his choice of terms be taken seriously: "[W]hen I talk about being an exile or a refugee I'm not just using a metaphor, I'm speaking literally."[9] Although he argues, on the same occasion, that exile has bestowed on him a rare autonomy as an individual, he tends to portray such autonomy as a measure of his ostracism, that is, as symptomatic of a disadvantaged and marginal existence; the predilection resurfaces in his assertion that "I am a refugee in the sense that I am always peripheral."[10] This is self-portraiture at its most self-pitying. British and American critics show signs of having been won over by the dramatic appeal in Naipaul's accounts of his uprootedness, but I would urge a more skeptical and a more precise approach. The challenge here is to analyze the emotional advantage Naipaul draws from applying the rhetoric of displacement and alienation to his circumstances in a loose enough fashion to keep in play a cluster of distinctively inflected terms.

The word *exile*, in popular usage, is beset with ambiguities. The Oxford English Dictionary definition of the state of exile, however, is quite narrowly circumscribed: "Enforced removal from one's native land according to an edict or sentence; penal expatriation or banishment; the state or condition of being penally banished; enforced residence in some foreign land." Associated, in its original sense, with banishment, it classically entails, as Mary McCarthy reminds us, a punitive act of exclusion on the part of the state followed by a period of agonized waiting abroad on the part of the victim.[11] The pairing of coercion with waiting is pivotal: the exile longs for a change of government or an easing of restrictions; his or her existence is oriented towards that moment when a return to the homeland will be possible once more. Whether Cubans in Miami, South Africans in London and Lusaka, or Palestinians in diaspora, exiles share the pain of banishment or flight, a hankering after the past and a vision of the future. While exiles are people—often writers and intellectuals—who are granted individual definition, one conventionally speaks of communities of exiles cemented by their obsession with home, their memories, their grievances, and their idealism. But this sense of belonging is only partial and cannot entirely remedy the experience of exile as a personal condition of dislocation and solitude; indeed, the unsteady vacillation between affiliation and isolation appears altogether characteristic of exile. Exile in this rigorous sense is the focus of Edward Said's authoritative essay on the subject; he views it primarily as a condition of pathos, anguish, severance, and abandonment, a destructive and jealous state wherein the victim must endure circumstances that are felt to be provisional yet are often endlessly protracted.[12]

If this strict interpretation of the term is adhered to, exiles can be distinguished from expatriates on two scores: first, by the ratio of violence to choice in the prompting of their departure; second, by their attitude to the native land. Henry Miller, Henry James, Ernest Hemingway, Graham Greene, Lawrence Durrell, Karen Blixen, and Katherine Mansfield were all, at one time or another, expatriate writers who voluntarily undertook to reside abroad. The expatriate life is comparatively untraumatic. It is a less painful, vulnerable, and extreme state than exile; it is more privileged and also less obviously political. While renouncing their native lands as the ideal places to inhabit, expatriates tend to retain a secure sense of national identity and frequently return home when they tire of life abroad. Naipaul, on a couple of occasions, has tried to distinguish his own position quite sharply from the relative privilege of the expatriate. And indeed, the very notion of the expatriate writer smacks so of First World opportunities and privileges that the idea of an expatriate emanating from the Third World does seem anomalous.

Even if Naipaul's departure from Trinidad was uncoerced, he feels very intensely that returning to his natal land has not been an option and that this impossibility has effectively curbed his freedom.

The terms *émigré* and *emigrant,* as opposed to *expatriate,* assume a much stronger sense of renunciation, of breaking with the past in the hopes of starting a new life and adopting a new national identity. Furthermore, where *expatriate,* like *exile,* affords a sense of individual definition, emigrants and émigrés are more anonymous; they often arrive and tend to be thought of en masse. This association is felt even more acutely in the case of refugees: the word seems seldom to appear except in the plural form. Refugees enjoy neither the individual definition of the exile nor the range of choices open to the expatriate and the émigré. The notion of a refugee writer or politician seems improbable—that would elevate him or her to the status of an exile.[13] Refugees tend to be powerless, anonymous, voiceless people who, as the etymology suggests, are in flight. They are described as swarming on borders, as coming in waves, as threatening to swamp. Others regularly speak on their behalf; if they themselves are said to speak at all it is through their numbers. Refugees, as Brecht recognized, are "messenger[s] of ill-tiding"; by virtue of their association with tyranny and catastrophe and by virtue of their numbers, they are both the most forlorn and the most threatening of displaced people.[14]

What happens, then, when this array of terms is brought to bear on Naipaul's dislocation? On the one hand, the English critic Andrew Gurr makes an unpersuasive attempt to set up a firm opposition between Naipaul as an exile and the New Zealand–born Katherine Mansfield, whom he designates an expatriate; on the other hand, as the title *V. S. Naipaul: A Study in Expatriate Sensibility* signals, others assume a more skeptical stance towards Naipaul's claims to the status of exile.[15] These very different responses to Naipaul's displacement are symptomatic of the distance between the dominant Anglo-American and Third World interpretations of his biography and ideological outlook.

But in order to probe the reasons for this distance, it is advisable first to observe Naipaul's own style of invoking the language of displacement to articulate his predicament:

> . . . one must make a pattern of one's observations, one's daily distress; one's lack of representation in the world; one's lack of status. These, for me, are not just ideas; when I talk about being an exile or a refugee I'm not just using a metaphor, I'm speaking literally. . . . Because one doesn't have a side, doesn't have a country, doesn't have a community; one is entirely an individual.[16]

The emotional logic of this passage warrants scrutiny. Naipaul's sketch of himself as literally both an "exile" and a "refugee" allows him to keep in play two quite distinctive, even contradictory, sets of resonances. As a refugee, he is bereft of privileges and representation; as an exile, he is solitary, a pure individual uncorrupted by the kind of communal affiliations that, in his terms, produce interested political commitments. He is drawn to *refugee* because it flatters his sense of destitution, but he is emphatic that this is not the destitution of faceless huddled masses, but the kind that elevates the individual above national affiliations, above partisan politics. The emotional focus of the passage, with its mounting negatives, is on a condition of loss, but by the end this has been quietly transformed into grounds for superiority. While the opening sentence of the statement accents his duress and abandonment, the closing sentence transforms this into an assertion of his self-contained individuality. In this manner Naipaul's disavowal of any national identity fortifies accounts (his own and others') of his status as a detached, disinterested, even apolitical writer.

For reasons of publishing, audience, and education, there was substantial pressure on Caribbean authors of Naipaul's generation to move abroad if they wished to survive as writers. Liberally interpreted, this pressure could be read as a form of coercion. But there remain two ways in which Naipaul's displacement jars with the notion of exile, and in these he differs from other displaced writers of Caribbean birth. Naipaul has asserted, repeatedly, that he is not only physically removed from his natal land but also emotionally disengaged from it. He declares that the possibility of being at home has not merely been deferred, but never existed in the first place, charging that even as a child he felt Trinidad to be an alien environment. Moreover, as the passage above intimates, Naipaul dissociates himself from any community of exiles. A pessimist and a quietist, he has no truck with those whose mutual ideals bind them to an image of an alternative, improved future for the land of their birth. And so the characteristic experience of exile as a wavering between supreme solitude and more collective passions is not his; he writes only of the isolation. Given this almost principled aloofness from any polity, Naipaul's position is perhaps most appositely characterized as, to borrow Auerbach's phrase, one of "willed homelessness."[17]

The assumptions behind Naipaul's rhetorical posturing on the matter of his displacement can be illuminated by a remark by the South African writer Breyten Breytenbach. Because his spouse is Vietnamese, Breytenbach was barred for many years under South Africa's Mixed Marriages

Act from returning to his natal land. But interviewed in Paris in 1986, Breytenbach balked at a reference to him as an exile:

> I've a split mind about the notion of exile. I reject it because there's the immediate tendency when one mentions exile to self-dramatize or to self-pity. It's a very sterile category to be fitted into. A very foreclosed one too. . . . The political or social exile is often a very sad person, whereas a literary exile may choose to live somewhere for his work.[18]

Elaborating on Breytenbach's wariness of the term, I would contend that *exile,* in the domain of literary history, possesess a very specific genealogy that by this stage has less to do with banishment and ostracism than with a powerful current of twentieth-century literary expectations in the West. Writers domiciled overseas, regardless of the circumstances of their removal from their native lands, commonly imagine and describe themselves as living in exile because it is a term privileged by high modernism and associated with the emergence of the metropolis as a crucible for a more international, though still European- or American-based culture. The phrase *in exile* resonates with a sophisticated anxiety that fits tidily with a certain conventional perception of the writer's lot in society. By choosing *exile* over the bland and anonymous *immigrant,* the all too confortable *expatriate,* and the even more hedonistic-sounding *cosmopolitan,* Naipaul can trumpet his alienation while implicitly drawing on a secure, reputable tradition of extratraditionalism. As Breytenbach is all too aware, exile as a literary state is susceptible to a lurking theatricality.

When one views Naipaul's "exile" from the larger perspective of twentieth-century literary history, it becomes apparent that in removing himself from a national tradition he linked himself to an aesthetic one. From his earliest years as a writer, he suffered not from any anxiety of influence, but from the fear of being cut adrift from a strong literary tradition. While his friend and fellow travel writer Paul Theroux praised him for being "wholly original . . . maybe the only writer today in whom there are no echoes of influences," Naipaul himself viewed originality as an ambiguous virtue: to be wholly original was to be wholly isolated.[19] Writing about Port of Spain required that he reconstruct the place from the foundations up for a Western audience almost entirely unacquainted with it, and he envied the securely metropolitan writers the ease with which they could draw resonance from the literary density of London, Paris, and New York. He feared, then, that his thematic attachment to marginalized societies had destined him to become a marginal writer.

Yet shortly after Theroux's study appeared, Naipaul qualified the image of himself as a marooned, extratraditional writer by choosing to affiliate himself with Conrad. I elaborate on the consequence of this elective affinity in a subsequent chapter analyzing the quite profound impact of *Heart of Darkness* on Naipaul's work. But with specific regard to his displacement, one should at least observe in passing how his alignment with Conrad has helped ease Naipaul across a threshold and into the company of the many celebrated twentieth-century authors whose hallmark is the by now normative estrangement of the déraciné or, at least, of the outsider. Part of Naipaul's felt kinship with Conrad has been thematic: The Polish émigré was someone "who sixty or seventy years ago meditated on my world, a world I recognize today."[20] But the alignment went beyond that. For by ignoring Conrad's English patriotism, Naipaul could read him as a prior exile who was "missing a society" and, by implication, as his primary point of contact with a tradition of breaking with tradition.[21]

If the term *exile* highlights the pathos of the outcast and plays down the security of belonging to the modern literature of the outsider, references to Naipaul's homelessness resonate with a slightly different, though related, ambivalence. Here the sense of destitution is fused to a lofty, existential, and constitutionally modern melancholy, perhaps most familiar in the form of Georg Lukács's "transcendental homelessness." Scanning the titles of articles on and interviews with Naipaul, one can get an inkling of how reiteratively homelessness or exile is taken to be definitive of his being and his work, and how insistently Anglo-American critics characterize his displacement in terms of the pathos of loss: "Writer Without a Society," "V. S. Naipaul, Man Without a Society," "Without a Place," "Writer Without Roots," "Historicity and Homelessness in Naipaul," "Exile's Story," "V. S. Naipaul's Negative Sense of Place," "No Place: V. S. Naipaul's Vision of Home in the Caribbean," "Nowhere to Go."[22] This prevailing view of Naipaul's biography seldom accommodates the degree to which he has capitalized on what Hollywood would call his "high profile" as irremediably wounded by history and dogged by the curse of marginality. By now, it would seem appropriate to address the disparity between the energetically defended image of Naipaul as one of history's rejects, someone condemned to concentrated alienation, and his standing as among the two or three most lionized writers resident in England. Given his forty years in that country, his thirty-five-year old marriage to an Englishwoman, and the dimensions of his trans-Atlantic reputation, to what extent can he continue to be portrayed with any legitimacy as cast out from and ill-fitted to metropolitan life?

The rhetoric of displacement that Naipaul has deployed is crucial to any understanding of his influence because it has set the terms for critical discussion of his life and work. Once the dominant spatial motif has been established, it can be lifted unobtrusively from the realm of personal geography and applied to inquiries about his political, moral, and empirical standpoints. So the question "Where is he coming from?" though metaphoric in such contexts, has invariably been answered by Anglo-American critics with a very literal reference to his life's trajectory of displacement. If he is known to be physically without a nation or a home, he can be readily depicted as removed from politics, morally elevated by an aloofness from any interested constituency, and detached or disinterested as an observer.

For the myth of Naipaul's detachment to be sustained, it is essential that he appear unassimilable, awkwardly placed, hopelessly oblique in his relation to the West; his authenticity as the metropole's favorite Third World interpreter of the Third World would be jeopardized were he no longer to appear as one of the castoffs of history. Naipaul's presumed neutrality is so prized because, in the guilty aftermath of colonialism, he seems to satisfy the need for the history that has "hitherto been written from the standpoint of the victor, . . . to be written from that of the vanquished.[23]" But he allows the West to have it both ways: listening to what the other world (in the guise of Naipaul) has to say, the West finds itself consoled, not troubled, by the upshot of this apparently inverted perspective. For while seeming to diversify quite radically the origin of reporting about the 'periphery', Naipaul does little to change its content.

From the standard critical viewpoint, the remarkable correspondence between Naipaul and the dominant Western perceptions of the 'periphery' derive not from the possibility that he might be an Oxford-educated English acculturate, but from the evidence that his objectivity is superbly uncompromised by national interests. If critical opinion in Britain and the United States hymns Naipaul as the consummately neutral observer he purports to be, and shares his personal preoccupation with his checkered provenance, this state of affairs is evidently to the advantage of both parties. As a racial East Indian and a natal West Indian, and—in terms of the polarities of the Brandt Commission—as one of the wretched of the South exiled in the North, he is treated as qualified to speak as a "universal man" in whom all the vectors of geographical bias are perfectly canceled. Unencumbered by the embarrassment of a white skin, born in and associated with the globe's margins, Naipaul can be strategically invoked as a Third World counterweight to opinions that prove discomfiting to the Western hegemony. That much is intimated by claims that Naipaul possesses "an eye without prejudice as well as an eye unclouded by fear that he might be prejudiced, a timidity common enough among a number of English writers" or that he owns a "moral advantage over English writers, by having lived on that frontier, so long veiled from English view."[24] Behind both these assertions stands the assumption that a dark-skinned writer deriving from a formerly colonized society can speak his mind with impunity as no white outsider could, especially one from a former imperial power. Yet even if insiders enjoy a greater license to be outspoken, it remains questionable why Naipaul should be singled out and given a moral advantage over other less ambiguously Third World authors.

If the Anglo-American tendency to defer to Naipaul as a semiinsider is manifestly partisan, it is also flawed in its assumptions. In one decisive sense, Naipaul's position in visiting, say, the Ivory Coast, Mauritius, Uruguay, Zaire or Malaysia, or even Trinidad and India, is much closer to that of a Western tourist than to the condition of an inhabitant of any of those lands. He is free to terminate his trip as he pleases, then to withdraw, brandishing his British passport, to the security of a metropolitan residence and reputation. In a quite material sense, England provides Naipaul with a home. Insiders in Third World countries, people without a refuge from their immediate circumstances, have to root their daily lives and ambitions where they find themselves. If, as is often the case, those circumstances are deplorable, the insiders cannot survive without hope, without envisioning improvements. This necessity may spawn a variety of shaky utopianisms, but one should nevertheless acknowledge the difference it makes when, lacking an alternative nationality, people can only escape to an improved future version of their native land. By such standards, Naipaul's litany of doom takes on the aspect of an outsider's luxury—he can afford to be unstintingly derisory because he rests secure in the knowledge of escape. And that knowledge relieves him of the pressure to inhabit one of those countries as the permanent, ineluctable site of his ambitions. By this account, it seems a little specious to claim that Naipaul can automatically approximate an indigenous perspective wherever he goes.

The Critical Response

The logical drift of Naipaul's remarks on exile, nationality, and impartiality has been rehearsed with great fideility by British and American critics. Paul Theroux was one of the first to endorse the persona Naipaul has fashioned for himself as someone wholly original, unprecedently alienated, and therefore a citizen of nowhere and everywhere. Echoing Naipaul's lexicon of displacement, Theroux restates the main stages of the argument with precision:

> [Naipaul ranks among the] former colonials, transplanted people who can claim no country as their own. They travel because they belong nowhere; they cannot settle, they are constantly moving—in a sense they never arrive—and much of their travel is flight. Rootlessness is their condition; it is the opposite of those for whom being metropolitan is a condition. The homeless are not calm; their homelessness is a source of particular pain, for as with all travellers, they are asked, "Where are you from?" and no simple answer is possible: all landscapes are alien.[25]

Later in the same study, addressing the issue of Naipaul's "unique condition," Theroux declares:

> . . . he is in his own words 'without a past, without ancestors', 'a little ridiculous and unlikely'. His is a condition of homelessness. It has the single advantage of enabling him to become a working resident—as much a resident in India as anywhere else—and allows him a depth of insight that is denied the metropolitan. For the rootless person, every country is a possible temporary home; but for Naipaul, there is no return, either to a past or a place. . . . Naipaul is the first of his line, without a tradition or home.[26]

Some six years previous to writing these words, Theroux had been befriended and inspired by Naipaul in Uganda; shortly after writing them, he followed Naipaul's example and produced his first travelogue set in the Third World. The most striking feature of Theroux's commentary is the clear, unequivocal confidence with which he contrasts the insecurity of the nomadic Naipaul with the easy stability of the metropolitan writer. By this stage, Naipaul had been out of Trinidad for twenty years; for all but a couple of those he had been domiciled in England. But Theroux's prudence prevents him from complicating the image of Naipaul's alienation; those twenty-odd years are treated as maintaining his homelessness on an even keel without drawing him closer to metropolitan interests and values. Significantly—and this is characteristic of Anglo-American treatments of Naipaul—Theroux portrays him not as an amalgam of three national traditions (Trinidad, India, and England), but as equally alien and therefore equally resident everywhere. This sweepingly negative formulation obviates any precise analysis of the triple heritages that nourish Naipaul's identity, sharpen the pathos of his condition, and, most importantly, extend very generously the domain of Naipaul's authority as an observer. Instead of possessing an insider's advantage in three cultures, and with it an insider's partialities, Naipaul is declared to possess a categorical advantage over others wherever he goes. Theroux, moreover, for all his initial generalizations about up-rooted former colonials as a category, ensures by the end of the second passage that Naipaul stands utterly alone and nonpareil—in pain, authority, and originality.

The critical tendency to adapt the geographical motif of Naipaul's exile for the purposes of accrediting him with singular powers as an observer is grounded, in the first instance, in some of the author's own remarks. Here two of his statements may illuminate, in complementary fashion, Naipaul's perspective on his own "objectivity." In the same interview where he claims to be a pure individual utterly without a side, a country, or a community, Naipaul explains how this occurred: "I come from a small society; I was aware that I had no influence in the world; I was apart from it. And then I belonged to a minority group, I moved away, became a foreigner, became a writer; you see the degrees of removal from direct involvement."[27] This remark should be set alongside Naipaul's contention that he sees from a vantage point outside of ideology, a claim he supports, a little self-consciously on the above occasion, by twice emphasizing that England is alien and can never furnish him with any sense of home. "I think," he reflects, "that one reason why my journalism can last is because I never had any such ideas about Left or Right. One just looked at what had happened. There are no principles involved in one's vision."[28] In moving between these two statements, one recognizes how Naipaul's early lack of influence, his claim to be a permanent foreigner, and his remoteness from any "direct involvement"—all evidence of powerless-ness—clear the way for the very empowering claim that he is unmappable in terms of ideological positions.

Mel Gussow's review-interview "Writer Without Roots" offers exem-plary support for the prevailing myth of Naipaul's neutrality. Gussow avers that "wherever he goes, it is a foreign country. For Naipaul, home has lost its meaning"; likewise, "in Trinidad, and wherever he has gone, he has been an outsider."[29] But the language of exclusion and wher-everness appears primarily to back up the truly bold claims: Naipaul's life and work are distinguished by a "detachment, emotional as well as geographic," and "the fact that he is beyond partisanship." Given this context, when Gussow charges that "with Naipaul, his tradition begins with him," one senses a determination to preempt any suggestion of either literary or ideological forerunners.[30] Naipaul's neutrality can be rendered incontestable by designating it a fated neutrality: The man has no choice but to write out of a free original space untrammeled by traditions or constituencies of interest. Alfred Kazin tenders a similar argument in concluding that "as a documentary reporter . . . Naipaul is totally without ideology."[31]

Naipaul remains as sanguine about his capacity to see all sides as he is about his status as a permanent foreigner everywhere; the two qualities are tightly bound. When an interviewer suggested that *Among the Believers* might be contoured by a partisan vision of Islam, Naipaul parried by laying claim to universal powers of empathetic insight:

> Nothing was falsified. I'm very, very scrupulous about that. And I have seldom been misled by people because in every new situation I'm always with the other man, I'm always looking at the world through his eyes. . . . It's a matter of observing where people are made by false hopes, political beliefs, tribal causes.[32]

This seems sufficient to have thwarted the critic's inchoate skepticism, for he proceeded to commend Naipaul for the " 'charity' in even his darkest books—the charity of looking. He refuses not to see."

The connection between Naipaul's purported clear-sightedness and his purported homelessness has been stated emphatically and often enough for these two defining qualities of his persona to have become practically indissociable. Irving Howe's pronouncements on this subject merit reflection. Declaring Naipaul to be "the world's writer," Howe argues that his "deracination . . . enables a steely perspective, the scraped honesty of the margin. It spurs him to a cool precision, trusting his own eyes."[33] By associating honesty with marginality and Naipaul with both, Howe becomes party to the myth of Naipaul as outmarginal- izing the margins themselves. Plainly, Howe does not mean that simply anyone from the periphery is capable of such probity and precision; Naipaul is singled out in this regard. He could perhaps be seen as some- what liminal to the metropolitan cultures of the Anglo-American world (and only then at a push), but if marginality is the measure of "scraped honesty," surely on a global scale, we can expect more concentrated honesty elsewhere?

For a summation of the Anglo-American critical tendency to defer to Naipaul's carefully crafted persona of himself as nonaligned, clear- sighted, and honest, one can turn to William Walsh's assessment of Naipaul's empirical expertise:

> That air of detachment which many have noted in Naipaul, and which sometimes may seem, and indeed be, evidence of an intention to keep his

distance from the world, is more frequently, and certainly at its best, a discipline of scrupulous accuracy, the effort to define the fact and refine the feeling. *Spectator ab extra:* Coleridge's words about Wordsworth, are peculiarly appropriate to the nature of Naipaul's sensibility. He has the telescopic sight of an unattached observer. . . .[34]

Walsh follows a predictable tack when he proceeds to depict Naipaul as "a remarkably free, untethered soul, an expatriate in his birthplace, an alien in his ancestral land, a disengaged observer of Britain and other countries." Rather less predictable is this assertion:

> The paradox of Naipaul's Indian journey was that he brought to bear upon the Indian scene a refinement of that superior, detached, Brahmin tradition drawn from India itself. . . . He is intent and focussed as a bird, as unsympathetic as a hawk and as high above the object. Naipaul's cool gaze sweeps over the subcontinent from Bombay to Kashmir, its capacity for observing unaffected both by his troubled soul or by the deadening poverty on every side.[35]

The pitch of Walsh's resolve to confirm and account for Naipaul's detachment is apparent from the farrago of evidence he calls into play. His appeals are fivefold: an association, through Coleridge and Wordsworth, of detachment with a romantic sensibility; the quite different appeal, with the reference to Naipaul's "telescopic" authority, to detachment as an ideal in the tradition of scientific empiricism; the standard, plangent account of Naipaul's homelessness; the Indian tradition of distance as expressive of a caste-based elitism; and a return, with the figure of the hawk, to a more romantic evocation of Naipaul's visual command. This last image is staged in a manner redolent of that pervasive colonial motif for centralizing observational authority that Mary Louise Pratt has dubbed "the monarch of all I survey," the imperial perspective of "looking in and down upon what is other."[36] All but one of these figurative arguments for Naipaul's detachment intersect with categorically Western traditions.

If numerous American and British critics have foreclosed the question of Naipaul's ideological entanglements by appealing, quite routinely, to the non sequitur of detachment following from an ill-defined exile or homelessness, the incoherence of such logic becomes manifest whenever they try to ground this abstract argument in the body of Naipaul's work. John Lukacs launched just such an attempt during an exchange between Edward Said and Conor Cruise O'Brien over the nature of Naipaul's constituency. Rising to Naipaul's defense, Lukacs interjected that:

"Naipaul hasn't spared anyone in his writings. He has had harsh things to say about people in Argentina and in Trinidad, about Africa and Pakistan. He's not at all selective in the manner of most intellectuals I know."[37] This remarkable assertion of Naipaul's evenhandedness depends on defining "anyone" with reference solely to the ranks of the Third World. Lukacs's obliviousness to his own naked bias is symptomatic of just how deeply Naipaul criticism—at least in Britain and the United States—has become party to the contradictory notion of selective universality.

However, most sponsors of the idea that Naipaul neither spares nor favors any particular group are at least sensitive to the need to stress his repudiations of the West. And so his scorn for the students he taught at Wesleyan will be recalled, or it will be suggested that he is an Anglophobe or that he is convinced of the West's decline. Eugene Goodheart's observations are in keeping with this current of opinion:

> It doesn't matter whether the scene is the half-developed or "mimic" societies of the Caribbean or the abysmal material squalor of India or the cruel places in Africa where revolutions are being made or, for that matter, the advanced societies of the West. Naipaul encounters one and all with a cold-eyed contempt. . . . It is always valuable for a writer from an underdeveloped country to refuse the ideological role that is usually conferred on literature about the colonies, whether on the side of the colonists or on the side of the natives.[38]

These passages articulate, quite crisply, two prevalent variants of the same argument. The first, cast in geographical or spatial terms, contends that Naipaul, the global scourge, treats every place the same. The second, phrased in terms of polarized ideologies, discovers Naipaul to be neither this nor that—even the equipoise in the syntax speaks of his capacity to balance the leanings of colonist and 'native'. In short, Naipaul appears as a still point in a world swirling with ideologies.

The recurrent style of reasoning about Naipaul's disinterestedness as outlined above is almost purely an Anglo-American phenomenon; South Asian, Indian, Caribbean, Latin American, Arab, and African critics invariably resist it. They are more likely to attempt to map his predilections off the very specifics of his life that are eclipsed by abstract talk of homelessness and of him as "the world's writer." Such critics are thus more partial to finding in Naipaul's writings strains that they trace back to his Brahman ancestry; to his middle-class standing in Trinidad; to that island's racial politics, with its deep-seated tensions between the Indian minority and the black majority; to a prevalent Hindu antipathy towards Muslim cultures; to Naipaul's Oxford education; to his lengthy attachment to London; and to his exalted standing in Britain and the United States. Many of these critiques are glancing and incidental rather than fully developed, but the pattern is insistent: most writers in publications like the *Trinidad Guardian* and the *Literary Half-Yearly* (Mysore) perceive very little detachment in Naipaul's work and make many references to his partisanship. In a predominantly sympathetic analysis of Naipaul's *A House for Mr. Biswas,* the West Indian critic Kenneth Ramchand has charged that the book is marred by the author's "one-sided compassion" for Trinidad's Indians.[39] Derek Walcott, in a related observation, has suggested that Naipaul's simplistic vision of the Caribbean and his tendentious ethnic politics are symptomatic of deep strains in West Indian societies.[40] The oeuvres of both V. S. and his brother Shiva are dotted with instances of them rallying to the defense of the Indian diaspora, whether in Trinidad, Guyana, Surinam, Kenya, Uganda, or England. Analogously, in writing of India itself prior to his 1989 trip, V. S.'s rare touches of compassionate understanding are largely reserved for members of the Brahman caste to which he is ancestrally connected. These predilections are scarcely surprising. And when they surface, they often provide focal points of interest, precisely because they are so keenly felt. But it is difficult to square such tendencies with the durable image of Naipaul as a nonaligned individual whose exile, homelessness, and alienation has transported him beyond the bounds of partisan observation.

Certainly, some of the claims of Naipaul's admirers can be quickly dispatched. The assertion, for example, that he has on occasion found fault with the West is quite accurate; to charge that he is "just as likely to criticize the West as the Third World" is demonstrably untrue. For many hundreds of pages in his nonfiction alone he has berated and ridiculed the inhabitants of postcolonial India, Trinidad, Jamaica, Martinique, Belize, Guyana, Surinam, Grenada, St. Kitts, Anguilla, Mauritius, the Ivory Coast, Zaire, Argentina, Uruguay, Iran, Pakistan, Malaysia, and Indonesia. Over thirty-seven years his criticisms of contemporary England and the United States—mainly of England—amounted to less than twenty pages. And when finally—in *The Enigma of Arrival* (1987) and *A Turn in the South* (1989)—he engaged with the English and American worlds that have provided his primary readership, the books he produced were unprecedently benign. So the most cursory attention to the weighting of his work should be sufficient to explode, once and for all, the stubborn and convenient myth of his neutrality and clear-sightedness.

Naipaul's Metropolitan Identity

To bring Naipaul's work down from the ether of detachment, one must proceed beyond exposing the pervasive myth and undertake the more positive endeavor of characterizing his alignments. I would contend that the crucial task here is to specify his relation to England and, more exactly, to metropolitan London. Naipaul tends to play down the significance of his lengthy residence in England and, concomitantly, to assert the absence of any clearcut national affiliations to that country, without reflecting on the depth of his commitments to the London–New York metropolitan axis that dominates the publishing and media cultures of the English-speaking world.

Prior to *The Enigma of Arrival,* the impact of England on the character of Naipaul's postcolonial ideology was almost directly proportional to his reluctance to address the subject. While he has written at length of the Trinidadian and Indian prongs of his identity, his reflections on England have been spare and begrudging, a remarkable circumstance given that he had spent more time in that country than anywhere else, including Trinidad. Early in his career, he wrote two brief essays on his feelings about England. The first, "London," appeared in 1958, eight years after his arrival there; the second, entitled "What's Wrong with Being a Snob?"—an altogether more confident and more acid piece of writing—was published in 1967.[41] For twenty years thereafter, he seemed loath to reflect on his position in England, portraying himself as a reluctant, debilitated, suffering resident impatient to flee the land he had fled to and providing scant acknowledgment of how his metropolitan vantage point empowered him. This tendency to edit England out of his life's narrative surfaced most obviously in interviews. When questioned about how he was adapting to England, he typically deflected the inquiry with more self-commiserating talk of homelessness, estrangement, rootlessness, and restlessness. Or, in disclaiming any significant attachment to England, he would insist on characterizing the country as neutral territory, as no specific place at all, simply a good place to write. Only in 1987, with the appearance of *The Enigma of Arrival,* a blend of autobiography and fiction, did he break that lengthy silence.[42]

If Naipaul has not often found fault with his country of residence, those few criticisms have been memorable: "It isn't only Africans who are bow-and-arrow people, it's so many people here living at a very high level who have allowed their minds to go slack. The English bourgeoisie are mimicking their former roles."[43] Even here, his choice of metaphor is calculated to isolate Third World 'primitivism', not middle-class English decadence, as the real object of his scorn. There are moments, however, when he openly laments the faded grandeur of the English middle class—the result, he contends, of the destructively egalitarian ideology of the welfare state:

> . . . the classless state had in fact become the proletarian state, where old aspirations had been abandoned and old sanctions shown to be without value, and where as in a colony just after independence, there was an atmosphere of holiday, revenge, self-destruction.[44]

The final phrase bespeaks Naipaul's real horror: that of the brutes—be they English working-class or decolonized Third World subjects—unshackled. In the same essay, Naipaul declares baldly that difference should be recognized but shown its place; to refuse to range one's citizens in terms of superiority and inferiority is to will a society run by those he dubs "mini-men," the metropolitan variants of the "mimic-men" with whom he populates the periphery. Plainly, when Naipaul finds occasion to criticize England, he does so not to tax it with the imperial past or with abuses of metropolitan power, but to lodge contrary complaints—that the democratic ambitions of the postimperial welfare state betray the best English values and hasten national decline towards a Third World level of degeneracy.

Naipaul's affection for the values of the English bourgeoisie in their imperial prime is expressive of an only half-concealed colonial nostalgia. But sometimes the nostalgia bursts forth. In a notable instance of this, Naipaul would have us believe that the augmentation, since the Victorian age, of the leveling languages of pluralism has been particularly damaging for writers, who now have to suppress their most deeply felt prejudices. It is with palpable nostalgia that he looks back at Anthony Trollope's *The West Indies and the Spanish Main* (1861), a book that strongly influenced his own Caribbean travelogue, written one hundred years later; in which, however, most partisan judgments had to be curtailed. Naipaul delightedly observes:

> The Victorians were, of course, privileged: they were free to express their most outrageous prejudices. Trollope could write, for instance: "I hate Baptists like poison," and not bother to say why; he could describe a West Indian island as a "Niggery-Hispano-Dano-Yankee-Doodle place": he simply meant, of course, that it was not British. It is Trollope's triumph that we would not have him without one of his prejudices; for through them he can be seen as a humane and devout and humorous and altogether enchanting person.[45]

Similarly, it was the absence of any pressure on Trollope to qualify his ethno- and Anglocentrism that enabled "what he saw as the idleness of the West Indian Negro" to become "the subject of some of his warmest vituperation."[46] To these quotes we might juxtapose a third: "The Victorian Age has been badly treated in Socialist propaganda. It was an age of constant constructive endeavour."[47] The author in this instance, however, is not Naipaul, but Margaret Thatcher, whose speeches are riddled with nostalgic Victorianism; indeed, it has been one of the mainstays of her ideology. The difference between the two invocations of that past age should not be blurred: Naipaul (or V. S. Nightfall, as Derek Walcott has dubbed him) long ago earned his black belt in pessimism and views the grand old days of Victorianism as irrecoverably past, while Thatcher— most strikingly during her first term—has expressed confidence in the possibility of reviving the Victorian spirit, reversing the course of history, and reinstating British pride.[48] Despite this difference in conception, a common problem binds Naipaul's and Thatcher's nostalgia: neither has thought through the consequences of idealizing that particular age, glibly sliding over the brutality and suffering inflicted—whether in domestic industry and homes or in the colonies—in the name of Victorian ideals. Trollope's voice sounds so assured only because it rings as much imperial as it does imperious.

Naipaul has always saved his fiercest invective for postcolonial governments and regimes; by comparison, his criticisms of the colonial rule, which hobbled those lands and shaped the enduring North–South imbalance of resources and of cultural and economic power, seem lightweight and occasional. Naipaul's nostalgia for the bourgeois culture and ethos of the heyday of British imperialism and for the apparently unfettered travel writing of mid-Victorianism, along with his relative vindication of that imperialism as an endeavor elevated by "ideas," simply cannot be squared with any consistent antipathy to colonialism. Such stances give the lie to claims like Irving Howe's that Naipaul's work is devoid of "any trace of Western condescension or nostalgia for colonialism."[49]

I would venture, then, that one reason why Naipaul speaks of his alienation from postcolonial England is that he feels more at home in the idealized imperial England of his imaginings. Steeped in adolescent readings of the nineteenth-century novel and made intimate through his colonial education at Queens' Royal College with a version of the Mother Country that was both literary and anachronistic, Naipaul makes it clear that his disappointment with the London he arrived in resulted from his passion for the splendor of the old imperial capital:

So I grew to feel that the grandeur belonged to the past; that I had come to England at the wrong time; that I had come too late to find the England, the heart of Empire, that (like a provincial from a far corner of the Empire) I had created in my fantasy.[50]

Paradoxically, this London of the past was an idealized future he was traveling to, so that, when the material metropolis of the 1950s fell short of his ideal, Naipaul consigned his vision of greatness to an earlier era. And there it seems to have remained for the duration of his career. As a consequence, he has held to a sentimental image of the English past that not only initially colored his adolescent expectations but, once those were dashed, persisted in shaping his posture towards both imperial and postimperial England.

Yet Naipaul's indulgence of an older imperial England cannot fully explain the way he bridles at questions about his relation to that country today. What, for instance, is one to make of these self-consciously off-hand, dismissive remarks?

Well, I come back to England because I have all my friends here now, in London. It's the place where I operate, and my publishers are here, the magazines for which I write are here. But again I must make the point that it's not a place where I can flourish completely.[51]

Even Naipaul's acknowledgments that London has played a critical role in shaping his career come across as impersonal and unimpassioned: "I couldn't have become a writer without London—the whole physical apparatus of publishing, of magazines, the BBC. This apparatus enables a man to make a living."[52] By talking of London as a place to "operate," of a "physical apparatus," of making a living, Naipaul casts his position there in the most dourly mechanical, utilitarian terms. Such phrasing is, of course, perfectly consistent with his jealous protection of his reputation for "perpetual ostracism."

While in the 1950s and early 1960s such expressions of an angular relation to England may have been valid, Naipaul, with assistance from his Anglo-American commentators, has succeeded in freezing that tangent, so that the question of his growing assimilation to and endorsement by mainstream British literary culture continues to be ignored. Though he can be seen to work out of the metropolis, Naipaul cannot be thought to inhabit it; any sign of identification with England would erode his value as a writer privy to Third World thinking to a degree unattainable by anyone English, and would also compromise the other prevailing interpretation, that of his universal detachment. For these reasons, the fact that England (supplemented in the past two decades by America) has provided him with his warmest, most receptive audience—that is, the fact that he is writing for the English—tends to go unstated. The closest Naipaul comes to admitting the bond between himself as a writer and his two nationally specific, politically sympathetic readerships appears in inverted formulations: "I do not write for Indians, who in any case do not read. My work is only possible in a liberal, civilized Western country. It is not possible in primitive societies."[53] The choice of prepositions is not gratuitous: his denial that he writes for Indians gives way not to an assertion that he writes for Westerners, but instead to the more ambiguous statement that he writes in a Western country.

On one noteworthy occasion, in the course of dissociating himself from England, Naipaul edged toward acknowledging the metropolis as a place where he felt secure, even if he avoided confronting the metropole's impact on his outlook:

> I've been living in England, but really I think it's truer to say that I've been attached to London, these few square miles which make an international city, a great metropolis. As soon as I move out of that little enchanted area, I'm in a foreign country in which I'm not terribly interested.[54]

As I have suggested, Naipaul has stimulated and capitalized on the critical habit of treating him as either unique or universal, with the consequence that his political affiliations have commonly been obscured. This critical pattern follows, I propose, from a category mistake: by accepting the nation as the unit of identification and concluding that Naipaul is not Trinidadian, Indian, or English, Anglo-American critics have overlooked—sometimes willfully—the possibility that his fundamental affiliations might be to London as a metropolis and, beyond that, to the London–New York metropolitan axis around which literary culture revolves in the English-speaking world. To provide an account of Naipaul's ideological commitments, it is thus necessary simultaneously to track the specifically Trinidadian, Indian, and English components of his identity—a task certain critics, notably Edward Said, John Thieme, Chris Searle, Selwyn Cudjoe, and Angus Richmond, have begun—and to supplement these with an understanding of his vantage point as a preeminently metropolitan writer.

The introduction of the category 'metropolitan' helps dispel the myth of Naipaul's homelessness; it also remedies the habit of seeing him in either hopelessly general or excessively individual terms. For 'metropolitan' can supplant the vagueness of the all-licensing 'universal' (a term with which it is certainly not synonymous), as well as tempering the image of Naipaul's uniqueness. On this last score, one may agree with

Naipaul that "to be an Indian from Trinidad is to be unlikely," but one should add, not so unlikely that he can secede from history. Although Naipaul is apt to be isolated as a special case, as someone who so obviously does not fit that he exists as a free-floating individual, I would counter that his life and work can be accommodated—more than he ordinarily admits—to a broader but historically specific pattern of former subjects of the British Empire gravitating to metropolitan London during the overlapping eras of decolonization and postcolonialism.

Beginning in 1945, the sharp influx into London of West Indians, and subsequently Indians and Pakistanis, ensured that the city would become incrementally more multicultural. Naipaul himself arrived in England in 1950, during the early phase of this immigration. A few years later, his brother followed suit. Viewed against this backdrop, certain remarks by both Naipauls begin to appear ambiguous, almost as sleights of hand. Shiva, for instance, in reasserting his entrenched nomadism and the impossibility of ever belonging to a community, pronounced in 1985 that "the city, while exacting its price, did not confer a new identity: I do not consider myself a Londoner."[55] But "Londoner" is an elusive category and not nearly as centered as Shiva makes it sound. Because the city is comprised of an array of communities, especially first- and second-generation Britons from the former colonies, notions of dispersal and diversity are built into the very concept of postcolonial London—except, that is, for those diehards who cling to the anachronistic image of The City as the capital of an ethnically and culturally homogeneous nation. While marginality may not be the norm, metropolitan minorities exist in sufficiently large numbers to exert a centrifugal pull on the city's identity. The standard presence, in London, of such substantial marginalized communities further confounds talk of exile, homelessness, and rootlessness.

The cultural role of the metropolis in global terms is complicated by its paradoxical position. On the other hand, it stands at the cultural crossroads: nationalisms intersect there, mingle and become disordered, while cultural identities and forms, likewise, get dismantled and are recombined. On the other hand, the metropolis exerts an international influence in the service of a particular nation. So a city like Naipaul's London exists as a place where a unitary national culture is broken up and diffused yet also as a concentrated site of national power: from an international perspective, it is imposing, in both senses of the word. The habit Naipaul exhibits of dissociating himself from surrounding society and being obsessed by his eccentric status induces him to play down his relation to the wider currents of cultural mixing in London and equally to underestimate the degree to which he is empowered, in global terms, by writing out of a strong metropolitan base.

Only rarely prior to *The Enigma of Arrival* (and even there only obliquely) did he display a curiosity about the cultural consequences of the intersection of immigrant and English national ideologies. He did demonstrate an inchoate fascination with these consequences in a 1963 review of C. L. R. James's *Beyond a Boundary*. Naipaul's decision to pair the Trinidadian-born author's book (at once an encomium to cricket and the autobiography of a prominent West Indian's relation to England) with Nirad Chaudhuri's *Autobiography of an Unknown Indian* signaled his alertness to those national components in his own identity and, beyond that, an incipient feeling for the transformation of English culture by ex-colonial immigrants. In a gifted turn of phrase, Naipaul wrote of James's and Chaudhuri's books as "part of the cultural boomeranging from the former colonies, delayed and still imperfectly understood." Sadly, particularly in his nonfiction, Naipaul has not followed through on this suggestive insight and, retreating into the self-intoxicated perspective that has become his trademark, has done little to further our understanding of the cultural boomerang or to return his own circumstances to that considerable phenomenon.

In this regard, *The Enigma of Arrival* represents a heartening advance over his previous nine books of nonfiction. Describing himself for the first time as a metropolitan, he looks back remorsefully at his obliviousness—as a callow would-be writer of eighteen—to the immense subject that lay all around him, a subject that could have been his own. Here, finally, he betrays hints of a more open, generous fascination with London's multicultural character. But it is a response he cannot sustain, as he withdraws into the security of his customary racial condescension towards those arrivants who have been pulled from the periphery to the metropolis:

> Because in 1950 in London I was at the beginning of that great movement of peoples which was to take place in the second half of the twentieth century—a movement and a cultural mixing greater than the peopling of the United States, which was essentially a movement of Europeans to the New World. This was a movement between all the continents. . . . Cities like London were to change. They were to cease being more or less national cities; they were to become cities of the world, modern-day Romes, establishing in the eyes of islanders like me and people even more remote in language and culture the pattern of what great cities should be. They were to be cities visited for learning and elegant goods and manners and freedom by all the barbarian peoples of the globe—people of forest and desert, Arabs, Africans, Malays.[57]

These sentences bespeak a rift in Naipaul, for a tolerance of diversity does not sit easily with him. He exhibits, in turn, a fascination with the metropolitan phenomenon of cultural mixing and an abhorrence for the same: in the end, the loathing that triumphs with his sardonic insinuation that mixing brings the barbarians. "Islanders like me" is the pivotal phrase in the passage. By tacitly designating himself a former barbarian, he travels out of range of reproof, his ethnic and geographical background once more licensing him to invoke "barbarian" for the purposes of racial slander and to do so with a directness that few white Westerners—even archconservatives—would dare, at least in print. Not that Naipaul is given to taking risks. He provides here a pat performance of the Third World Against Itself by someone secure both in his Third World credentials and in the knowledge that his words delight a ready audience in the metropolis, making those holding the center more secure in their presumptions of centrality. "All the barbarian peoples of the globe": at such moments, far from being set adrift, Naipaul seems quite safely anchored by a metropolitan way of seeing to a metropolitan audience.

Instead of complicating his values, Naipaul's longstanding experience of London's multicultural society has encouraged him, bolstered by a considerable reputation, to assert a unitary notion of civilization. Drawing a mental moat around the metropole, he has declared everything inside, Civilization; everything outside, Bush. This crudely binary division of societies mars his thought: "[My vision] came from living in the bush. It came from a fear of being swallowed up by the bush, a fear of the people of the bush, and it's a fear I haven't altogether lost. They are the enemies of the civilization which I cherish."[58] Such talk of fear and marginality, heard from another angle, resonates with the tones of privilege and metropolitan centrality, that is, with the assurance of someone confident that the might of the civilization is banked up behind him. Shiva Naipaul, even more extravagantly, played off his self-characterization as someone alienated everywhere, and achieved an almost pathological metamorphosis of his relative privilege into an expression of victimization. Suppressing his relation to London, Shiva was apt to caricature the postcolonial Third World by melding racial slander with bottomless self-pity: "A new marginality has been thrust upon people like myself by the assorted wogdoms that have come into being during the last twenty-five years—those penitential states of mind that are equated with 'liberation.' Marginality is sad. But, in my case, it is a sadness beyond my control."[59]

V. S. Naipaul's failure to contextualize his marginality by assessing his relations to the British capital has the effect of scaling down the advantage he draws from his metropolitan position and also of segregating him unduly from an immigrant tradition and a literary one, both associated with London as a metropolis. It would be profitable to ponder those intertwined traditions by adapting Perry Anderson's, Raymond Williams's, and Paul Gilroy's analyses of immigrant contributions to the creation of British metropolitan culture.[60] This would entail tracing how, even as—in Williams's words—the intellectual contributions of European immigrants to Britain between the wars "began in isolation and exposure [and] ended, at many levels, in an establishment," so, too, the post–World War II black immigrants have begun to reshape British culture and, in the specific domain of literature, have started digging a grave for the venerable assumption that "British writer" is an ethnically specific designation.[61] Most of these authors, unlike Naipaul, are not scandalized by the pronoun *we* and identify themselves with the struggles of first-, second-, and earlier-generation black residents in Britain to shake off the stigma of being termed "immigrants" and "New Commonwealth" people, euphemisms that testify to the legislators' calculated disowning of black Britons. The irony here ought not to be missed: Naipaul, secure, esteemed, and integrated into the high culture of metropolitan England, asserting his homelessness, while considerable numbers of genuinely disowned people battle to be acknowledged as legitimate members of the society he is at liberty to reject rhetorically, although he depends on it in every way.

2

Naipaul and the
Traditions of Travel

It's hard to conceive of, say, an Indian Paul Theroux becoming
obsessed with the railways of the United States, or a black African
Karen Blixen heading for Scandinavia.

Salman Rushdie, "Adventures and Epics"

Travel and travellers are two things I loathe—and yet here I am, all
set to tell the story of my expeditions.

Claude Lévi-Strauss, *Tristes Tropiques*

When Martin Amis asserts that Naipaul "remains our most exhilarating
explorer, with a corpus of travel writing that now surpasses that of D. H.
Lawrence and Graham Greene," his possessive "our" stakes a British
claim.[1] Yet, as we have seen, Naipaul himself reacts allergically to the
first-person plural and to any suggestion of his Britishness. Against both
he asserts his ostracism, his homelessness, and the honesty of his autonomy, suppressing in the process the complex participation of his work in
literary, political, and national traditions. In the ensuing chapter, I seek
to offset Naipaul's avoidance of questions of tradition by considering his
relation to the generic legacies of travel writing.

This endeavor requires that one consider his reaction to prior, particularly British, exemplars of the form. One needs to investigate, in addition, the political affiliations that emerge from his stance toward the
genre's shifting historical contexts and capacities. To what degree does
Naipaul dissociate himself from, or extend, the colonial legacy of the
discourse of travel? How, for instance, is one to interpret his impassioned rejection of the terms *colonialist* and *imperialist* for the purposes
of historical explanation?[2] Any attempt to probe Naipaul's relationship
to the colonial dimensions of travel writing is, moreover, inseparable
from the question of the historical moment at which he inherited the

genre. How is his stance toward the formal legacy affected by the fact that he writes at a time when the sun has set both on the British empire and, if one accepts the logic of Paul Fussell's *Abroad,* on "real" travel?[3] In other words, what is Naipaul's status as a postcolonial traveler who writes in the high era of tourism?

Naipaul and the Victorians

Opening Naipaul's first travelogue, *The Middle Passage,* one immediately enters the *Weltanschauung* of a secular Hindu West Indian would-be-Victorian. Naipaul pronounces his opinions with a strident bravura and is obsessed with finding confirmation for his judgments in Victorian assertions about the West Indies. Before encountering a word from Naipaul, one has to cross two epigraphs from the most shrilly racist of Caribbean travel books, James Anthony Froude's *The English in the West Indies* (1887), and at one point Naipaul quotes Anthony Trollope's *The West Indies and the Spanish Main* (1859) approvingly five times over the course of three pages.[4] Together with Froude and Trollope, Charles Kingsley's *At Last: A Christmas in the West Indies* (1871) serves as the third major source of Victorian authority for the sentiments of *The Middle Passage.* Indeed, Naipaul is so set on "confirming" his observations by quoting from this trio that his travelogue becomes shrouded in an atmosphere of colonial atavism.

The effect of such rhetorical maneuvers is to support his contention that "no attitude in the West Indies is new" and, more dangerously, his insistence that the West Indies are permanently "half-made" societies, devoid of history and sealed against the possibility of change.[5] Trinidad he declares to be irrevocably "unimportant, uncreative, cynical," and he uses Trollope's yearning to see Jamaica dispatched to oblivion as the occasion to dismiss the region en masse: " 'If we could,' wrote Trollope, 'we would fain forget Jamaica altogether.' The West Indies, he might have said."[6]

To grasp more fully the origins and function of Naipaul's Victorian obsession, one has to understand his frame of mind in setting out on the seven-month Caribbean journey that produced *The Middle Passage.* One has to consider, too, the place of that book in the trajectory of his career. The idea that he attempt a nonfictional work on the West Indies was the brainchild of Dr. Eric Williams, prime minister at the time (1960) of newly independent Trinidad and Tobago. Not only did Williams arrange for government sponsorship, but he also launched Naipaul, who hitherto had only written fiction, on his career as a travel writer and journalist.

The Middle Passage is—despite sponsorship—a very unofficial-looking book. As it constituted Naipaul's first attempt at travel writing, Williams, unlike later publishers, was in no position to anticipate and therefore bank on a characteristically Naipaulian cast of responses. All he had to go on were the three volumes of fiction—*The Mystic Masseur, The Suffrage of Elvira,* and *Miguel Street*—that had appeared in the three years preceding the visit. They, however, would have provided a poor gauge of what was to come, because in branching out into nonfiction Naipaul departed from his old tone: the relentless negativity of *The Middle Passage* separates that volume (and the bulk of his subsequent writing) from the often empathetic satire of the earlier fiction.[7] Although *A House for Mr. Biswas* had been completed before Naipaul embarked on his return voyage to the Caribbean, the writing of the novel left its mark on *The Middle Passage.* For the journey was born of an immense fatigue, after the breakdown Naipaul suffered in bringing his epic novel to its conclusion.[8]

So Naipaul traveled back from England to the West Indies in a state of mental fragility and, moreover, apprehensive of the long-term imaginative consequences of diversifying from fiction into nonfiction. His sense of insecurity was exacerbated by his panic at the possibility of sinking back into "the void of non-achievement" which the West Indies had always symbolized for him.[9] To top it all, he had, at this stage, before the publication of *Biswas,* only a limited readership in Britain and the United States and remained uncertain of his potential audience. These, then, were the circumstances that helped produce the odd phenomenon of a West Indian, traveling home to his native land in 1961, deciding to route his narrative of that journey through the anachronistic, imperial accounts of the region furnished by Trollope, Froude, and Kingsley.

Emotionally and culturally, Naipaul's childhood had prepared him for a Victorian Britain that had long since passed. He never fully recovered from that chimera. Thus, when he speaks of being educated toward the Old World, the epithet *Old* takes on a particular resonance:

> Coming from a place like Trinidad, which I always felt existed on the edge of the world, far away from everything else, not only physically but also in terms of culture, I felt that I had to try very hard to rejoin the Old World.[10]

In his symptomatic phrasing, "rejoin" testifies to the ease with which he confuses the feeling that he *ought to have belonged* to the Old World with the illusion that he once did. And in fantasy, his bond is not to contemporary England, but to the bygone grandeur and cultural self-confidence of Victoria's empire.

In *The Middle Passage* it is precisely that Victorian tone of self-assurance that Naipaul strains after, through quotation and rhetorical echoes. As they are worked into *The Middle Passage,* Naipaul's invocations of the Victorians stand uninflected with irony and strategically stripped of historical distance. He is so set on asserting his ideological kinship with the Victorians that one could be forgiven from assuming that he had no other accounts to build on and, in particular, that there were no indigenous, anticolonial interpretations of West Indian cultural and political history.

This problem is brought to the fore by one of his invocations of Froude:

> The natural graces of life do not show themselves under such conditions. There has been no saint in the West Indies since Las Casas, no hero unless philonegro enthusiasm can make one out of Toussaint. There are no people there in the true sense of the word, with a character and purpose of their own.[11]

Naipaul never attempts to offset this and allied Victorian dismissals of the West Indies with alternative readings of the region's culture and history. Why, for instance, is he silent about the "philonegro enthusiasm" of C. L. R. James, who, in *The Black Jacobins,* celebrated Toussaint's brilliance in helping liberate Haiti from French, British, and Spanish imperialists?[12] Even more pointedly, why are the frequent invocations of Froude not at least played off against quotations from Froude's contemporary, the West Indian, J. J. Thomas, who in 1889 published a book-length rebuttal of *The English in the West Indies*? Ironically, some of the very cultural prejudices that Naipaul most admires in Froude had been challenged by Thomas seventy years earlier.[13] It is as if, in attempting to win himself an English audience through habits of Victorian association, Naipaul cannot risk jeopardizing the purity of his allegiance to the imperial vantage point and, concomitantly, the purity of his account of West Indian immutability.

As an Englishman by acculturation rather than by birth, Naipaul seems to feel the need to out-Anglicize the English, hence his reinvention of an archaic literary style of patriotic racism. In an encomium to "that mid-Victorian certainty" so apparent in *The West Indies and the Spanish Main,* Naipaul reflects enviously on Trollope's "unapologetic display of outrageous prejudices":

> Who today, discussing race relations, will begin a paragraph: "But to get back to our sable friends"? Who will suggest that America should take

over Cuba to put an end to the slave trade, and will end his argument: "On the whole I cannot see how Englishmen can refrain from sympathizing with the desire of the United States to become possessed of this fertile island"?[14]

Naipaul's indulgence of nineteenth-century racial prejudices and imperial ambitions surfaces prominently in his discussion of such stalwart Victorian subjects as "Negro idleness" and evolutionary backwardness.[15] He manages to vindicate Trollope's attack on "Negro idleness" on the grounds that he possessed "humanitarian" motives:

> Trollope arrived at his humanitarianism almost, it seems, through a contemplation of the unpleasant. His anger at this refusal to work is grounded not in racial feelings, but in his religious sense of duty and in his Civil Servant's sense of what helps to balance a budget.[16]

Thus Naipaul dissociates Trollope's "sense of duty" from its consequences for the empire's West Indian subjects and presents it as a legitimate value in its own right.

Naipaul does not stop at indulging Victorian prejudices; he assumes them as his own, to the point where, as Abrahams and Szwed have noted, he begins at times to sound like Trollope.[17] This tonal spillage from the Victorians to Naipaul is evident, for instance, in his account of the rivalry between Indian and black Trinidadians:

> 'The two races,' Froude observed in 1887, 'are more absolutely apart than the white and the black. The Asiatic insists the more on his superiority in the fear perhaps that if he did not the white might forget it.' Like monkeys pleading for evolution, each claiming to be whiter than the other, Indians and Negroes appeal to the unacknowledged white audience to see how much they despise one another.[18]

By way of the self-consciously Victorian trope of the evolving monkey, Naipaul blends his voice with Froude's as if the seventy-four years of Caribbean history that lie between *The English in the West Indies* and *The Middle Passage* were irrelevant.

But there is a more astonishing aspect to this passage. Naipaul himself is a Trinidadian Indian and hence, to use his own terms, among the monkeys "pleading for evolution." One might never have guessed from the ease with which he harmonizes his voice to Froude's that in the 1880s, the very decade when Froude was penning his anti-Indian poison, Naipaul's grandfather was being shipped from Uttar Pradesh to Trinidad as an indentured laborer. Naipaul's remarks thus throw into relief a dangerous rift in his attitude toward his own West Indian origins, as Naipaul alias Froude peers down at Naipaul alias evolving monkey.

Despite the intensity of the Victorian echoes, they cannot quite drown out the periodic note of autobiographical panic:

> The years I had spent abroad fell away and I could not be sure which was the reality in my life: the first eighteen years in Trinidad or the later years in England. I had never wanted to stay in Trinidad. When I was in the fourth form I wrote a vow on the endpaper of my Kennedy's *Revised Latin Primer* to leave within five years. I left after six; and for many years afterwards in England, falling asleep in bedsitters with the electric fire on, I had been awakened by the nightmare that I was back in tropical Trinidad. I had never examined this fear of Trinidad. I had never wished to.[19]

His ill-preparedness for the strains of returning renders *The Middle Passage* more than a neo-Victorian travelogue; it is also the personal record of an exorcism. But the link between the two should not be lost: the gesture of articulating his experiences through a Victorian tradition of travel is symptomatic of his need to rid himself of the West Indies by ventriloquizing an English identity.

Twenty-five years later, Naipaul himself came to reflect on the symptomatic confusions of *The Middle Passage*:

> I knew and was glamoured by the ideas of the metropolitan traveler, the man starting from Europe. It was the only kind of model I had; but—as a colonial among colonials who were very close to me—I could not be that kind of traveler, even though I might share that traveler's education and culture and have his feeling for adventure. Especially I was aware of not having a metropolitan audience to 'report back' to. The fight between my idea of the glamour of the travel-writer and the rawness of my nerves as a colonial traveling among colonials made for difficult writing. When, the traveling done, I went back to London with my notes and diaries, to do the writing, the problems were not resolved.[20]

This helps account for Naipaul's reliance on the Victorians as well as the outbursts of fury and the raw malice that, for the first time, enters his humor. They become measures of the difficulties he experiences in redefining, as a traveler, his relationship to the West Indies; they become indicative, likewise, of his struggle as a writer to locate and feel at home in an appropriate tone.

While observing that, for these reasons, Naipaul's elective affinity with an imperial vantage point peaked in *The Middle Passage,* one should recognize that the connection persisted, sometimes almost as overtly, in his later work. For instance, as I discuss in Chapter 4, Conrad's *Heart of Darkness*—a text that lies on the cusp between the Victorian and Edwardian eras, has proved a decisive presence in Naipaul's

African writings. In addition, it is fair to say that whether asserting his distance from literary traditions or aligning himself with them, Naipaul has continued to favor, as his measure, a British colonial lineage—from Sir Walter Ralegh to Graham Greene.

What he has continued to carry with him from the Victorian training ground of *The Middle Passage* is a tone of outrageous superiority that blends easily into racism. One hears it in his assertion that " 'prime Asiatic mind' doesn't say as much to me as 'dumb Asiatic mind' " and that "it takes a long time in India to come to the simple conclusion that, by God, these people are just extraordinary stupid."[21] In keeping with his line of abuse, he observes of the *bindi:* "The dot means: my head is empty."[22] The tone resurfaces in his insistence that Argentinians are "in fact living on a borrowed culture; they had created nothing; and when the British Empire that protected them withdrew, the whole thing just fell apart. It will not be put together again."[23] And his response to a lecturer at Uganda's Makerere University is redolent of the venerably imperial stance toward the *évolué:* "Those are the ones that frighten me. . . . He's carrying a book. The ones that carry books scare the hell out of me, man."[24]

Nor can one ignore the timing of some of these provocations. In 1958, a year marked by a surge of physical and political brutality against West Indian immigrants in Britain (indeed, the year of the Notting Hill riots), Naipaul's contribution to the nation's racial mood included: "[T]here will soon be two million Jamaicans. It is hard to see what anyone [in Britain] can do except eat more Jamaican bananas without complaining. And perhaps—who knows?—a banana a day will keep the Jamaican away."[25] Twenty-three years later, in 1981, he simultaneously promoted *Among the Believers* and capitalized on the anti-Arab hysteria that followed the Iranian Revolution and the hostage crisis by declaring: "I'm interested in civilizations. If Arabs piss on my doorstep in South Kensington, I can't *not* notice. It's silly to pretend they're not barbarians."[26] As the counterpointing of civilizations and pissing Arabs makes obvious, Naipaul's aim here is not to target individuals but to add his trendy impugnment of an entire civilization on the evidence of isolated public urinations. Such remarks point up the inaccuracy of claims, like Conor Cruise O'Brien's, that "there is no trace of a racialist bias in Naipaul."[27] In the decisiveness and scope of his racism, Naipaul concedes little to Trollope and Froude.

I have argued that Naipaul turned to the Victorians for several intersecting reasons. First, his colonial upbringing prepared him for a grandly imperial, romanticized England that was largely distilled from his nineteenth-century reading and his anachronistic schooling. Second, a cluster of insecurities—including his lack of an audience, his desire to purge himself of his West Indianness, and his image of writing as a fundamentally British vocation—prompted him to view literary tradition as a lifeline rather than (as later) the hangman's noose. At the time of writing *The Middle Passage,* his fear of exclusion overshadowed his fear of belonging. The third reason for his Victorian affiliation is more specific. Because of his own shaky identity, he envied Froude, Trollope, et al. their authorititive tone, the supreme imperial confidence that came, quite literally, from being on top of the world. It is this superior tone that Naipaul continues to emulate in his later writings. Finally, he admired the way the Victorians, unlike many of their twentieth-century successors, had turned travel writing into a vehicle for substantial political and moral commentary. The Victorians, Naipaul suggests, expected more from the genre than simply whimsical or bizarre adventures; their travel writers had also to be intensely opinionated about the places they visited.

This last affinity is pivotal, for on it balances one of the great contradictions in Naipaul's approach to travel writing: to take a society seriously has come, for him, to mean giving free rein to cultural and personal expressions of arrogance. That is, the depth of one's engagement with a country can be read off the certainty with which one dismisses it.

Naipaul and the Georgians

Naipaul displays significantly less tolerance toward the Georgian travel writers of the 1930s than toward the Victorians. His stance here is complex—a mixture of legitimate criticism and a tendency to exaggerate his own extratraditionalism. Indeed, while he sought to quote his way toward a Victorian ancestry, in responding to the Georgians he demonstrates his later, more durable fixation with seeming an oddity unaccommodated by tradition.

In 1968, Naipaul travelled to Antibes to research an essay he was devising on Graham Greene for *The Daily Telegraph Magazine.* His encounters with Greene evince a modicum of fellow feeling. Naipaul recalls that, when setting out as a writer, he had read Greene in bulk. He shares Greene's impatience with the claustral insularity of post-WW II English writing and one senses his guarded empathy with the older man's fidelity to "the larger movements of events," with his desire (like Naipaul's, achieved under Conrad's influence) to "remain committed to the whole world."[28]

Yet in contrast to the imperial purposefulness of Froude and Trollope, and in contrast to his own earnest sense of his travels as "missions," Naipaul ultimately finds the methods and assumptions of a writer like Graham Greene both trivial and blinkered. Naipaul has, on several occasions, spoken slightingly of the kind of expatriate travel writer who flourished best between the wars, producing a literature that "moves out of one protected, enclosed world and sets itself abroad, pretends it is having adventures and fails to see that it has assumed such security for itself."[29] He thus seeks to distinguish between writers (including himself) who derive from weak, unstable societies and those, like Greene and Waugh, who "walk around the world without ever wondering why they can do it and others can't."[30] His own travel, he contends, is distinctive because it is psychologically more perilous and concomitantly more serious.

How accurate are these criticisms, and what light do they shed on Naipaul's own conception of the genre's possibilities and responsibilities? To approach these questions requires that one consider the crucial position of the Georgians in the trajectory of British travel writing and, thereby, the reasons why Naipaul would single them out for the purposes of contrastive self-definition. For in Naipaul's dissociation of himself from Greene and company one discerns, on the one hand, a justifiable impatience with the sheltered risk-taking and self-involvement of many Georgian travelers and, on the other hand, Naipaul's reflex insistence on exaggerating his displacement from tradition and characterizing himself as a uniquely embattled writer. It is imperative to keep both these dimensions of his relationship to the Georgians in play.

During the era between the wars, and particularly during the 1930s, travel writing grew in stature and popularity to the point where, as Samuel Hynes has argued, it overshadowed other prose genres.[31] The revival in the genre's standing that began with figures like Norman Douglas, D. H. Lawrence, and Aldous Huxley, peaked with the succeeding generation of Greene, Byron, Fleming, and Waugh. Opportunities for travel had expanded between the wars, and a literary generation's wanderlust was aroused by the recent privations of World War I, whether experienced in the trenches or through a claustral, garrisoned, rationed life back in Britain. The Depression, dampened by a sodden climate, added to the seductiveness of warmer parts. After World War I, moreover, borders were still relatively porous, and travel cheap.

Although the adventurers of the thirties exercised a privileged mobility that was enabled by empire (and often, by an Oxbridge background), they did not attempt nearly as conscientiously as Froude and Trollope to

legitimate the imperial endeavor. More commonly, they sought to escape a civilization that seemed mechanistic and soulless and to have
come adrift from the causes of progress and power. In an atmosphere of
national apprehension and faltering imperial resolution, travel writing
tended to become more self-absorbed, inward, capricious, and drained
of the element of missionary purpose that Naipaul recognized and admired in some of the Victorians. Naipaul's intolerance toward this shift
in the focus of travel writing is understandable, for whatever else his
travelogues undertake, they do not chronicle escapism of the global
playground sort. However, as a consequence, he ends up being more
indulgent of the decisive racism of Froude and Trollope than of the
indecisive bohemian wanderlust of the Georgians.

A sense of why Naipaul derides the literary adventurers of the thirties can be best achieved through a brief consideration of Fussell's
Abroad, an account of travel writing between the wars. Fussell's peculiar book is useful here for several reasons. Written in a popular prose,
it has proved influential not just in characterizing one era of travel
writing but in attempting to define that era as the last great literary
flowering of the form before it was trampled beneath the surge of
tourism. Precisely because Fussell is nostalgic for the thirties and emotionally involved in the era's "spirit of adventure," his account throws
into relief some of the legitimate aspects to Naipaul's quarrel with the
travelers of that period.

Fussell identifies so completely with the spirit of the travel writers of
the twenties and thirties that he is apt to idealize their motives and to
equate, with undue rigidity, their formal predilections with the generic
requirements of the travel book in its "pure" state. On this view, the
genre should be whimsical, romantic, irreverent, eccentric, superficially
enthralled by the "primitive," scathing of industrial societies, and disdainful of politics. Fussell's tone is elegiac (he speaks, for instance, of
the "pleasant relics of this lost age of travel"), and his intolerance of
tourism profound.[32]

Fussell isolates a Georgian variant of a romantic conception of travel
and elevates, unquestioningly, the values it esteemed. Thus the interwar
period, which saw a late variant of a particular historical tendency in the
genre, becomes frozen for Fussell as *the* age of travel, while prior and
subsequent experiments in the form—experiments engaged in under the
pressures of quite different social values and historical contexts—are
derogated as impure. Yet, remarkably, he manages to do so without
reference to the imperial prerogative that facilitated interwar travel.
Many of the regions Waugh and company visited were under British

sway; others were not. But in nearly all instances, the footloose cocki-
ness common among Fussell's travelers was backed by a combination of
male class privilege and Britain's global authority.

Because of this blind spot in Fussell's analysis, it is not surprising that
the "discovered" or exotic peoples only appear on stage to assume bit
parts in a European pastoral. The single instance where Fussell entertains a speculative, "native" point of view deserves a full context:

> . . . travel books are not merely displaced quest romances. They are also
> displaced pastoral romances. If William Empson is right to define tradi-
> tional pastoral as a mode of presentation implying "a beautiful relation
> between rich and poor," then pastoral is a powerful element in most travel
> books, for, unless he's a *Wandervogel* or similar kind of layabout (few of
> whom write books), the traveler is almost always richer and freer than
> those he's among. He is both a plutocrat *pro tem* and the sort of plutocrat
> the natives don't mind having around.[33]

Fussell proceeds by taking for granted that "the cash nexus" between
traveler and "native" is "a beautiful relation" and by lyricizing interwar
travelers' frequent pursuit of the Golden Age.[34]

The interwar travelers whom Fussell extolls were, in a sense, the
obvious figures for Naipaul to define himself against. As the allure and
prominence of the genre declined in Britain during the forties and fifties,
the thirties provided him with the most authoritative recent examples of
high-profile travel literature. Furthermore, because on several fundamental points the mood of thirties travel writing did differ from his own,
he could invoke it to sharpen the image of his extratraditionalism.

Among the most obvious of these differences is the absence of the
pastoral reflex that marks many of the interwar travelogues. Naipaul's
skepticism toward such nostalgia for "unspoiled" places surfaces on the
final page of *In a Free State*, one of his bleakest books.[35] There he
recounts how, touring the pyramids, he was prompted by an ancient
artist's rendition of the Nile to treat skeptically the idea of a modern fall
from a more innocent past. In general, Naipaul does not admit any
remedial, purer realm outside the West in space or time and is unable to
harbor dreams of an idealized organic society. He is a stranger to the
diverse disillusionments with the industrial, "mechanistic" North that
inform the travel writings of Huxley, Douglas, and Lawrence, and thereafter Greene and Waugh as well. Where Greene was apt to hymn Liberian or Mexican pastoral, Naipaul prefers to see unliterary peasants
enveloped by a backwardness without prospects. When the word *primitive* occurs in his travel writings, it does so, not in the context of a last-

gasp romantic desire to salvage a purer past, but as a straightforward term of abuse.

Relative to most of the interwar travelers, Naipaul is, then, positively unromantic about non-Western societies and more hesitant to criticize any aspect of Western cultures. But he can also legitimately set himself apart in terms of the motives for his travels. He does not journey to escape; there are no signs of him seeking to swap smoggy gloom for sun, boredom for adventure, a workaday world for sumptuous freedoms. His opinion that "travelling is often only glamorous in retrospect" is a familiar one.[36] However, I know of no other author equally committed to travel who regards his or her ventures, even retrospectively, with such conscientious displeasure.

Naipaul does not engage in the customary rewriting of the traveler's misfortune as an exercise in recreational masochism. He will often lament having undertaken a journey and become lastingly angry with the countries he visits—as if they had imposed themselves upon him. This antitraveling tendency can be traced back to the early pages of his first travel book, *The Middle Passage:* "As soon as the Francisco Bobadilla had touched the quay, ship's side against rubber bumpers, I began to feel all my old fear of Trinidad. I did not want to stay."[37] He stays but cannot quell his dislike for the journey and the region. His next trip, to India, produced similar regrets. He recalls wishing "that Bombay was only another port such as those we had touched on the journey, a port that the freighter passenger might explore or reject."[38] He arrives at the conclusion that the "journey ought not to have been made; it has broken my life in two."[39] And again, his judgment of the society becomes entangled with his personal discomfort: "You mustn't go. You mustn't," he urged on returning from that second voyage, "India is a dead country."[40] Other destinations fare little better: "Earlier this year I was in the Congo—it's not a journey I recommend."[41]

Impatient with the "spirit of adventure" and apparently scornful of the places he visits, why does Naipaul travel? In the previous chapter I considered the questionably self-serving dimensions to one of the responses he gives—that he is a genetic nomad. A second response emerges in the course of one of his attacks on Greene and his peers:

> They're travelers in a world that's been made safe for them by empire. They write books in which they can imagine the Europeanness of their characters against the native background. The primary difference between my travel and theirs is that while they travel for the picturesque, I'm *desperately* concerned about the countries I'm in.[42]

On other occasions, likewise, Naipaul insists that his travel writings are distinctive because of their seriousness, their concern.[43] Compared to the Georgians, they do appear serious insofar as their freight of political commentary is considerably weightier than anything Waugh, Norman, or Byron took on board. It seems improbable, moreover, that Naipaul's approach would be countenanced by Fussell, as politics, in his view, corrupts the form.

However, one should not confuse political interest with concern nor lose sight of the fact that, as the above quote indicates, Naipaul can use legitimate criticism of the interwar travelers to deflect attention from his own advantaged circumstances. If irreverant Georgian adventurers took their risks in a world made safe for them by empire, aren't Naipaul's more earnest, more political travel writings supported by a legacy of colonial attitudes that he can assume are already in place? In other words, by calling into question the "rebelliousness" of Greene and company and by then distancing himself from that lineage, Naipaul creates an exaggerated image of himself as a risk taker who operates outside the protective fence of imperial assumptions. Yet, while his formal responses to the genre do distinguish him from the interwar set, in ideological terms he travels armed with cultural and racial attitudes that have a long, imperial history in British-based travel writing and beyond.

This ulterior dimension to Naipaul's critique of the Georgians is evident in his choice of phrase: "[T]hey can imagine the Europeanness of their characters against the native background." Now manifestly, in ethnic terms, Naipaul cannot speak of his Europeanness, but this obscures the manner in which, ideologically, his vantage point is quite Eurocentric. Thus his critique of the interwar travelers distracts attention from the common ground that he shares with them as a British-based visitor who refracts the global margins through a national tradition of travel.

So despite the origins of their author, none of Naipaul's travelogues reverses the dominant direction of what, from a Western point of view, remains a centrifugal genre. His initial journey, undertaken at eighteen in 1950, was indeed from the known colony to the unknown metropolis, but that was to prove atypical in its trajectory, for Naipaul as for travel writers in general. From then on, England was no longer to be his destination, but the fixed, assumed, seldom described point of his departures and returns. And because he soon adjusted himself to a predominantly metropolitan perspective, he has contributed little to the tradition of inverted travelogues produced by Third Worlders or colonial subjects who have sought to write up the foreign peculiarities of Britain and the United States. One has only to contrast the angle of vision and cultural assumptions of any of Naipaul's travel writings with what one finds in Ham Mukasa's *Sir Apolo Kagwa Discovers Britain,* John Pepper Clark's *America, Their America,* or the lineage of Arab writing about Europe documented by Ibrahim Abu-Lughod to realize the limitations of any approach to Naipaul that treats him as alienated from a Eurocentric, and more precisely British, tradition of travel.[44]

Naipaul and Post–World War II Travel

I have sought thus far to provide a discursive context for Naipaul's travel writing by considering his reaction to earlier British exemplars of the form. In so doing, I have explored the literary and political implications of the Victorian strains in his approach to the genre and, in addition, his complex hostility toward the Georgians. But to situate his travel writings adequately, one has to come to terms with the altered historical circumstances in which he has operated. For, along with a substantial group of post–World War II English-speaking travel writers—among whom one would rank Eric Newby, Jonathan Raban, Bruce Chatwin, Shiva Naipaul, Edward Hoagland, Paul Theroux, Colin Thubron, Peter Matthiessen, Patrick Marnham, Martha Gellhorn, Jan Morris, and Patrick Leigh Fermor—Naipaul has helped rehabilitate the genre while, at the same time, altering it to accommodate the amplitude of the global changes since the rush of travel literature during the thirties. Specifically, Naipaul and the others now travel in a world that is post–World War II and postcolonial and belongs to the high age of tourism.

In seeking to assess the effect of these altered circumstances on Naipaul's adaptation of the genre, one can turn quite appropriately to 1945 and Evelyn Waugh for a pronouncement on the prospects for a post–World War II literature of travel. If in the thirties Waugh had hungered for adventure, by the end of World War II he looked back with remorse and a sense of finality at the peripatetic youth that he shared with Greene, Byron, and Fleming:

> Had we known, we might have lingered with 'Palinurus'; had we known that all that seeming-solid, patiently built, gorgeously ornamented structure of Western life was to melt overnight like an ice-castle, leaving only a puddle of mud; had we known that man was even then leaving his post. Instead we set off on our various stern roads; I to the Tropics and the Arctic, with the belief that barbarism was a dodo to be stalked with a pinch of salt. . . . We have most of us marched and made camp since then, gone hungry and thirsty, lived where pistols flourished and fired. At the

time it seemed an ordeal, an initiation into manhood. . . . My own travelling days are over, and I do not expect to see many travel books in the
future. When I was a reviewer, they used, I remember, to appear in
batches of four or five a week cram-full of charm and wit and enlarged
Leica snapshots. There is no room for tourists in a world of 'displaced
persons.' Never again, I suppose, shall we land on foreign soil with a letter
of credit and a passport (itself the first faint shadow of the great cloud that
envelops us) and feel the world wide open before us. . . . The very young,
perhaps, may set out like the *Wandervogels* of the Weimar period; lean,
lawless, aimless couples with rucksacks, joining the great army of men and
women without papers, without official existence, the refugees and desert-
ers, who drift everywhere today between the barbed wire. I shall not, by
my own wish, be among them.[45]

Waugh's words are spoken out of the public exhaustion of a half-
destroyed Europe and the personal fatigue of an aging, increasingly
stay-at-home writer. His is a classic end-of-an-era pronouncement, sig-
naling the death of a secure notion of civilization and anticipating that
the travel literature that ventured out from that "seeming-solid structure
of Western life" would necessarily also crumble away. Thus for Waugh,
there is something symbiotic about the strength of the civilization and its
capacity to generate travel writing. The double decline that he foresees
stems in part from Europe's acknowledgment of its own capacity for
"barbarism," as if the travel genre could only flourish in circumstances
where there is a clearcut split between civilized home and barbarous
abroad. Waugh rebukes himself and his generation for the naïveté of this
assumption: Their conception of "barbarism" as exotic and remote
blinded them to its presence as an adjacent, imminent threat.

But there is a second related reason why Waugh overhastily predicted
the demise of travel literature: his sense that travel is incongruous "in a
world of 'displaced persons.' " He seems to imply that in the post–World
War II context of mass statelessness, the traveler becomes an embarrassing figure whose movements parody that suddenly widespread mobility
that is freedom's antithesis.

Yet, contrary to Waugh's expectations, the travel genre has recovered
since World War II, particularly since the sixties. In so doing, the form
has accommodated both the loss of Western civilization's sense of invul-
nerability and the increasing normality of human displacement. Naipaul
has not only proved a pivotal figure in the genre's post–World War II
revival, but because of his fixation with the issues of civilization and
displacement, he has come to assume a symptomatic centrality. He has
succeeded in admitting into his travel writings something like Waugh's

sense of the precariousness of Western civilization, though for quite different historical reasons and without compromising on his conviction that the West is the repository of civilized values. The historical and cultural differences between the two writers' perceptions of Western vulnerability are critical: Waugh lived through Europe's self-subversion; Naipaul grew up in Trinidad with the sensation that civilization was foreign and far-off. He has spoken of how, despite his long residence in England, he remains haunted by the fear of Western civilization as vulnerable to the predations of the encroaching bush. Where for Waugh European fascism was the new internal barbarism, Naipaul locates the threats to civilization in the impoverished nations of the postcolonial world. And he does so in a way that can sometimes seem anachronistically imperial—as if Europe's experience of its own destructive powers had not begun to complicate the terms of travel between civilization and barbarism.

Ironically, Waugh's sense of the traveler as superannuated by the massing of "displaced persons" can be read as an index of how little he could anticipate the post–World War II emergence of a travel writer like Naipaul, whose life is marked by the expanded mobility and multiple affiliations that have become increasingly ubiquitous metropolitan conditions. Nor, from the vantage point of 1945, could Waugh have anticipated how someone like Naipaul was to rework the travel genre so as to place at its thematic fulcrum the syncretic and sometimes bewildered social identities that have emerged from the accelerated traffic in displaced people, commodities, and ideas.[46]

Adjusting to Tourism

I have suggested that Naipaul's travel writings contain a paradoxical and sometimes explosive mixture of rearguard imperialism along with a very contemporary response to the disorienting changes in the social fabric and cultural identities of the post–World War II, postcolonial era. Thus, in considering his relation to the traditions and shifting historical inclinations of travel writing, one has to balance an alertness to his attempts to redeem the old Eurocentric certitudes with an equal awareness of the manner in which, as a member of the postcolonial generation of travel writers, he has had to rethink the genre so as to absorb the altered relations between the metropolitan West and the new nations of the Third World.

From a travel writer's perspective, one the most pressing of these changes has been the incremental expansion of tourism. It has a special pertinence for Naipaul, given his ties to the tourist heartland of the Caribbean. One of the recurrent concerns of his Caribbean writings is the power of American tourism since World War II to reorient the region psychologically and economically away from Britain and toward the United States. Naipaul reflects, likewise, on tourism's erosion of indigenous cultural styles, such that what might have been deemed authentically West Indian now has, built into it, the touristic expectations of what constitutes that authenticity.

The relationship between cultural authenticity and cultural difference has emerged as a central issue in post–World War II travel writing, providing a thematic focus not just for Naipaul, but for figures as diverse as Theroux, Marnham, Chatwin, Hoagland, Morris, Shiva Naipaul, and Lévi-Strauss, as well as for critics and theorists of tourism like Dean MacCannell, Fussell, and Jean-Paul Dumont. If a primary motive of travel has been a quest for the experience of "real" difference, in the age of tourism, the traveler is increasingly exposed either to the manicured difference of the self-consciously exoticized or, at the other extreme, manageable difference, that is, a careful blend of the ambiences of home and abroad. Yet ironically, post–World War II travel writers' preoccupation with the decay of authenticity has helped revitalize the genre, sustaining it well beyond its projected death at the hands of tourism.

Whether it be Theroux in *The Great Railway Bazaar* or Lévi-Strauss in *Tristes Tropiques,* the commonest response to the decline in authenticity is to assume an unequivocally nostalgic posture toward the pretouristic era, when cultural difference had not been been blurred by the scale of cultural interpenetration. Indicative of this tendency is Lévi-Strauss's remark that he "should have liked to live in the age of *real* travel, when the spectacle on offer had not yet been blemished, contaminated, and confounded; then I could have seen Lahore not as I saw it, but as it appeared to Bernier, Tavernier, Manucci. . . ."[47] The phenomenon of cultural mixing could, of course, be portrayed in quite different terms; certain postmodernist thinkers, for instance, might register the changes with excitement, perceiving a rich proliferation of new syncretic cultural forms. But in post–World War II travel writing the prevailing tendency has been to reach for the imagery of contagion, diminution, and decline.

As one of the great chroniclers of decrepitude, Naipaul assumes a special and, in one sense, unusual importance here. He is obsessed with the issue of cultural mixing yet refuses to view it as a decline from a purer past; the pursuit of the vanishing is, to his mind, a sentimental exercise and an intolerable reason for traveling. He has cherished the image of a time when Britain was great, but abroad in the Third World he closes off both avenues to pleasure, impatient with nostalgic quests for traces of cultural authenticity and at the same time disliking the culturally hybrid present.

Naipaul assails in unsparing terms the preservationist impulse in contemporary travel literature. Reviewing Hamilton Basso's *A Quota of Seaweed*, he draws attention to the hypocritical, self-defeating dimensions of the phenomenon:

> Mr. Basso suggests that he is the last American to see the unspoiled Spain, the last white man to see the unspoiled natives. Soon, he tells us sadly, the American tourists will come, and all that is quaint and dark and unspoiled will be so no longer. No one despises the American tourist more than the American tourist; and Mr. Basso doesn't see that the straw-hatted, dark-glassed, camera-hung, bermuda-shorted American in the tropics, looking for calypso and safe kicks, has been primed and conditioned by scores of vapid professional writers like Mr. Basso himself.[48]

Naipaul is asking the unreflecting Basso to acknowledge that it is in the nature of his denunciations of tourism to feed the very industry he denounces. Indeed, one might suggest that the rhetoric of antitourism is one of the surest ploys for enticing tourists. It is a tradition continued by the current "Sophisticated Traveler" series in *The New York Times*—articles that are effectively literary advertisements, simultaneously dispatched to millions of readers, for solitary spots and uncorrupted, "authentic" cultures.

It follows that the relationship between tourism and antitourism that suffuses post–World War II travel writing functions less as an opposition than as a dialectic. The most useful point of departure for an understanding of this dialectic is provided by the sociologist Dean MacCannell, in *The Tourist: A New Theorist of the Leisure Class*.[49] The unorthodoxy of MacCannell's approach stems from his refusal of the standard evaluative distinction between the authentic (and endangered) traveler and the tourist, seeking rather to explain the dynamics of tourism as an institution, in its semiotic (and to a lesser extent) its economic aspects. Indeed, for MacCannell, theorists' uncritical participation in the language of authenticity is the crux of the problem. One of modernity's primary characteristics is its preoccupation with the increasing rarity of "true," "real," "original," "natural," and "authentic" objects and experiences. Tourism is symptomatic and constitutive of the inexhaustible quest for these attributes, a quest that is also a form of conquest.

By considering the relations among the three requisite elements for the social construction of a tourist attraction, namely, the tourist, the sight, and the marker, MacCannell describes the process of what he calls "sight sacralization."[50] A sight is isolated as special, as a "must," as a "real experience," as free from inauthenticity. Markers verifying this—on-sight and off-sight ones—proliferate around it: signposts, guides, postcards, effigies, advertisements, and, although MacCannell does not mention them specifically, travel books. Ironically, however, the very proliferation of pointers to the authentic precludes the place or object sustaining that aura. That is, in striving to make contact with the "real thing" tourists become participants in the self-subversive gestures of a staged authenticity, the act of veneration doubling as an act of devaluation.

MacCannell's analysis of the dynamics of tourism bears directly on Naipaul's impatience with Basso's contradictory gesture of disdaining tourists yet disseminating markers to "pure" sites, thereby helping keep alive the dialectical movement between authentication and the subversion of that announced authenticity. Naipaul himself avoids this deadlock; he rhapsodizes neither about "unknown" beaches nor about the overdetermined wonders of the Taj Mahal. His books are, if anything, bad for business, as he pretty much restricts himself to what MacCannell has termed "negative sight-seeing."

However, if Naipaul avoids playing into the hands of the tourist industry, I would contend that there remains a semiofficial dimension to his travel writing. This contention may be approached by way of Hans Magnus Enzensberger's essay "Tourists of the Revolution."[51] Enzensberger's subject is the type of radical Western tourist committed to reporting back positively on communism in the Eastern bloc. Such a figure has been in decline since the sixties as the East has become less isolated from the West and, concomitantly, as the number of Western defenders of the Soviet system has dwindled. The verdicts typical of this literature of radical tourism are largely framed in advance and delivered by people who purport to communicate the essence of the system yet live outside of it. Enzensberger is alert to the limitations of such a perspective:

> No one who returns from a sojourn in socialism is a genuine part of the process he tries to describe. Neither voluntary commitment nor the degree of solidarity with which one behaves, no propaganda action, no walk through the cane fields and schools, factories and mines, not to mention a few moments at the lectern or a quick handshake with the leader of the revolution, can deceive about the fact. The less the traveler understands this and the less he questions his own position, the greater and more

justified will be the animosity that the voyager into socialism encounters from the very onset—from both sides.[52]

Naipaul's travel writings have met with animosity from the people he describes partly because he has proved insufficiently self-conscious about the limitations of his visitor's perspective. Where Enzensberger's radical tourist reports back from across the East–West divide, Naipaul reports back from across the gulf separating North from South, but in both instances the writers are given to confirming prior views. The one's will to idealize is matched by the other's commitment to negative tourism; Naipaul's inability to empathize with local predicaments is almost as complete as some tourists of the revolution's capacity for blind identification. To be sure, the Soviet state's delegation system was a brazen style of sponsorship more direct and inhibiting than anything that contours Naipaul's judgments. Yet it would be misleading to focus only on official, internal sponsorship provided by the nation visited. Naipaul may be unofficial in relation to the countries he travels to, but he has come to assume a semiofficial status in relation to the British and American publications that, in furnishing him with advances, invest in the predictable ideological tenor of his responses. In the United States in particular there is a veritable network of publications, editors, and literary personalities who have collaboratively shored up his reputation: Joan Didion, Irving Howe, Elizabeth Hardwick, Michiko Kakutani, Mel Gussow, Hilton Kramer, Robert Boyers, and Conor Cruise O'Brien, all prominently placed in publications like *The New York Review of Books, The New York Times Book Review, The New Criterion, Salmagundi,* and *Dissent.*

The Middle Passage and Tourism

Given the Caribbean's status as a heartland of tourism, it is appropriate that *The Middle Passage* should contain Naipaul's most sustained reflections on that phenomenon, particularly in relation to the combined cultural consequences of tourism and emigration in the post–World War II era. This concern is made prominent from the outset of the book. The vessel that conveys him from Southampton to the West Indies, the *Francisco Bobadilla,* assumes an iconic significance in terms of his obsession with the enhanced global mobility experienced, though in utterly different ways, by the privileged and the underprivileged alike. The tourist and emigrant serve as his two poles of reference: traveling south from England, the ship carries first-class and tourist-class passengers whom it offloads in the West Indies, taking on board, in exchange, emigrants heading north to England. These two poles also come to express Naipaul's somewhat altered status: ten years earlier he himself had emigrated to England, but now, in his aloofness and separation by deck from the "immigrant-type West Indians," he is noticeably closer to the condition of the tourist.

Yet he does not fit the mold entirely. After seven months of travel in the West Indies, he closes his journey with a spell in a luxury hotel on Jamaica's north coast, the tourist strip of the island. He finds himself incapable of relaxing in the quarantined paradise: "I couldn't be a tourist in the West Indies, not after the journey I had made."[53] "It was as though one had driven out of Jamaica, as though, to find the West Indies of the tourist's ideal, one had had to leave the West Indies."[54]

However, in a peculiar way, Naipaul's antitourism fuses with his uncompromising hostility toward the region itself. His condemnation of the tourist society is harsher than his judgment of either the tourists or the inequities in North–South economic relations that have provoked tourism. That much is apparent when he decries the reorientation of calypso toward tourist tastes: "For this bastardization Trinidadians are as much to blame as anyone. Just as they take pleasure in their American modernity, so they take pleasure in the ideals of the tourist brochure."[55] He later pronounces, along similar lines, that "every poor country accepts tourism as an unavoidable degradation. None has gone so far as some of these West Indian islands, which in the name of tourism, are selling themselves into a new slavery."[56] His decision to see the problem only from the perspective of Caribbeans' self-bastardization and self-enslavement, while ignoring the lengthening shadow of American hegemony in the region, is indicative of his determination to interpret the problems of postcolonial nations as primarily self-inflicted rather than as substantially induced from without. Nor, given the roots of the West Indies in those people who (to recall Aimé Césaire's phrase) arrived as "nontourists of the triangular circuit," is his elected image of self-enslavement tasteful or historically apposite.[57]

Naipaul's position, then, emerges as an peculiar one. While he insists on exploring the underbelly of the Caribbean, which the tourists evade, he is sympathetic neither toward the indigenous cultures that are being eroded by tourism nor toward the new, Americanized cultural values for which tourism is a primary conduit. So ironically, while, on the one hand, he regrets "how strong and ineradicable the wish is, among the bongo islanders, to act up to the tourist image," on the other hand, it is not at all clear what to his mind this process damages, given his dismissiveness toward endemic cultural forms. As is often the case in Naipaul's travel books, one is left suspended between two categorical negatives, the old and the new, without any positive recommendations.

Even if he does explore dimensions of the West Indies that the tourist refuses to confront, Naipaul suffers from a version of the tourist's ailment. His future is not invested in the region, and he is free to treat it as a pseudoplace, severed from the world of substance to which he returns. Both the orthodox tourist and Naipaul locate the islands on the far side of reality, if for different reasons. For the former they represent a fantasy paradise, an ornamental retreat from the world of work and obligations, while for Naipaul the insubstantiality of the islands derives from their philistinism, etched as they are in his childhood memory as the antithesis of real culture.

Hence, ironically, traveling to the region where he is in the best position to overcome the limitations of the visitor's perspective, to declare confidently not just "I was there," but "I am from there," he feels the strongest need to undo that advantage by aligning himself with a British literary tradition of travel. For in his own mind, his identity as a West Indian is incompatible with the identity to which he truly aspires—that of the writer. And so, through his overdetermined dialogue with the Victorians, he attempts simultaneously to allude his way into a literary tradition and to disengage himself from the Caribbean. As he was to observe many years later: "[I]t was as if, then, having won through to a particular kind of fear, my relationship with my island had come to an end. Because after this I never found in myself any particular wish to go back."[58] *The Middle Passage* can thus be read as a threshold text in which affilliation to one tradition entails the exorcism of another. It is as if, to rid himself of the West Indies, he had first to face it and then to write it out of his system, thereby freeing himself to become a truly metropolitan writer. The book that emerges shares more affinities with the Georgian tradition of travel than Naipaul might care to admit, for ultimately *The Middle Passage* is most intelligible as a journey of rage into the *terra incognita* of the self.

3

At the Generic Crossroads: Travel Writing, Ethnography, and Autobiography

There is no foreign land; it is the traveller only that is foreign.
ROBERT LOUIS STEVENSON, *The Silverado Squatters*

I recognized my own instincts as a traveller, and was content to be myself, to be what I had always been, a looker.
V. S. NAIPAUL, *Finding the Centre*

With perfectly appropriate indecision, Edmund Leach once described Lévi-Strauss's *Tristes Tropiques* as an "autobiographical ethnographic travel book."[1] James Clifford, more broadly, has depicted travel writing as a "para-ethnographic" genre.[2] Manifestly, nothing in Naipaul's oeuvre is as professionally ethnographic as stretches of Lévi-Strauss's hybrid book; nor would Naipaul ever speak of himself as a purveyor of anthropological knowledge. However, the further one delves into his travel books, the more one recognizes affinities in his work to ethnographic modes, particularly those variants of ethnography that have grown more self-consciously accommodating to the personal. The importance of these affinities is accentuated by the fact that Naipaul's lines of travel follow the well-worn anthropological routes from Europe to the so-called traditional or primitive societies of the former colonies. "The West," S. P. Mohanty quips ruefully, "possesses a history and a sociology, the Third World merely an anthropology."[3] Indeed, the pervasive image of Naipaul as a neutral explainer of non-Western cultures to Western audiences has sometimes prompted critics to view him as a relative of the native informant or indigenous ethnographer.[4]

Because he attempts to anatomize the cultures he visits (rather than simply embarking on an adventure), there are few travel writers who invoke the discourses of cultural representation in as sustained or earnest a fashion. Conversely, Naipaul has often remarked that he views travel less as a series of interludes in his life than as an autobiographically motivated enactment of his origins and identity.[5] Hence, most of what one learns of his life is gleaned from his travel narratives, in transit, as it were, rather than within the confines of formal autobiography.

To come to terms with the rhetoric and political allegiances of Naipaul's travel writings, one should therefore complement historical inquiry into his imperial affinities and his status as a postcolonial voyager with an investigation into the formal capacities of the travel genre. Such an inquiry can, I believe, best be launched from recent ethnographic debate. From that basis one can proceed to analyze virtually any of Naipaul's travel writings; those I have elected to focus on include *India: A Wounded Civilization* (1977), *Among the Believers* (1981), "The Crocodiles of Yamoussoukro" (1984), and in particular, Naipaul's first Indian book, *An Area of Darkness* (1964).

Of crucial concern here is the status of travel literature as a versatile form that entertains both ethnographic and autobiographical possibilities. Because the genre admits these rival centers of authority, travel writers are repeatedly confronted with the choice between analyzing the society surveyed and foregrounding their authorial personalities. The presence of two competing foci of interest makes travel literature generically unstable, but it also grants the writer radically different styles of authority. Naipaul deploys this versatility to great advantage. Reminiscing on Trinidadian carnival, for instance, he remarks:

> I have never cared for dressing up or 'jumping up' in the streets, and Carnival in Trinidad has always depressed me. This year, too, the 'military' bands were not so funny: they vividly recalled the photographs of the tragic absurdities in the Congo. With this Carnival depression I flew north over the Caribbean.[6]

Here Naipaul chooses to subordinate the phenomenon of carnival to a narrative focus on his own personality—his moods, his movements, his memories. The thrust of his rejection of carnival is more temperamental than analytical; it relies, for its authority, on an emotional rapport between reader and traveler.

In a disquisition on the "underdeveloped ego" of the Indian, Naipaul deploys a markedly different rhetoric:

> Caste and clan are more than brotherhoods; they define the individual completely. The individual is never on his own; he is always fundamentally a member of his group, with a complex apparatus of rules, rituals, taboos.

> Every detail of behaviour is regulated—the bowels to be cleared before
> breakfast and never after, for instance, the left hand and not the right to be
> used for intimate sexual contact, and so on. Relationships are codified.[7]

Here Naipaul the moody traveler is withheld from view and Indian
cultural practices are brought center-stage. He comes closer to a style of
ethnography: the language is unemotive, diagnostic, nonnarrative, and
he strives to sound formal and impartial.

The rhetorical strategies in these passages could readily have been
inverted. One can imagine Naipaul providing a more distanced account
of Trinidadian carnival as a cultural practice, suppressing his own opinionated presence and deploying the distant tones of the ethnomusicolo-
gist. Conversely, one can picture Naipaul criticizing the "underdeveloped ego" that the extended family and caste system putatively generate
but staging his critique as an autobiographical experience of exasperation at a meal or on a train. In that case, his cultural observations would
function as an expression of his personality or at least exist in a state of
tension with it. The facility with which Naipaul moves between these
rival styles of authority helps him keep in play the image of himself as
someone so personally concerned about Third World societies that he is
unable to achieve emotional distance from them, as well as the inverse
portrait of himself as an aloof, objective analyst of those same societies.

To date, inquiry into the literature of travel remains spare, especially
on the question of the genre's mixed styles of authority. The only sustained theoretical attempts to address such issues have arisen, ironically,
out of the decay of ethnographic authority in the postcolonial era. Particularly in the United States, anthropology's disciplinary soul-searching
has grown more intense since the 1960s; some of this has proved self-
serving, some genuinely self-critical. Either way, the discipline's frenzied interrogation of its formal assumptions has helped bring to the fore
insights that bear directly on the rhetorical strategies of a travel writer of
Naipaul's ilk.

Particularly pertinent is the way anthropological doubt has expanded
inquiry into issues of textuality and power: the distribution of the authority to represent non-Western cultures; the generic conventions that buoy
up that authority; the apportioning of interest between the personality
of the observer and the culture of the observed; and the rhetorical
strategies for transforming fieldwork into text, that is, the shift from
looking down at a society to writing it up. Furthermore, if one places
Naipaul's nonfiction alongside some of the postcolonial ethnographic
experiments, it becomes possible to discern a generic affinity between a

more assertive travel literature and a more tentative, less stable, social science, in other words between travel writing that aspires to self-confident cultural description and ethnography awakening to the rhetoric and empirical limitations of its customary methodologies.

Travel and Self-Reflexive Ethnography

"The church of anthropology is in trouble," Eric Wolf has opined. "The sacraments have been stolen. People have looked behind the altar and found nothing there."[8] Others have spoken of "the disintegration of 'Man' as *telos* for a whole discipline" or of the deep exhaustion of anthropological paradigms.[9] A small minority of cultural anthropologists have responded to their disciplinary anxieties by experimenting at the primary level with new modes of writing about cultures. More commonly, they have embarked on the endeavor of shaping alternative critical approaches for analyzing the methodological assumptions that circumscribe the composition of an ethnography.[10]

The loosening of ethnographic conventions since the 1960s and a correspondent burgeoning textual self-consciousness get foregrounded in the work of, amongst others, Renato Rosaldo, Vincent Crapanzano, Michael Fischer, George Marcus, Deborah Gordon, Marc Manganaro, Paul Rabinow, Steve Webster, James Clifford, and Johannes Fabian, the last three being, in their distinctive ways, the most incisive. It is important to observe that this recently prominent fascination with ethnography's formal predicaments is a revitalized concern rather than a wholly novel one: versions of the current anxieties have shadowed earlier figures from Bronislaw Malinowski to Michel Leiris. But the unraveling of the discipline's self-assurance has been hastened by global decolonization, by the growth of interest in linguistic or discourse theorists (notably Ferdinand de Saussure and Mikhail Bakhtin), and by a line of influence running from Paul Ricoeur through Clifford Geertz to figures like Vincent Crapanzano and Paul Rabinow.[11]

It is Webster who articulates most crisply the critical feature of this generic fracturing, namely, the convergence of aesthetic and social scientific conceptions of culture.[12] This development, I would tender, assumes a special salience for travel literature, for it admits an ethnographic rapprochement with both travel writing and autobiography, such that hitherto suppressed links among these nonfictional forms can be addressed more openly. Rabinow marks the coordinates of this generic confluence most precisely in the introduction to his *Reflections on Field-work in Morocco,* where, invoking Ricoeur, he describes the ambition of his text as "the comprehension of the self by the detour of the comprehension of the other."[13] Associations from all three tributary genres converge in Rabinow's phrase: the graphic self of autobiography, the process of travel, and the graphic "other" of ethnography. While Rabinow's subsequent evocation of his Moroccan trip shows scant evidence that this more personalized writing, on its own, can either democratize or decolonize the ethnographic form, his prefatory remarks do give focus to an alternative approach. For the text indulges—rather than suppressing in the name of social science—autobiographical and traveler's insights.

So, on the one flank, expanded curiosity about the textual dimensions of ethnography—the gestures of the writing self—throws into relief areas of possible intersection with autobiography.[14] On the other flank, ethnography and travel writing have also shown signs of convergence. This latter development assumes unusual historical interest because anthropology gathered force as a social scientific endeavor in the early twentieth century partly by defining itself *against* amateur travel writing, which, along with the reports of colonial officials and missionaries, had theretofore provided a significant basis for Western knowledge about non-Western cultures.[15] It would be inaccurate to imply that in the nineteenth century no distinctions existed between travelogues and cultural descriptions with more "scientific" ambitions, for there were textual pointers (for example, the presence of indices and footnotes) to different levels of scholarly intent. However, the distinction was considerably firmed up once anthropology sought to secure its credentials as a social science by segregating itself from travel writing and other less disciplined (in both senses) modes of cultural representation through the formalizing of institutional and stylistic constraints.

As Webster has observed, the generic conventions of ethnography began to solidify in the 1920s with the publication of key texts by Malinowski and Radcliffe-Brown.[16] At this time, in the wake of World War I, the British intellectual climate was, to a noteworthy degree, polarized into a radical skepticism, on one hand, and an emerging logical positivism. This helped sharpen the divide between scientific and nonscientific discourses. British anthropologists, wishing to win admission for their fledgling discipline into the sciences, came under pressure to purge their writing of rhetorical conventions that might smack of amateurism or subjective impressionism. At the institutional level, fieldwork and the monograph became the primary forms of accreditation that were to distinguish the professional anthropologist from the amateur traveler. But at the textual level, the stylistic controls were also tightened. The naked fallibility and subjectivism of the first-person voice became stigmatized, and just as the personality of the ethnographic narrator tended to be effaced, so, too, individual informants were apt to disappear into generalized types—the prepubescent male, the tribal elder. Ethnography developed a strong antinarrative tendency, a tendency to edit out the sequence in which information was acquired in the field. Furthermore, figurative, connotative, and impassioned language was generally eschewed, and there was a strong partiality for the ethnographic present, a tense that freezes a culture in time.

These pervasive tendencies have, of course, never been utterly binding. And earlier ethnographers, from Elenore Smith Bowen (*Return to Laughter*) to Michel Leiris (*L'Afrique fantôme*) have sought, on occasion, to accommodate more of their fieldwork experience through personalized forms.[17] However, in the 1970s and 1980s, the limits of the traditional stylistic controls came to be flexed rather more frequently in works like Rabinow's *Reflections on Fieldwork in Morocco,* Crapanzano's *Tuhami: Portrait of a Moroccan,* Jean-Paul Dumont's *The Headman and I,* and Karla Poewe's *Reflections of a Woman Anthropologist: No Hiding Place.*[18] Works of this ilk sought, through more personalized or dialogic forms, to dramatize the complex contingencies of the knowledge they produced.

By foregrounding their personalities, ethnographers like Rabinow and Dumont replaced the appeal to methodological authority with a contrary appeal to the staged fallibility of felt experience. This shift can be interpreted as a reaction against a mode of cultural description that has encouraged the suppression of personality as well as the suppression of how the material may be contoured by, for instance, the sequence of the ethnographer's moods and by his or her emotional relationships with members of the culture observed.

Efforts to integrate greater theoretical self-consciousness into ethnographic practice can be too readily construed as automatically redressing the imbalances in power that have haunted anthropology. The new evocativeness can become self-glorifying; textual sensitivity is no substitute for analysis of the material, institutional conditions that continue to sustain such texts.[19] However, the dilemmas around the role of personality admit a fundamental link between the representational modes of self-conscious ethnographers and those of a travel writer like Naipaul. C. D. Narasimhaiah, for instance, finds Naipaul's representations of India "obtrusively personal," Edward Said expresses a general skepticism about

"Naipaul the phenomenon, the celebrated sensibility on tour," and Benedict Anderson designates Naipaul the doyen of the kind of travel writing

> wherein the celebrity is, with luck, much better known than the politics
> with which he or she is holidaying. . . . [This type] expects to show events
> in the great shadow of himself. For these purposes, the best events are
> those which, by artful chiaroscuro, contrast the tourist as violently as
> possible with the political landscape.[20]

From Naipaul's predominantly positive reception by his British and
American constituencies, one concludes that the textual staging of his
personality has not had the effect of complicating or subduing his authority as a social interpreter but rather of boosting it—remote peoples
become worth "learning about" through the mediation of his celebrated
personality.

   D. J. Enright, in a review of Naipaul's second travel book, *An Area
of Darkness,* provides a somewhat different perspective from Anderson's on the generic relationship between self-presentation and cultural
description:

> A travel book by an author of little personality is likely to be plain dull; a
> travel book by an author with a pronounced personality (like Mr. Naipaul)
> is likely to tell us more about the author than about the country. Heads,
> the country loses; tails the author wins.[21]

On Enright's view, the travel book is predicated not on two equal centers of interest but on one: the personality of the traveler, which ought
therefore to be as enunciated as possible. Hence Enright tolerates more
readily than Anderson the subordination of cultural and political representation to the dramas of the self. Naipaul, however, makes it clear that
he wishes to salvage more authority as a cross-cultural interpreter than
Enright admits as appropriate to the genre. This ambition Naipaul
shares with writers of self-reflexive ethnographies who seek to replace
the traditional ethnographic personality, which is dull to the point of
invisibility, with a more pronounced presence in the hopes that cross-
cultural knowledge gets enhanced, not diminished, by a stronger focus
on the dynamics between observer and observed.

The Contingency of Travel Narrative

I have suggested that the discourses of cultural description are haunted
by dilemmas of voice: what level of subjectivity will boost the observer's
authority and credibility, and at what point does this fade into egocen-

trism or subjective whimsy? This fundamental quandary is coupled to a second formal decision: how to reconcile, through narrative, the traveler's or ethnographer's often random experience of the observed culture with the desire to give a representative sense of that culture.

The question of arbitrariness arises perhaps most dramatically at the point when the writer has to invent a written shape for the voyage. Superficially, a travel book might appear to have a natural structure—to be plotted by the journey itself. And there are indeed ritual moments: the sea voyage in, the clearance at customs, the search for a hotel, the train ride from Y to Z, customs again, the airport lounge, and flight out. In broad terms, travel writing is a genre of mobility, whereas ethnography has traditionally tilted toward stasis; in the latter, movement tends to go undescribed rather than being thematically foregrounded. But, particularly given the strains of formal innovation prominent in some current ethnography, the distinction cannot be categorical. Rabinow's *Reflections on Fieldwork in Morocco,* for example, provides a more detailed record of the author's movements and the effect of those movements on his relationship to the society than does Naipaul's *India: A Wounded Civilization.*

This last book, born of Naipaul's visit to India during the 1975 Emergency and classified by Penguin as Travel/Current Events, exemplifies the genre's polymorphic possibilities as well as the random degree to which the form adheres, for its plotting, to the shape of the journey. Naipaul embarks on his account as follows:

> The lights of Bombay airport showed that it had been raining; and the aeroplane, as it taxied in, an hour or two after midnight, blew the monsoon puddles over the concrete. This was in mid-August; and officially (though this monsoon was to be prolonged) the monsoon still had two weeks to go. In the small, damp terminal building there were passengers from an earlier flight, by Gulf Air.[22]

After this conventionalized, almost paradigmatic arrival scene, Naipaul proceeds to delineate his autobiographical motives for the trip and his convoluted relationship to India: he cannot travel solely for the sights; the land is not home, yet he seems intimate with it; he still feels the ancestral tug. By the third page, he has taken the reader through three beginnings: the airport scene that inaugurates the journey, the announcement of his lines of cultural investigation into Indian society, and the personal departure—"the starting point of this inquiry . . . has been myself."[23] As the narrative advances, one senses some jostling among these three impulses—the traveling, the ethnographic-political, and the autobiographical. Without a doubt, in this particular book the second of these dominates: the primary concern is with rituals, cultural attitudes, institutions. The autobiographical component recedes after the first few pages, and Naipaul loses interest, too, in plotting his observations along the chronological nodes of the journey or at least finds that such a form does not serve. The book ends without any record of his departure. As such, *India: A Wounded Civilization* is less decisively about the experience of travel than are *The Middle Passage, An Area of Darkness, Among the Believers,* and *A Turn in the South.*

But even prior to addressing the considerable formal openness of the genre, a travel writer has to come to terms with the extreme selectiveness of his or her experience of the culture. Enright, in his reading of *An Area of Darkness,* is particularly alert to the relationship between the contingencies of cultural contact and the personality and status of the traveler:

> To write a travel book, . . . leaves the author dependent on the confrontation of his personality with the small minority of facts which happen to come his way; with the beaten-track or hit-and-run traveller the facts will be merely touristic, and even with the more enterprising or more privileged, they will still be a small minority and inevitably limited in kind by the fact that he *is* a traveller.[24]

Naipaul himself describes quite atmospherically the psychological pressures of coping with the arbitrariness of his points of entry into the society he seeks to represent.[25] In so doing, he emphasizes his lack of a methodological approach in a manner that would not be out of place in the preface to any number of self-reflexive ethnographies, for Bowen, Crapanzano, Rabinow, Dumont, and Poewe have all sought to retrieve a sense of contingency from the ravages of methodology:

> To arrive at a place without knowing anyone there, and sometimes without an introduction; to learn how to move among strangers for the short time one could afford to be among them; to hold oneself in constant readiness for adventure or revelation; to allow oneself to be carried along, up to a point, by accidents; and consciously to follow up other impulses—that could be as creative and imaginative a procedure as the writing that came after. . . . Always, at the beginning, there was the possibility of failure—of not finding anything, not getting started on the chain of accidents and encounters.[26]

The problem Naipaul thus faces is how to metamorphose, in moving from experience to text, "the chain of accidents and encounters" into a set of representative observations about the society.

The first page of his Islamic travelogue, *Among the Believers,* points up the contradictions that can result. In need of an interpreter for the voyage from Tehran to Qom, Naipaul has no idea where to look but is given Sadeq's name by an embassy official. The record of their first encounter proceeds as follows:

> He came some minutes before eight. He was in his late twenties, small and carefully dressed, handsome, with a well-barbered head of hair. I didn't like him. I saw him as a man of simple origins, simply educated, but with a great sneering pride, deferential but resentful, not liking himself for what he was doing. He was the kind of man who, without political doctrine, only with resentments, had made the Iranian revolution.[27]

From the first page of *Among the Believers* it thus becomes apparent that, as a travel writer, Naipaul values the element of arbitrariness and is eager to convey the sensation of being a prisoner of fortune in a strange land. Yet, as a polemical travel writer given to broad cultural generalizations, he feels a strong impulse running counter to the first: the urge to transcend the limitations of the chance encounter. For that reason, Sadeq has to do double duty as an example of Naipaul's vulnerability to contingency and as an embodiment of a cultural essence: Islamic "resentment." In such incidents, one detects Naipaul engineering a shaky bridge between the unpredictable and the essential.

Typifying Procedures in the Ivory Coast

Naipaul's ability to manipulate the generic options of travel writing in the interests of cultural essentialism is perhaps most explicit in his record of his trip to the Ivory Coast, "The Crocodiles of Yamoussoukro." The travelogue illustrates, in the process, the political ramifications of such formal choices. The example of "The Crocodiles of Yamoussoukro" assumes a special significance because Naipaul prefaces it with some sustained self-reflexive commentary on what it means to be a travel writer. *Finding the Centre,* his title for the volume incorporating the Ivoirian essay, suggests the drift of these reflections.[28] How is he to position what he calls "the traveller's I"?[29] And how he is to center his evocation of an unfamiliar culture?

At one point, Naipaul describes his sense of the formal alternatives open to him, remarking:

> I would have liked in 'The Crocodiles of Yamoussoukro' to take the reader through all the stages of my adventure in the Ivory Coast. I would

have liked to begin at the very beginning, with the blankness and anxiety of arrival. But it didn't work as narrative. And narrative was my aim. Within that, my travelling method was intended to be transparent. The reader will see how the material was gathered. . . .[30]

As in his Islamic book, he wishes to proceed from the blank sensation of arrival to the creation of a narrative arranged around a central conception of the society. If, in *Among the Believers,* the idea of resentment serves this function, in "Yamoussoukro" he establishes the icon of the crocodile pit as the embodiment of an African essence.

The political implications of this essay get shaped by two choices, one formal, the other social. Instead of adhering to the structure of the journey as he had projected, Naipaul decides to center his narrative on the phenomenon of the title: the crocodiles housed by President Houphouet-Boigny in an artificial lake. The crocodiles eat live chickens; the crocodiles look spectacular. Yet Naipaul makes them do a great deal of figurative work: they become emblematic of the ineluctable ills of the Ivory Coast and, beyond that, of all Africa. For it is Naipaul's thesis that Africa can achieve only a veneer of modernity because magic and make-believe are the real rulers of the continent. He therefore interprets the existence of the croc-pit as testament to the futility of African quests for social development; it provides, moreover, "a glimpse of an African Africa. . . ."[31]

How Naipaul achieves his insider's perspective is not at all apparent. For his decision to invest the crocodiles with a centripetal force in the narrative was preceded by a social decision taken during the trip itself: he sought out the company of European, American, and Caribbean expatriates as he felt drawn to people who maintained a tangential relation to the society. Some of them moved between continents, "one place always made bearable by the prospect of departure for the other"; for others, Africa held the charm of sharpening their sense of identity by allowing them to stand out.[32]

If Ivoirian opinion is thin on the ground, expat opinion and anecdote are not. In support of his crocodile magic thesis Naipaul quotes a European who declares that in the hinterland dignitaries are welcomed by having their feet bathed in blood.

> Usually it was the blood of a chicken or an animal. But to do a chief the highest honour, his feet should be washed in human blood, the blood of a sacrificed person, a child. And the child could be eaten afterwards. I believed what this man said.[33]

Another expat tells of sacrificial heads refrigerated for export.

A pattern emerges in the distribution of Naipaul's skepticism and credulity: he dismisses the Ivoirians as fantasists while indulging the residual colonials in their efforts to recycle the hoariest myths of the imperial encounter. The notion of cannibalism, of course, fits tidily with the symbol of the croc-pit and the general pathology in the Ivory Coast essay (and imperial discourses generally) around fears of engulfment.

This particular travelogue raises, quite graphically, questions of representativeness: what image or incident from among random encounters does the travel writer elect to define the society visited, and how is that choice arrived at? In "The Crocodiles" one witnesses the political consequences of a clash between Naipaul's choice of company in his travels and his formal choice in writing up the journey. For, on the one hand, he affords the croc-pit (and the spinoff, salable theme of sacrificial magic) a totemic centrality: that is the real Ivory Coast and, moreover, the real Africa. Yet, on the other hand, he penetrates to the purported center of the society by way of those who are extraneous to it.

If the cultural essentialism one encounters in "The Crocodiles" derives from a contradiction between his peripheral experience of the Ivory Coast and his centralized explanation of it, this tension, in turn, is best explained by a contradiction in his self-image. Naipaul's own accounts are helpful here. Speaking of the expatriates with whom he fraternized, he observes: "[T]he people I found, the people I was attracted to, were not unlike myself. They too were trying to find order in their world, looking for the center. . . ."[34] Yet he offers a quite different account of why he was drawn to the Ivory Coast in the first place: "[If] I go to places where people live restricted lives, it is because my curiosity is still dictated in part by my colonial Trinidad background. I go to places which, however alien, connect in some way with what I already know."[35]

So, using the language of the natural, autobiographical attraction, Naipaul claims a privileged understanding both of the uncentered expatriates, who are free to roam the world, and of their opposites, the Ivoirians, whose identities are claustrophobically centered in a restricted environment. He thereby endows himself with a global persona in whose being the most fundamental contradictions of cultural description are resolved: he is the visitor and the visited, the observer and the observed. If, in these terms, his polymorphic identity grants him an international authority, this authority in turn allows him to move with arrogant speed from his random experiences as a traveler to the cultural essentialism of his pronouncements on the African personality. Thus a direct link appears between Naipaul's preemptive familiarity with the places he visits and the typifying procedures he employs to define them.

Naipaul and Indigenous Ethnography

In analyzing Naipaul's cognitive style as a travel writer, I have sought to trouble the notion that he reconciles, in his person, the roles of autobiographical participant and semiethnographic observer. The broad issue of the unreciprocal relations between knower and known, as well as Naipaul's own fascination with insider–outsider dynamics, can be usefully approached through the quest, in some recent ethnographic thought, for modes of dispersed authority.[36]

In the personalized ethnographies referred to earlier, one finds a heightened sensitivity to the angle of observation and a growing recognition of the need to relinquish the commanding vantage points of yore. For those who wish to render this angle less acutely imperial, one general goal has been to abolish the steep hierarchy between the professional outsider and the amateur native informant, whose observations are conventionally subordinated to the larger textual designs of the authorial outsider. In this regard, two alternative models to the hierarchical one have surfaced. First, there have been attempts to introduce a more egalitarian relationship and informant through dual authorship. This seems to be the possibility Michael Fischer has in mind when he presses for a "more fully bifocal cultural criticism."[37]

The second model for reducing the discrepancy between the representational power of the invariably Western ethnographer and the generally non-Western informants entails jettisoning the Western ethnographer altogether. This occurs when the figure who might in an earlier era have featured as a native informant rises, through a (usually Western) disciplinary training to the status of indigenous ethnographer. The entry of so-called indigenous ethnographers into the discipline may sometimes entail a generic shift toward autobiography if professional distance cedes some ground to the subjective expertise and intuitions that derive from the ethnographer's experience not as a visitor to the culture, but as a lifelong member of it.

Because of its prominence in postcolonial debate around more egalitarian styles of representation, the idea of the indigenous ethnographer provides a comparative context for Naipaul's cross-cultural reputation and methods. To what extent is he in a position to reduce the dichotomy between the foreign and the local? How does he measure up against the view of the indigenous ethnographer as a Janus-faced figure who can claim—though not uncontentiously—to command the insider's authority to represent his or her culture while simultaneously taking advantage of the powerful representational assumptions of an established Western genre? To what degree is he a privileged informant?

The closest Naipaul comes to the mixed tones of the insider's personalized ethnography occurs, unpredictably, in his account of the cremation of his younger sister, Sati, who died prematurely of a brain hemorrhage.[38] Evoking the memory of that occasion in *The Enigma of Arrival,* Naipaul turns the cremation into an informal, but quite detailed study of historical changes in Trinidadian Hindu death rites. Drawing on memories of the ceremonial practices of his youth, he assumes an intense interest in the gestures and beliefs of the pundit who presides over the ceremony: his conception of the Hindi scriptures, the balls of rice and balls of earth, the flower arrangements, the brass places of consecrated food, the earth altar, the miniature pine pyre.

Throughout this episode, there is a strong sense of Naipaul's presence and of the depth of his understanding of Trinidad's Hindu community, although his representation of the cremation is curiously distant, as if the intensity of his methodical observations provided an outlet for repressed yet powerful familial feeling. This degree of inside access to the dynamics of a culture cannot, however, be equaled in his accounts of other societies and ethnic groups.

Yet, as we have seen, American and British critics often seek to credit Naipaul with an insider's intuitions. I would argue that their readiness to do so, while partly willful, is also in large part the result of the asymmetry in representational power between the West and the so-called Third World. Talal Asad, in his discussion of indigenous ethnography, and Aijaz Ahmad, in writing more generally of Western responses to non-Western intellectuals, have both pointed out that because relatively few indigenous accounts reach the West, those that win through are often too quickly generalized as representative.[39] As Ahmad observes:

> The retribution visited upon the head of an Asian, an African, an Arab intellectual who is of any consequence and who writes in English is that he/she is immediately elevated to the lonely splendour of a "representative"— of a race, a continent, a civilization, even the "third world."[40]

Hence the absurd generality of the *New York Times'* description of a Salman Rushdie novel as "a Continent finding its voice."[41]

But what is a burden of representativeness to some is a boon to others, Naipaul being a case in point. Despite the tenuousness of his links to any Third World society (with the exception of Trinidad), he has been allowed a high profile in the American and British media on the grounds of his "special knowledge." Because he writes in English and has a neocolonial orientation easily assimilable to the dominant London–New York media axis, Naipaul can shoulder out others who, on the subject of Grenada, Pakistan, or Zaire, possess a more precise, intimate expertise and who can more plausibly claim an intuitive dimension to their comprehension of their societies.

I would therefore argue that questions of cultural difference and identity should not be separated from the more institutional question of the distribution of representational power. When Naipaul enunciates his "I," his voice is not that of a polymorphous indigenous authority assured of some common experience with sundry non-Western nations or communities. Rather, he speaks a language that resonates with traditions of discursive power that assert the visual and political ascendancy of metropolitan knowers over the peripheral and underrepresented known.

Self-Fashioning in *An Area of Darkness*

I have suggested, then, that the ideal of the indigenous ethnographer is founded on the dream of reconciliation, a dream of blending the distinctive accents of the participant insider and the observant outsider into a voice that can speak with a uniquely resonant yet flexible authority. Just how far—and why—Naipaul falls short of this ideal is well illustrated by one of his most fraught travelogues, *An Area of Darkness,* the record of his first trip to India, undertaken in 1961.

Of all his travel books, *An Area of Darkness* contains his most sustained attempt to become self-conscious about his projection of an autobiographical persona: "To get anywhere in the writing," Naipaul observes, "I had first of all to define myself very clearly to myself."[42] The difficulty and instability of his efforts turn this book into a forceful instance of the potential for interference between the goals of self-portraiture and cultural description. The tone swings between naked rage at India and anguished bouts of self-scrutiny. Naipaul's desire to belong yet simultaneously to retain an outsider's "take" on the society lies at the root of this anguish. However, his dual fantasies of immersion and elevation ultimately subvert each other; indeed, both the flair and the confusion of the book are intimately connected to the unsettling effects of his efforts to harmonize such discordant voices.

The poles of the semiethnographic and the autobiographical first manifest themselves in the ambivalent title. As an aloof observer, Naipaul's final judgment on India is overwhelmingly negative: he sees it as a bleak, hopeless land, blanketed by a moral and historical darkness. Over the course of the journey he becomes obsessed with his visual authority and specifically with the gulf between his own clearsightedness and the putatively dimmed perspective of Indians. As he remarks late in the book: "I had learned to see; I could not deny what I saw. They remained in that other world."[43] The titular area of darkness thus alludes to his perception of his trip as a journey by one of the seeing through the country of the blind.

Running counter to this retrospective, distanced assessment of India is a more personal, involved perspective that produces less secure judgments. For the area of darkness is, on one level, also the dark landscape of his childhood imagination, a region he had been pointed toward by his grandfather's stories, a region that had shadowed his life but had yet to assume the precise hues of memory and experience. It was the yearning to realize more intimately the personal promise of India that had prompted him to travel there in the first place. One can thus also read *An Area of Darkness* as the record of a man who had intended to travel toward a sense of his Indian identity, but instead finds himself recoiling from the land and assuming an aloof, semiethnographic posture toward the culture. It is a posture Naipaul cannot sustain with any equanimity, and it periodically crumples before the force of a very personal anger.

From the outset, the contradictions begin to open up between his areas of darkness. On the one hand, he approaches the trip as a traveler sanguine about his ability to penetrate to the "real" India, to see it detachedly, free from local blindnesses and obsessions. To this end he invokes empirical experience mixed with bouts of informal ethnographic, political, and historical inquiry. On the other hand, his notion of the "real" India is overdetermined by his lifelong mythologizing of it; he requires of this other, personally abstracted country that it complete his identity, allowing him to become (to use a term he favors) a "whole man."

Naipaul evokes the autobiographical roots of his imaginary India in great emotional detail. When his Brahman grandfather left India's Uttar Pradesh region to teach and labor in Trinidad's cane fields, he "carried his village with him."[44] Naipaul's father's denial of Trinidad was less complete, but he, too, transmitted to his son a preoccupation with the all-Indian world of isolated Hindi-speaking, rural villages. His short stories brought that world—which V. S. had never known—to life and were decisive in enabling his son to acknowledge that, despite their provinciality, Trinidad's Indian communities held potential as literary material. The upshot of this was the imaginative pull Naipaul felt back toward India:

> To me as a child the India that had produced so many of the persons and things around me was featureless, and I thought of the time when the transference was made as a period of darkness, darkness which also extended to the land, as darkness surrounds a hut at evening, though for a little way around the hut there is still light. The light was the area of my experience, in time and place.[45]

And so, in embarking for India, Naipaul anticipated that the powerful though as yet featureless land that had first stirred in his childhood imagination would finally take on an empirical aspect, allowing the myth and the reality to harmonize. And with such harmonizing of the imaginary and the immediate, he hoped to secure a sense of belonging. Trinidad had seemed "the interlude, the illusion"; England had furnished him with a "fantasy of nobility," that is, the dream of embarking on a career as a writer; the "fantasy of home," however, he had reserved for India.[46]

Yet that first trip to the subcontinent was to dash his expectations in a manner that recalls André Gide's disillusionment with the Soviet Union after his pilgrimage there in 1936. In Brecht's words, Gide

> set out like someone who is looking for a new country, tired of the old one, doubtlessly eager to hear his own yelp of joy, but what he was really looking for was *his* new country, not an unknown but a known country, not one that others but one that he himself had built, and in his head at that. He did not find this country. It apparently does not exist on this planet.[47]

Looking back on his Indian journey, Naipaul blames it for having broken his life in two. The record of the voyage becomes, under the strain of contradictory ambitions, similarly riven. In India he feels at times empowered by the sense of aloofness that he associates with being both a writer and an outsider; it feeds, too, into a style of anthropological elevation. From this vantage point, he discerns "Indian myopia" everywhere; it becomes an *idée fixe*. His preoccupation with this notion suffuses his writings on India: *An Area of Darkness,* the essays in *The Overcrowded Barracoon,* and *India: A Wounded Civilization,* as well as several of his interviews. What Naipaul calls the Indian "defect of vision" is the source of a national degeneration as, in his opinion, "when men cannot observe, they don't have ideas; they have obsessions."[48] Moreover, if Indians' incapacity to see themselves objectively promotes obsessions, these in turn encourage unruly political movements and what he ultimately describes as Indian "barbarism." In this way, Naipaul presents "the defect of vision" not as an arbitrary failing, but as the fundamental flaw in the national character.

Indian and other non-Western critics have been quick to throw this particular charge back at Naipaul. As Fouad Ajami notes, "It has been a Naipaulian assumption that only men who live in remote, dark places are denied a clear vision of the world."[49] More specifically, for Nissim Eze-kiel, the Naipaul of *An Area of Darkness* "argues too exclusively from revulsion and anger to *see* (his favourite word) the problem in the round," while H. H. Anniah Gowda declares the visitor "has chosen to shut his eyes to the India which is not defecating," a sentiment shared by Raja Rao, among others: "The defecating processes seem somehow to draw Mr. Naipaul's attention a great deal."[50] These are charges to which Naipaul is vulnerable, for *An Area of Darkness,* even more than most of his travel writings, is a deeply obsessive book. One should add that his insistence on his direct visual access to India masks the fact that he knows no Indian language other than English and that his aural and oral relation-ship to the society is heavily mediated. All the same, in his outsider's persona, Naipaul considers it his "mission" to apply his unhampered vision to exposing the blindnesses congregated in the subcontinent.

The imperiousness of his vantage point is manifest in his remark that

> It is well that Indians are unable to look at their country directly, for the distress they would see would drive them mad. And it is well that they have no sense of history, for how then would they be able to continue to squat amid their ruins, and which Indian would be able to read the history of his country for the last thousand years without anger and pain? It is better to retreat into fantasy and fatalism.[51]

The tone here situates Naipaul outside the Indian reliance on fantasy. But because of his divided sense of purpose, his perception of his rela-tion to the observed culture as one of a dependable visiting empiricist pitted against the local fantasists is in danger of being subverted by his own experience. That much is evident when, in writing of the Hima-layas, he records how he

> felt linked to them; I liked speaking the name. India, the Himalayas: they went together. In so many of the brightly coloured religious pictures in my grandmother's house I had seen these mountains, cones of white against simple, cold blue. They had become part of the India of my fantasy. . . . The pictures I knew to be wrong; their message was no message to me; but in that corner of the mind which continues childlike their truth remained a possibility.[52]

And so, intermittently, the hard-edged empiricism of the traveler who lectures on the need for direct vision dissolves before the power of his private fantasies. The triumph of the observer over the participants is never quite complete or satisfactory, even to the observer himself. Part of Naipaul craves a fuller participation, wants, in short, to belong. But he discovers that the visible, immediate land remains out of reach; "India" is most accessible by way of his childhood fantasies, an eccentric route that, paradoxically, further isolates rather than integrating him. This, then, is one source of the angry frustration that characterizes his portrait of the society.[53]

Yet if India disappoints him by resisting his expectations, this experience of exclusion is matched, on Naipaul's part, by an active decision to withdraw from its inhabitants. In a revealing passage he records how, stripped in India of his ethnic distinctiveness, he had to cast around for alternative ways to assert his difference:

> . . . for the first time in my life I was one of the crowd. There was nothing in my appearance or dress to distinguish me from the crowd eternally hurrying into Churchgate Station. In Trinidad to be an Indian was to be distinctive. To be anything there was distinctive; difference was each man's attribute. To be an Indian in England was distinctive; in Egypt it was more so. Now in Bombay I entered a shop or a restaurant and awaited a special quality of response. And there was nothing. It was like being denied part of my reality. Again and again I was caught. I was faceless. I might sink without a trace into that Indian crowd. I had been made by Trinidad and England; recognition of my difference was necessary to me. I felt the need to impose myself, and didn't know how.[54]

This is one of those redeeming moments in *An Area of Darkness* where Naipaul allows us access to the fundamental contradiction in his identity as a travel writer, as he recognizes that the projected pleasure of identifying with a group is diminished by the accompanying threat of anonymity. He often laments his homelessness and expresses the aspiration to belong yet recoils from all collective association.[55]

If his image of himself as homeless—and concomitantly as a natural traveler—crystalized during that first trip through India, the journey also confirmed his far deeper dread of facelessness. And in his terms, facelessness and homelessness become opposites: homelessness is a way of standing above the crowd, of, in Naipaul's phrase, imposing himself. One should add that, increasingly, Naipaul was to professionalize this need for self-imposition. In exposing the dimensions of his psychological dependence on his difference, India also allowed him a clearer sense of how that dependence could become a vocational principle.

One can return to Naipaul's childhood for the beginnings of this jealous individualism—to his early sense of having to forge an identity in opposition to a community hostile to individuation. He admired his father largely because Seepersad rebelled against the group norms, and he resented his mother for capitulating to convention. Naipaul's most sustained nonfictional reflections on these experiences appear in his commentary on his father's collection of stories, in his "Prologue to an Autobiography," and in the foreword to *A House for Mr. Biswas*.[56] But they are evoked splendidly through the fictional extended family of the Tulsis in *Biswas,* the kind of family Naipaul once described as "a microcosm of the authoritarian state."[57] There is nothing arbitrary about this image: one senses in Naipaul a continuous line of autocracy from the family, through the village, the cause, the political movement, and the party, to the state. The group for him is never an achieved condition but rather an expression of failure; community marks the absence of individualism on a mass scale. Here one faces a fundamental contradiction in his psychology: The same childhood that equipped him with the fantasy that he might one day belong in India also bred in him an insurmountable suspicion of group identities.

If the individual vision, the individual achievement, and the individual freedom are the only ones Naipaul can entertain, how does this conviction mark *An Area of Darkness* in particular and, more broadly, his approach to cultural representation? Nissim Ezekiel is one critic who has sensed some of the disabling consequences, particularly for a travel writer who has chosen Third World societies as his stamping ground:

> My quarrel is that Mr. Naipaul is so often uninvolved and unconcerned. He writes exclusively from the point of view of his own dilemma, his temperamental alienation from his mixed background, his choice and his escape. That temperament is not universal, not even widely distributed, that choice is not open to all, *the escape for most is not from the community but into it.* To forget this is to be wholly subjective, wholly self-righteous, to think first and last of one's own expectations, one's extreme discomfort. (Emphasis added)[58]

Gordon Rohlehr issues a related complaint against Naipaul's antipathy toward West Indian cultural practices, which are predicated on the flight into, not away from, community:

> Naipaul's hatred of the steel band and all it indicates is no mere rejection of West Indian culture, but a rejection of the single common ground where Trinidadians of all races meet on a basis of equality. Carnival in Trinidad, dominated by steel-band calypso and costume, is more than a time of

general merry-making. One can, without naively propounding a West Indian version of the myth of the happy Negro, recognize Carnival as one of the few symbols, however tenuous, of a oneness in the Trinidadian people.[59]

Ezekiel and Rohlehr discern, then, an incompatibility—at once epistemological and temperamental—between Naipaul's fixation on the individual and the collective cultural forces in the societies he portrays.

Yet at least in the Indian context, Naipaul issues an unexpected retort. For at one point he contends that, despite the evidence, he does in fact see the society from the inside because his negative predilections are paradigmatically Indian:

> It is only now, as the impatience of the observer is dissipated in the processes of writing and self-inquiry, that I see how much this philosophy had also been mine. It had enabled me, through the stresses of a long residence in England, to withdraw completely from nationality and loyalties except to persons; it had made me content to be myself alone, my work, my name (the last two so different from the first); it had convinced me that every man was an island, and taught me to shield all that I knew to be good and pure within myself from the corruption of causes.[60]

Thus in the gap between his experience of India and his written response to it, Naipaul comes to reconceive his flight from the crowd, which he had first seen as a rejection of India, as an expression of his Indianness. He thereby attempts to pass off his alienation from India as a measure of his intimacy with it.

This move allows him to maximize his authority. For in satisfying his desire to stand out, to be unrepresentative, he can also act in ways that are representatively Indian. So, again, one witnesses him striving to describe his cultural identity as a fusion of the insider and the outsider. However, unquestionably, over the course of his temperamental voyages to India, he positions himself more frequently as the disdainful outsider than as the would-be insider. The tone he favors is the one that expresses how "the absurdity of India can be total. It appears to ridicule analysis. It takes the onlooker beyond anger and despair to neutrality."[61] His preference, in this kind of assessment, for the term *neutrality* rather than, say, *indifference,* is significant, because the notion of neutrality is inseparable from his projection of an autobiographical persona who remains an impartial onlooker. Hence despite his efforts to lay claim to an insider's vision of sorts, he is generally more comfortable exempting himself from the Indian refusal to see.

The way Naipaul's arguments turn on the division between seeing and not seeing and the correspondence between this split and an outsider's and an insider's perspectives render *An Area of Darkness* a classic instance of the fixation with visual authority that has governed the discourses of ethnography and travel alike. The most imperial of the senses, the eye becomes in *An Area of Darkness* less a conduit for empiricism than a controlling metaphor that is symptomatic of Naipaul's cognitive style. It is a style that he characterizes directly in the epigraph with which this chapter began: "My uncertainty about my role withered; a role was not necessary. I recognized my own instincts as a traveller, and was content to be myself, to be what I had always been, a looker."[62] Resting in the secure assumption of this correspondence between self and sight, Naipaul has dealt too lightly with fundamental questions of representativeness, above all, the relationship between the forms of representation and the power to represent.

4

Preparations for Travel: Naipaul's Conradian Atavism

> And I found that Conrad—sixty years before, in the time of a great peace—had been everywhere before me. . . .
>
> V.S. Naipaul, "Conrad's Darkness"

Accumulatively, Naipaul's reliance on normative traditions of discourse—many of them manifesting imperial affinities—calls into question the routine accounts of his embattled extratraditionalism. I have proposed that Naipaul favors the multivalent language of exile as a means of attaching himself to a tradition of ostracism, that Victorian travel writing emerges as one of his principal adoptive ancestries, and that he invokes the travel genre's semiethnographic and autobiographical styles of cultural description in ways that tend to affirm dominant metropolitan preconceptions about Third World societies.

The rhetorical cycles of prefiguration and confirmation that characterize Naipaul's allegiance to such traditions are best exemplified by his relation to Conrad. As a displaced writer, an immigrant, an international wanderer turned Englishman, and moreover as someone fascinated by the psychological dimensions to colonial experience and by notions of primitivism, Conrad has provided Naipaul with his most direct point of entry into mainstream British literature. The three regions that have most preoccupied Naipaul—the Caribbean, India, and Africa—have all been shadowed to some degree by Conrad's presence. In one essay, Naipaul ranks Trinidad as "one of the Conradian dark places of the earth"; in another he reads the island's Black Power revolt as a reenactment and fulfilment of "An Outpost of Progress."[1] More subtly, India, too, becomes a semi-Conradian *Area of Darkness*. However, it is when Naipaul turns, in the 1970s, to write repeatedly about Africa that his work becomes scored most deeply with this inscription: in the essays "Conrad's Darkness" and "A New King for the Congo," in *A Bend in the River,* his Central African novel, and in *A Congo Diary.* These last two titles, twinned in a manner that repeats Conrad's pairing of *Heart of Darkness* and *The Congo Diary,* were born of a river voyage that retraced the Pole's famous venture. This affiliation, moreover, runs very much through the male line of the Naipaul family: Seepersad drew encouragement from Conrad's example, and *Heart of Darkness* became a determining presence in *North of South,* brother Shiva's record of his East African journey.[2]

Indeed, one cannot understand Conrad's hold on Naipaul without observing the lines of transmission, how an Anglicized Polish author came to assume pride of place in a Port of Spain family. To do so one must return to one of Naipaul's early memories, the moment of his induction into modern literature:

> [Conrad] was, I suppose, the first modern writer I was introduced to. It was through my father. My father was a self-taught man, picking his way through a cultural confusion of which he was perhaps hardly aware and which I have only recently begun to understand; and he wished himself to be a writer. He read less for pleasure than for clues, hints and encouragement; and he introduced me to those writers he had come upon in his own search. Conrad was one of the earliest of these: Conrad the stylist, but more than that, Conrad the late starter, holding out hope to those who didn't seem to be starting at all.
>
> I believe I was ten when Conrad was first read to me. It sounds alarming; but the story was "The Lagoon"; and the reading was a success.[3]

This incident presents a fantasy of male genesis through a convocation of authors: the celebrated émigré modernist, the thwarted Trinidadian, and his son, the ten-year-old writer-to-be sprung from the possibilities represented by both Conrad and Seepersad. The timing of that reading scene—circa 1942—and the occasion of its essayistic recollection—mid-1974—acquire a critical significance. For that memorable convergence of father and son through Conrad occurred just a year before Seepersad published his sole book, the very year that Vidia first committed himself to becoming a writer. Thirty-one years later, Vidia composed "Conrad's Darkness" while preparing to select his deceased father's stories with a mind to publishing them abroad. The resulting volume, *Gurudeva and Other Stories,* contains a long commemorative introduction wherein Vidia recalls the decisive inspiration he drew both from Seepersad's reverence for books and from his tenacious, improbable dream of becoming an author.

Naipaul's two principal literary progenitors are thus evidently bonded in memory, each allowing him to reimagine what qualified as writing and to ratify the literary potential of his colonial experience. The men fathered him in complementary ways: Seepersad taught him that Trinidad could become fertile material for fiction, while Conrad the traveler suggested that an international range of experience could compensate for the absence of a profound knowledge of a single society. So although Seepersad transmitted an esteem for Conrad to his son, the two men approached the modernist seeking different kinds of precedent. The father, whose talent had begun to flower in obscurity and on the brink of the grave, required the consoling memory of a late, great bloomer; the precocious Vidia was drawn to the idea of a wandering, global writer. Conrad's example stands, for instance, behind Naipaul's remark that travel "broadened my world view; it showed me a changing world and took me out of my colonial shell; it became the substitute for the mature social experience—the deepening knowledge of a society—which my background and the nature of my life denied me."[4]

Yet, in the context of Naipaul's career, "Conrad's Darkness" needs to be read not just as recollection, but as preparation. The essay doubles as a reminiscence on Conrad's place in Naipaul's genesis as a writer and as Naipaul's way of equipping himself for the voyage to Zaire, undertaken a few months after completing the piece. Ironically, in the African writings that issued from that trip, the same Conrad who helped him cope with his early sense of unorthodoxy turns into a powerfully orthodox influence on him. Certainly, there is no more arresting example of Naipaul's conventionalism than his adherence, in "A New King for the Congo," *A Congo Diary,* and *A Bend in the River,* to the *Heart of Darkness* tradition of figuring Africa, the continent whose depiction in the West remains most centralized and undifferentiated.

Heart of Darkness has exerted a centripetal pull over Western representations of Africa unequaled in this century by the sway of any other text over the portrayal of any single continent. Journalists, historians, novelists, anthropologists, filmmakers, advertising hacks, and, most conspicuously, travel writers have drawn so routinely and with such license on the novella that the figure of Africa as a heart of darkness has become intelligible even to people who have never read any Conrad. The trope has accrued, in the process, a rhetorical force only distantly dependent on the context and form of its initial usage. The in-house tendencies of this figurative tradition have been fortified by their extension under certain circumstances to other, non-African regions of the tropical periphery, whether the Vietnam of Francis Ford Coppola's

Apocalypse Now and Philip Caputo's *A Rumor of War* or the Central America of Joan Didion's *Salvador.*[5] Yet such extensions have always seemed more whimsical, less peremptory: African nations remain most consistently and compulsively subjected to the novella's determining precedent.

Thus, at a certain point, Naipaul's familial, autobiographical attraction to Conrad converges with something else: the Western tradition of "doing" Africa via *Heart of Darkness,* an obvious shortcut taken by writers of nonfiction as varied as André Gide, Graham Greene, and Hannah Arendt during the colonial era and, during the postcolonial period, by the brothers Naipaul, Alberto Moravia, Patrick Marnham, Edward Hoagland, Nadine Gordimer, Paul Hyland, and Joseph Hone.[6] From this perspective, Naipaul can be seen to work out of and project a tradition wherein the governing figure, the "heart of darkness," and a cluster of reiterated phrases around it have passed from one fin-de-siécle fictional representation of the Belgian Congo into the factual rhetoric of both colonial and neocolonial writers. For in slipping from fiction to the literature of "fact," this trope and its constellation of phrases have accumulated a normative force, confining Africa to an invented consistency that militates against certain kinds of information, as well as historically and regionally more specific representations. The net effect is the image of a continent still debilitated by a measure of figurative arrest.

As we have seen, Naipaul's reflections on his elective affinity with Conrad are informed by his image of himself as an exile, a marooned, extratraditional writer who resides in England yet does not belong there. But his sense of affiliation goes well beyond that:

> Conrad's value to me is that he is someone who sixty or seventy years ago meditated on my world, a world I recognize today. I feel this about no other writer of the century.[7]

> And I found Conrad—sixty years before, in the time of a great peace—had been everywhere before me. . . . as a man offering a vision of the world's half-made societies as places which continuously made and unmade themselves, where there was no goal, and where always "something inherent in the necessities of successful action . . . carried with it the moral degradation of the idea."[8]

This statement hints at several dominant tendencies in Naipaul's appropriation of Conrad. First, to "recognize today" a world that Conrad wrote about sixty of seventy years back is to interpret that world as static—a central tenet of Naipaul's travelogues, from *India: A Wounded Civilization* to *The Loss of El Dorado.* On the "margins" of the globe, time is not of the essence; nations and cultures are impervious to change, bereft of history. One is therefore freer to represent such regions through Conrad's language because in those parts "then" and "now" are essentially interchangeable.

Relatedly, it is worth noting how Naipaul's syntax casts these societies—"places which continuously made and unmade themselves"—as the agents of their own cyclical destruction. Such places are without history and incapable of becoming full (as opposed to "half-made") societies largely because they are locked into a hermetic system of self-destruction.

The third point to be made here returns us to the epigraph of this chapter: "And I found Conrad—sixty years before, in the time of a great peace—had been everywhere before me. . . ." That "found" underscores an assumption basic not only to Naipaul's neo-Conradian writings but to the broader *Heart of Darkness* tradition as well. For on this view, to write about Africa through Conrad is not so much to choose him as an ancestor, as to discover him already in place. He may be back in time, but to spell out Naipaul's spatial metaphor, his imprint lies on the path ahead, waiting to be "found" on arrival. And so Conrad is presented as neither an invented nor a chosen starting point, but a natural one. Naipaul's statement, then, portrays in miniature how this particular intertextual tradition is dogged by circular, self-confirming tendencies.

The *Heart of Darkness* Tradition

The relationship between a travel writer's capacity to discover familiarity in a foreign land and the way he or she has been primed by certain accredited representations of that region may involve something more precise than preconception. As in the *Heart of Darkness* tradition, those ideas may not merely have been thought in advance but have taken form in very specific, predictable phrasing. That much is strikingly evident in appropriations of Conrad by European authors writing well before Naipaul: Graham Greene, for instance, in *Journey Without Maps,* André Gide in *Voyage to the Congo,* and Hannah Arendt in *Imperialism,* the second volume of her *Origins of Totalitarianism.* To recognize the shaping presence of *Heart of Darkness* in the rhetoric of such texts is to clarify our vision of Naipaul. For he ought to be viewed not simply as a writer with a personal allegiance to Conrad, but as someone who attaches himself to a broad, secure tradition of appealing to *Heart of Darkness* in an effort to render African history and travel intelligible. It is to Greene's and Arendt's earlier adaptations of Conrad, therefore, that I turn for a wider sense of Naipaul's placement within this tradition.

In *Journey Without Maps,* Greene offers an account of a 200-mile voyage he undertook on foot through Liberia in 1934. Greene, like Conrad before and Naipaul after him, voyaged down the Congo River and published a journal record of the trip,[9] but it is in Greene's Liberian travelogue that Conrad's pull is felt most strongly. Just how overdetermined a trope "heart of darkness" becomes in *Journey Without Maps* is apparent from a passage that throws into stark relief the process whereby the experience of recognition is most readily conveyed through the language of the literary forerunner:

> But what had astonished me about Africa was that it had never been really strange. Gibraltar and Tangier—those extended just parted hands—seemed more than ever to represent an unnatural breach. The 'heart of darkess' was common to us both. Freud has made us conscious as we have never been before of those ancestral threads which still exist in our unconscious minds to lead us back. The need, of course, has always been felt, to go back and begin again. Mungo Park, Livingstone, Stanley, Rimbaud, Conrad represented only another method to Freud's, a more costly, less easy method, calling for physical as well as mental strength. The writers, Rimbaud and Conrad, were conscious of this purpose, but one is not certain how far the explorers knew the nature of the fascination which worked on them in the dirt, the disease, the barbarity and the familiarity of Africa.[10]

Paradoxically, when Greene visits Africa for the first time he suddenly realizes that he has known it all along. But his explanation as to why there is this peculiar barbarity yet familiarity to Africa merits our attention. Greene charges that it is because " 'the heart of darkness' is common to us both," but this shared heart of darkness is not, as he would have us believe, a primitivism of the collective unconscious linking Europeans to Africa, but rather the heart of darkness as a core trope in the Western tradition of representing Africa. So I would venture that the primary bond between Europe and Africa here is discursive rather than more amorphously psychological and that Greene is able to rediscover Africa because of the force with which his culture has reiteratively prepared him for an Africa that is most intelligible as a variant of a literary figure.

The opening sentence of the excerpt, in which Greene marks Africa's astonishing lack of strangeness, is a variant of Marlow's experience of the continent. Faced with the incomprehensible howling of "savages,"

Marlow recoils from the prospect of his "remote kinship with this wild and passionate uproar." But he concedes:

> . . . if you were man enough you would admit to yourself that there was in you just the faintest trace of a response to the terrible frankness of that noise, a dim suspicion of there being a meaning in it which you—you so remote from the night of first ages—could comprehend.[11]

What Marlow and Greene share, then, is a perception of Africa as the site of human origins. But for Marlow that origin is vicious and monstrous, and to admit kinship with Africa is to risk anarchy and madness, to court social and psychological breakdown. For Greene, however, writing thirty-five years later, the encounter with African origins is not one of terror but of shame and yearning—shame that through materialism and industrialism Europeans have betrayed the ostensibly peaceable beginnings of the human species, and yearning for the uncorrupted state of existence that he considers to have been preserved quintessentially in Africa alone. Where Conrad sees Europeans as having ascended from African primitivism (if still vulnerable to its incursions), Greene regards Europeans as having fallen from the African state of prelapsarian harmony. Despite this important difference, however, the two authors share a perception of Africa as the essence of primitivism—regardless of whether that primitivism is negatively valued (as by Conrad) or positively (by Greene). Furthermore, they share a comparative interest that is also narcissistic: Africa is intriguing primarily insofar as it helps Europe gauge, by comparison, the status and condition of its own cultures.[12]

Greene ratifies Conrad's symbolic Africa most directly by keeping in play the psychological dimensions of the journey into the continent's interior. Here the pivotal notion is that of the voyage irrationally undertaken that becomes a voyage into the irrational. But even in borrowing the psychological motif from Conrad, Greene reworks his symbolism. Greene's narrative is loudly Freudian: time and again, he asserts that the expedition is a form of analysis, "a more expensive, less cosy alternative to Freud."[13] (In England in the 1930s it was a standing joke to ask if one was going to a psychoanalyst or to Africa.[14]) Thus, if the African voyage is held to be culturally remedial by furnishing an idyllic vision of Europe's preindustrial, prerational past, it is also, to invoke one of the narrative's most persistent metaphors, personally therapeutic. As is evident from the long excerpt quoted earlier, there are three irrational, mapless routes back: Freud's route, that of African exploration (Mungo Park, Livingstone, and Stanley), and the writer's method (Conrad and Rimbaud). In Greene's terms, all three allow one to feel one's way back to a compound origin, a racial and an individual childhood, the double "past from which one has emerged."

Greene's voyage to Africa enables him, in a sense, not only to recover, like Marlow, the first chapter of the biography of the human race, but to retrieve, in addition, the lost opening chapter of his autobiography.[15] The twin symbolism of the voyage is made explicit when, deep in the Liberian hinterland, he witnesses the ritual of the Bush Devils and announces emotionally that "one had the sensation of having come home, for here one was finding associations with a personal and a racial childhood."[16] That same ritual enables him to relive the sharp passions of his nursery years, especially the ecstasy and terror provoked by the witch Gagool in H. Rider Haggard's *King Solomon's Mines,* and, crucially, the ritual is described both as the "central darkness" and the very "heart of darkness."[17]

Hannah Arendt's powerful history of imperialism gets blown off course as soon as it approaches African shores. Citing *Heart of Darkness* as "the most illuminating work on actual race experience in Africa," Arendt allows Conrad's text to overwhelm both her language and her analysis.[18] She first uses it to feel her way into Afrikaner psychology:

> Race was the Boers' answer to the overwhelming monstrosity of Africa— a whole continent populated and overpopulated by savages—an explanation of the madness which grasped and illuminated them like "a flash of lightning in a serene sky: 'Exterminate all the brutes'."[19]

Yet Arendt is also content to mobilize Kurtz in defining the motives and character of a diametrically opposed group, the international adventurers, mostly British, who were drawn to South Africa by the lure of gold:

> Like Mr. Kurtz in Conrad's *Heart of Darkness,* they were "hollow to the core," "reckless without hardihood, greedy without audacity and cruel without courage." They believed in nothing and "could get [themselves] to believe anything—anything." Expelled from a world with accepted social values, they had been thrown back upon themselves and still had nothing to fall back upon except, here and there, a streak of talent which made them as dangerous as Kurtz if they were ever allowed to return to their homelands.[20]

Arendt proceeds to quote at length the core passage (which so influenced Greene) beginning: "We were cut off from the comprehension of our surroundings. . . . We could not understand because we were too far and could not remember, because we were traveling in the night of first ages. . . ."

Having established Conrad's primacy over several pages, Arendt becomes rather cavalier in her failure to demarcate quotations:

> Many of these adventurers had gone mad in the silent wilderness of an overpopulated continent where the presence of human beings only underlined utter solitude, and where an untouched, overwhelmingly hostile nature that nobody had ever taken the trouble to change into human landscape seemed to wait in sublime patience "for the passing away of the fantastic invasion" of man.[21]

Arendt leans so heavily on her neo-Conradian insights, and particularly on her sense of Kurtz-like adventurers driven demented by exposure to the pristine savagery of peoples bereft of culture or history, that she scarcely pauses to weigh the losses and suffering in Africa. Nowhere else in her three-volume account of totalitarianism does she allow the history of a region to be so comprehensively re-routed through fiction. And nowhere else does she capitulate so swiftly to the notion that a continent's precolonial peoples were incapable of working their world into cultural and historical form.

During the postcolonial era, *Heart of Darkness* has been subject to even more prolific adaptations. Conrad has retained his usefulness for those who wish to situate Third World cultures outside the bounds of history. This becomes explicit in two famous remodelings of *Heart of Darkness* that took shape in the 1970s: Naipaul's *A Bend in the River* and Francis Ford Coppola's *Apocalypse Now.* The most widely known adaptation of Conrad's novella in any medium, Coppola's film reveals with particular clarity the geographical and historical reach of neo-Conradian discourse. But it also exposes how, within that range, invocations of Conrad invariably segregate the world into those possessing and those denied history.

Coppola's attentiveness to Conrad was so direct that the publishers of a major study, *Conrad and Imperialism,* saw fit to display a still from *Apocalypse Now* on the book's cover.[22] Coppola himself felt obliged to include Conrad's name in the screen credits, but one of his jealous writers coerced him into removing it. *Apocalypse Now* differs from *Journey Without Maps* in that its visual rhetoric is fictional rather than documentary and, further, in that it remains more faithful to the structure of *Heart of Darkness.* For while the first half of the film is a spectacular evocation of the violence of Vietnam, the second half depicts the river as an escape hatch out of the disquieting morality of the American invasion and into a prehistoric world that appears to have more to do with evil in the abstract than with the particular historical questions raised by the American presence in

Vietnam. In Coppola's mind, "Willard [the film's Marlow figure] arriving at the compound to meet Kurtz is like coming to the place that you don't want to go—because it's all *your* ghosts and all *your* demons."[23] Those emphatic possessives are consistent with the film's pandering to Western narcissism, with the way it plays off the inward, psychological dimensions of *Heart of Darkness* in a manner closer to Greene (though without the nostalgia) than to Naipaul. The specific danger constituted by the American invasion is forgotten in the face of a generalized fear of "going native" that is cast as timeless yet rendered personal. Captain Kurtz's small-scale, low-tech atrocities committed in the company of his 'primitive' henchmen are allowed to become the real horror, while the massive napalming is made ethically peripheral, that is, ethically downstream from the true heart of darkness. In the words of one of the film's American officers: "Out there with those natives it must be a temptation to be God." So the brutality becomes dissociated from America's historical decision to intervene and is instead isolated in its quintessential form in the war-painted delirium of the Cambodian and Vietnamese 'savages'.[24]

Apocalypse Now, no less than *Journey Without Maps,* bespeaks the influential role of adaptations of *Heart of Darkness* in reinforcing the Western obsession with stripping other cultures of their autonomous or semiautonomous histories and identities so as to absorb them into a gigantic, continuous narrative of the West. Like Greene, Coppola introduces the figure of the heart of darkness to span his historical and psychological preoccupations, but on examination this proves to be a very rickety, illogical connection. That much is made clear by one of the director's most telling remarks:

> From the bridge on, I started moving back in time, because I wanted to imply that the issues and the themes were timeless—this was all going on when guys were throwing spears. As you went further up the river, you went deeper into the origins of human nature, which was the heart of darkness: what we were really like.[25]

Coppola's invocation of Conrad enables him to shift from the morality of America's historical actions in Vietnam to the timeless morality of the global species—as he says, "this was all going on when guys were throwing spears." By overlaying *Heart of Darkness* on Vietnam, Coppola is able to set in motion a perverse chain of logic whereby the inhabitants of an invaded country, metamorphosed into psychological ciphers, become the root cause of their own napalming. Quite simply, as the Cambodians and Vietnamese are not coeval with the Americans but become, in the second half of the film, emblematically prehistoric, their existence in history is entirely subordinated to their symbolic, psychological function. That way the real battle can be represented not as a military, historical, and international event, but rather as a conflict between two mythologized dimensions of America itself: between the civilized, orderly, high-tech, napalming self and the more threatening, barbaric spear-throwing self, that is, the self that could all too easily forget its advancement and lapse into Cambodianism.

An observation by the anthropologist Johannes Fabian on the importance of evolutionary time for rationalizing colonial endeavors can serve as a useful gloss to Coppola's remarks:

> The condition of an emerging anthropological praxis came to be linked to colonialism and imperialism. One cannot insist too much that these links were epistemological, not just moral or ethical. Anthropology contributed above all to the intellectual justification of the colonial enterprise. It gave to politics and economics a firm belief in "natural" i.e., evolutionary Time. It promoted a scheme in terms of which not only past cultures, but all living societies were irrevocably placed on a temporal slope, a stream of Time—some upstream, others downstream.[26]

Fabian's perception helps clarify the bond between an essentialist tradition of thinking that demands a single all-embracing narrative of human development and the figure of the river journey into the heart of darkness.

The cluster of tropes that has been borrowed persistently from *Heart of Darkness* has often provided an acceptable high literary front for evolutionary thinking and, as a result (to borrow an image that is Conrad's, Fabian's and Coppola's), Africans—and less reiteratively Cambodians and Vietnamese—continue to be seen widely as the 'tribes' at the remote source of the river, removed from the West not only in space but in time.[27]

From Conrad's "Darkness" to Mobutu's Zaire

Shiva and V. S. Naipaul both rediscovered Conrad in Africa during the 1970s, Shiva on the continent's East coast, V. S. on the West. I have written elsewhere at some length on Shiva's fondness for *Heart of Darkness* as a way of reducing African history to a showdown between Kurtz clones (following Arendt, he sees the Boers as Kurtz's heirs) and indigenous primitives.[28] But the extreme crudity of Shiva's version of this encounter is a mere shadow of the more subtle perversities of his older brother who, repeatededly during the 1970s, revived Conrad in his reflections on Zaire. It is to these that I now turn.

One critic of Francis Ford Coppola's *Apocalypse Now* has suggested that Kurtz is "the biggest, fattest temptation to generalization in English literature."[29] Certainly Naipaul succumbed to that temptation as he voyaged in commemorative fashion down the Congo River, with *Heart of Darkness* in the forefront of his mind.[30] On his 1974 trip Naipaul was drawn to Kurtz's magnetic allure and allowed it to tug his observations in the direction of a charismatic literariness that tries to confer intelligibility on Zairean corruption. But this resonant style of figurative explanation can only succeed if more mundane political, historical, and economic details are kept out of sight.

Naipaul's renavigation of the river generated three pieces: "A New King for the Congo: Mobutu and the Nihilism of Africa," *A Congo Diary,* and the novel *A Bend in the River.* In an extraordinary passage in the first of these, he reincarnates Kurtz in independent Zaire.[31] Writing of Pierre Mulele, a former minister of education who led a rebellion against the central government in 1964, Naipaul declares:

> To Joseph Conrad, Stanleyville—in 1890 the Stanley Falls station—was the heart of darkness. It was there, in Conrad's story, that Kurtz reigned, the ivory agent degraded from idealism to savagery, taken back to the earliest ages of man, by wilderness, solitude and power, his house surrounded by impaled human heads. Seventy years later, at this bend in the river, something like Conrad's fantasy came to pass. But the man with "the inconceivable mystery of a soul that knew no restraint, no faith, no fear" was black, and not white; and he had been maddened not by contact with wilderness and primitivism, but with the civilization established by those pioneers who now lie on Mont Ngamliema, above the Kinshasa rapids.[32]

Through this inventive legerdemain, Naipaul cancels in a gesture the entire twentieth-century history of Congo/Zaire and reaffirms what we have been schooled to believe all along: that time is not of the essence in Africa, for nothing new can really happen there anyway. African history, he implies, and later reiterates in *A Congo Diary,* is insistently repetitive to the point of stasis.[33]

In resiting "Conrad's fantasy" at "this bend in the river" the passage alludes back to *Heart of Darkness* but also forward to Naipaul's own fiction, erecting a "factual" bridge between the two and drawing both of them closer to an interrupted but apparently consistent narrative of actual African events. But to what events is Naipaul alluding? Mulele's followers did kill many people, often cruelly, as did other Zairean factions; as did the 8,600 Belgian paratroopers who invaded the country to shore up corporate interests in the copper-rich Katanga province in 1960; as did the Belgian, American, South African, and British mercenaries who battled left-wing secessionists in 1964. One should be emphatic here: "The process of restoring the authority of Kinshasa was often accompanied by massacres comparable in scale to the assassinations by the rebels."[34] And while the Mulelists' actions were violent, they were by no means without "restraint": they made a policy of respecting traditional chiefs, while attacking officials whom they considered to be neocolonial appointees.[35]

My point is not to vindicate the Mulelists' actions but to question the wisdom of equating Kurtz with the Zairean rebel leader in a fashion that sets up a causal relation between their locale and their morality, reinscribing that easy ethical geography whereby Kurtz's behavior and Mulele's become most intelligible as emanations of place. (Although, to be sure, while associating Kurtz with Mulele, Naipaul distinguishes them on one point: Kurtz was dragged down by African savagery, while Mulele, far worse, was destroyed by his inability to entertain the prospect of civilization.[36]) Naipaul's word for this apparently endemic African degeneration is "nihilism," a word he introduces in the essay's title and repeatedly uses to cement together Kurtz, Mulele, Zaire's President Mobutu, and ultimately the entire continent. Buttressed by invocations of Conrad, "nihilism" in turn fortifies Naipaul's thinking not only in the Mobutu essay, but in *A Congo Diary* as well. Mulele's rebellion is cited as an instance of this "African nihilism, the rage of primitive men coming to themselves and finding that they have been fooled and affronted"; the rule of Mobutu—"the great African nihilist"—embodies the same impulse but with less bloodshed.[37]

Naipaul's notion of African nihilism is nourished in this essay by its connection to an ill-used Conradian pessimism. Blending Conrad's two African tales, Naipaul finds contemporary counterparts to the weak colonials, "unredeemed by an idea, not a sentimental pretence but an idea; and an unselfish belief in the idea," people, in Naipaul's words, "too simple for an outpost of progress."[38] Reading "An Outpost of Progress" as a timeless "story of the congruent corruptions of colonizer and colonized," Naipaul is able to employ it here and elsewhere in the service of his leveling vision of nihilism, a vision that is scrupulously pessimistic precisely because he insists that the corruption in the former colonies is equally the fault of those who did the colonizing and those who were colonized.[39] Naipaul consistently downplays the sequence of corruption—a more nuanced historical analysis might jeopardize his grand perception of Africa as the site of nihilism and insanity.

In his view, the town prophesied in "An Outpost of Progress" did indeed appear and then vanish again for the want of "a deliberate belief."[40] Through a rhetoric of analogy that is invested with a determining force, the failures of contemporary Zaire are made to speak of "the great African wound," "self-wounding and nihilistic" actions that are "part of no creative plan."[41] Analogously, "the ideas of responsibility, the state and creativity are ideas brought by the visitor; they do not correspond, for all the mimicry of language, to African aspirations."[42] I would offset this litany by tendering that the "visitor" has brought other more damaging ideas.

One of these ideas was colonialism; another, the Cold War. To begin with, let it be stressed that the Belgian colonial legacy was particularly dismal. Of the 4,645 most senior executive positions in the Congolese bureaucracy in 1960, the year of the country's independence, only three were Zairean.[43] In such a sprawling country, a strong bureaucracy was essential for any hope of national cohesion. Nor were the departing colonial administrators readily replaced: Belgian educational policy had left the country with a total of seventeen university graduates and not a single doctor, lawyer, architect, or professor.[44] This dearth of trained personnel was felt as strongly in the new army for, at the moment of independence, the officers' corps was entirely European. In sum, an educational shortage of that order cannot be remedied in a decade or two.

The disarray occasioned by such paltry preparation for independence was compounded by the Cold War, which, in the opening years of the 1960s, was at its iciest, with American global policy also at its most interventionist. The United States quickly determined that Patrice Lumumba, the new republic's first prime minister, would be unsympathetic to American interests, so the CIA had him overthrown and assassinated.[45] Even one of his bitterest enemies, the Katangese foreign minister, Evaniste Kimbe, conceded that "only Lumumba might have been big enough to govern the Congo" and that there was no one to step into the breach.[46] American and Belgian mining interests also instigated and sustained the secession of copper-rich Katanga, the country's wealthiest province. Thus, for the first four years of its independence, Zaire juddered beneath a rush of largely foreign-sponsored secessions and uprisings and of accompanying incursions of foreign troops—Belgian paratroopers, international mercenaries, and United Nations forces.

As early as 1961, the United States had singled out Mobutu for support; ever since then Zaire has been a client autocracy under American patronage.[47] Mobutu simply could not have sustained his lengthy rule without American funds. A 1975 document from the AID (part of the World Bank) Development Assistance Program for Zaire expresses the objectives for this support quite candidly:

(1) to maintain U.S. accessibility to raw materials which are in abundant supply in Zaire;
(2) to foster U.S. investment in Zaire so that we will have access to the Zaire market; and
(3) to sustain our political interests in Central Africa, bearing in mind that Zaire is the "bellwether" for political stability in this part of the world.[48]

The same document flies in the face of all the data by deducing that "there is also evidence that President Mobutu has a desire to use his power for the benefit of all Zairians [sic]."

In sum, a more historical, less belleristic, and less atavistic account of the construction of Zairean nationhood than Naipaul admits might have exposed Mobutu's corrupt leadership as in large part an international phenomenon, not an expression of some African essence. Mobutu needs to be recognized as, to a significant extent, an interactive product of colonial and Cold War interventionism.

Nothing could be further from my purpose than to defend the squanderous, cultic, thoroughly heinous Mobutu, a man for whom the word *kleptocrat* might have been personally coined. Naipaul can be quite brilliant in cutting down Mobutu's ill-begotten, pretentious, and devastating efforts to impose his bogus notions of cultural authenticity upon his nation. And at moments—as when he remarks that "like Leopold II, Mobutu owns Zaire"—Naipaul hints at the possibility of an essay more responsive to those processes of neocolonialism that Fanon evoked so keenly.[49] However, on each such occasion Naipaul reverts to his basic thesis, which is that Mobutu (and Mulele and Idi Amin) express a timeless spirit of continental nihilism. If Mobutu fabricates a sentimental cult of African purity in his own image, Naipaul makes the same error in reverse by reaffirming the Western construction of a monolithic Africa that serves as civilization's necessary, impure other. With exemplary insight, Kwame Anthony Appiah has reflected on precisely this issue— the bankruptcy of inventing and counterinventing the "real" Africa:

. . . the very invention of Africa (as something more than a geographical entity) must be understood, ultimately, as an outgrowth of European racialism; the notion of Pan-Africanism was founded on the notion of the African, which was, in turn, founded not on any genuine cultural common-

ality but on the very European concept of the Negro. . . . Simply put, the
overdetermined course of cultural nationalism in Africa has been to make
real the imaginary identities to which Europe has subjected us.[50]

So while Naipaul rightly explodes Mobutu's ersatz claims to authenticity,
he does so by trundling out the very racist inventions against which
Mobutu sought to arm himself in the first place.

One should therefore question to what extent the derelict condition of
Zaire is best explained by creating a composite character of Kurtz-
Mulele-Mobutu and by elegant hop-skip-and-jumping between Conrad's Congo of the 1890s and the Zaire of 1975, with almost no stops in
between. To what degree do those imperious phrases—about outposts
of progress, about enterprises in want of a deliberate belief and unredeemed by ideas—stand in for other, less resonant but more complex
explanations? And to what extent is his perception of "a country trapped
and static" predetermined by his insistence on tailoring Zaire to Conrad's distant representations? Finally, precisely because Naipaul's fatal-
ism about Africa is also an accusation, that of being historically para-
lyzed and unable to adapt to the "visitor's" ideas of "responsibility, the
state, and creativity," one should insist that his identification of nihilism
as the continent's defining characteristic be tested, in this instance,
against an understanding of Zaire's historical and economic dependen-
cies, as well as against the sordid history of the invention of Africa.

In the closing words of the Mobutu essay, Naipaul writes:

> To arrive at this sense of a country trapped and static, eternally vulnera-
> ble, is to begin to have something of the African sense of the void. It is to
> begin to fall, in the African way, into a dream of a past—the vacancy of
> river and forest, the hut in the brown yard, the dugout—when the dead
> ancestors watched and protected, and the enemies were only men.[51]

But Naipaul matches this African atavism, which he reads into the very
landscape, with an atavism all of his own. He çan only make sense of his
strange environment by imagining himself back into the position of
Conrad in a reconstructed narrative wherein Mulele and Mobutu are
coerced into appearing as throwbacks to Kurtz. Recollecting his river
odyssey, Naipaul notes in his diary: "Hard to believe in that thousand-
mile journey—so repetitive the scenes, the dug-outs, the huts. The heart
of darkness. The effect on a man of 1975, a journey undertaken deliberately: yet still with its elements of the mysterious, the dark."[52] At just
such moments, when his perceptions and understanding are obstructed,
Naipaul is most apt to draw on a Conradian phrase in an attempt to give
definition to his experiences. For it is primarily his assurance in superim-

posing a deliberate, well-mapped itinerary of the imagination onto Zaire that enables him to interpret the place with any confidence.

It is not surprising, therefore, to discern a note of alarm when he deduces: "History has disappeared. Even the Belgian colonial past. And no one, African, Asian, European, [in Zaire] has heard of Conrad or *Heart of Darkness*."[53] For a Western outsider, Conrad's steamboat voyage is so obviously the route to follow—not just literally but imaginatively—through Zaire, that Naipaul's realization of the insiders' ignorance of Conrad and their capacity to do without Conrad's mediations removes them and their society from the bounds of comprehension. Yet the crowning irony is that this very incomprehensibility does not cause Naipaul any self-mistrust; it does not challenge him to reconsider his relationship to Zaire by throwing into relief the limitations of Conrad as an interpretive tool. Instead, he contains his alarm by recasting his estrangement not as a relationship but as an attribute of the environment. And by substituting incomprehensibility for alienation, he can conveniently take deeper refuge in Conrad, confirming that author's prescience by perceiving all about him an impenetrability that he interprets as an unchanging quality of place rather than as an expression of the distance between a traveler primed by Conrad and a society both ignorant of the latter's writings and bearing the scantiest relation to them.

As an appendix, it should be noted that Naipaul threatened to sue the magazine *Discovery* (distributed only to holders of the American Express Gold Card) on finding that one of its writers had lifted, unacknowledged, the passage cited above equating Kurtz with Mulele.[54] It strikes me as scarcely coincidental that the author of an article on Africa in a glossy travel magazine should have chosen to plagiarize precisely the bit of Naipaul that leans most heavily on *Heart of Darkness,* for it is exactly that handed-down Africa that Western tourists would find most exotic yet most consolingly familiar.

Contra Conrad

The Nigerian author Chinua Achebe has written forcefully about the immense labor of overturning Conrad's legacy, of negating that particular negation. Clearly, Achebe has felt the pressure of Conrad's assumed priority as the 'natural' starting point for a Western understanding of Africa. And in trying to circumvent that imposed, imported 'naturalness,' he is alert to the difficulty of inventing alternative points of departure that are nevertheless accessible to African writers' often predominantly Western audiences. In Achebe's words: "Whatever Conrad's problems were, you might say, he is now safely dead. Quite true. Unfortunately his heart of darkness plagues us still"; he speaks angrily of "the wilful tenacity with which the West holds this image to its heart."[55] Rethinking this last remark, he speculates that "although I have used the word wilful a few times to characterize the West's view of Africa, it may well be that what is happening by this stage is more akin to reflex action than calculated malice."[56]

Cedric Watts, responding to Achebe's attack, has defended Conrad on the grounds that "[i]f one 'heart of darkness' is explicitly central Africa, another is London, centre of a 'mournful gloom,' 'a brooding gloom.' "[57] But will that rejoinder do? I would question whether Achebe's charges can ever be decisively countered by a return to the text. For the Nigerian's ire is surely not directed at Conrad alone but at the effect of the novella as it has been commonly transmitted and put to work by Western cultures. If one attends to the way *Heart of Darkness* has been taken up by subsequent writers and has passed into a wider non-literary discourse, it becomes clear that there is scarcely ever any attempt at a counterpoise between the River Thames and the River Congo, between a European and an African heart of darkness. Instead, Africa is treated quite solidly as the locus classicus of primitivism and degeneration.

Where Achebe assails the heart of darkness tradition head-on, the Afro-Caribbean poet Derek Walcott tries to deflect and reroute the core trope by generalizing it away from Africa:

> Through Kurtz's teeth, white skull in elephant grass
> the imperial fiction sings. Sunday
> wrinkles downriver from the Heart of Darkness.
> The heart of darkness is not Africa.
> The heart of darkness is the core of fire
> in the white center of the holocaust.
> The heart of darkness is the rubber claw
> selecting a scalpel in antiseptic light,
> the hills of children's shoes outside the chimneys,
> the tinkling nickel instruments on the white altar. . . .[58]

Walcott's effort to establish the heart of darkness as a figure for a moral condition no longer predicated on an African, or even a Third World, locale seems a thin straw in a very strong wind. Third World intellectuals have, on occasion, partially succeeded in doing what Walcott has set out to do, that is, worked a Western canonical text against the grain. Here one thinks especially of the popular appropriation in the 1960s and early 1970s of Shakespeare's Caliban as the triumphant, resisting slave and hero of decolonization.[59] Yet despite such precedents for counter-hegemonic co-option, my sense is that *Heart of Darkness* has become so entrenched in metropolitan discourse about the globe's "periphery" that I am pessimistic about the capacity of Third World writers to appropriate this insistent trope by reversing it. Such an advance seems particularly unlikely so long as writers like Naipaul persist in launching themselves from Conradian assumptions.

In seeking to generalize *Heart of Darkness* away from Africa in particular and, more broadly, to sunder the abiding connection between Conrad's trope and the Third World, Achebe and Walcott have attempted to clear a path for alternative, more varied representations of those regions. In the case of Africa, indigenous literatures have proliferated since the late 1950s, and the bulk of these representations are noncomparative and nonreactive; to take up Appiah's phrase, they do not require "the reader to understand Africa by embedding it in European culture."[60] In recording cultural differences, they avoid ranking them up- or downstream, that is, they resist the pressure to integrate cultures into a single, essentialist narrative, evolutionary or otherwise.

These developments were not available to Gide writing in the 1920s, Greene in the 1930s, and Arendt in the late 1940s and early 1950s. For the process of Africans and the African diaspora writing back—that is, the counter-tradition of remedial, internal representations by Africans—had, at that time, even by 1950, achieved little momentum. The same does not hold true for the period in which Naipaul deployed Conrad. If *Heart of Darkness* has remained an influential Western representation of Africa and one that has persisted in shaping a wider discourse about the continent, there existed by the 1970s a rich alternative vein of writing from within African cultural traditions, by the likes of Leopold Senghor, Kwame Nkrumah, Jomo Kenyatta, Chinua Achebe, Wole Soyinka, Ngugi wa Thiong'o, and scores of other Africans, as well as influential writings by Afro-Caribbeans of the standing of Aimé Césaire, Frantz Fanon, C. L. R. James, and Walter Rodney. Given these expanded (if still suppressed) options, Naipaul nonetheless preferred to write out of, rather than against, the predispositions of his audience.

Even amidst the expanded range of representational options of the postcolonial era, the selectively transmitted, overdetermined components of *Heart of Darkness* have retained an aggregate force with the power to close off other discursive avenues. This major representational

option has become so favored primarily because of a common perception of Conrad as trailblazer, but also because Western literary travelers
in Africa are apt to pursue each other's tracks. Gide dedicates his travelogue to Conrad and journeys up the Congo; Alberto Moravia travels
both their routes (one of his pieces, "Congo on My Mind," is billed as "a
voyage upriver, in the spirit of Joseph Conrad," and a chapter in a
second of his African travelogues is entitled "In the Footsteps of Gide");
Shiva Naipaul, in turn, defers to Conrad, Moravia, and Huxley; and
Huxley applauds Shiva Naipaul's book in the *New York Times*.[61]

Some of these authors do, on occasion, edge toward recognizing the
implications of their tendency to use Conrad as a kind of base camp and
each other as lean-tos along the way. Moravia comes closest to interro-
gating the problem of prior representation, of what Evelyn Waugh once
called places that are "already fully labelled."[62] Moravia's account of his
third voyage up the Zaire River in the imaginary wake of Conrad's
steamer begins with an appropriate insight into the label's capacity to
stand in for the locale itself:

> A word gives a name to a place and can also transform the place into
> literature—which, in turn, is substituted for the place. After Homer, in
> certain parts of the Mediterranean you are no longer traveling in Italy or
> Greece but in the *Iliad* or the *Odyssey*. And it could be said that today,
> after Conrad, you are not just in Zaire, or Malaysia, but in *Heart of
> Darkness* or in *Lord Jim*.[63]

This substitution could be described as a literary relative of that process
whereby, in Dean MacCannell's terms, the marker of a tourist spot may
come to take precedence over the sight itself.[64] Once Western literary
travelers enter "Conrad territory," they are expected to legitimate their
experiences by invoking the verbal marker "heart of darkness," which
stands as a guarantor that they were in touch with the real thing.

Although Gide never reflects as directly as Moravia on the prefigu-
rative shaping of his experience through the literary labeling of the
places he visits, he at least ponders, in the Congo narrative, the impact
of his anticipatory imaginings about the voyage. Given how steeped he is
in *Heart of Darkness* and how self-conscious he is about Conrad's precedent, this form of self-scrutiny clearly includes the impact of the novella
upon his expectations. That much is suggested, for example, by Gide's
remark: "My imaginary idea of this country was so lively . . . that I
wonder whether, in the future, this false image will not be stronger than
my memory of the reality and whether I shall see, Bangui, for instance,
in my mind's eye as it is really, or as I first of all imagined it would be."[65]

Nearly half a century later, Naipaul displays less interest than Gide in quizzing his own predispositions, among which the rediscovery of Conrad in Africa ranks highly. One might have expected from his writings at least an awareness of the accretive force of prior representations, of the power of dominant images to bond together and thicken into stereotypes. It is these precisely phrased stereotypes that Naipaul fails to interrogate and that, as a traveler, he allows to become his controlling preconceptions.

In his essay on Conrad, Naipaul alludes to an analogous process of prejudgment, that of reading with set expectations. There he reasons:

> We take to novels our own ideas of what the novel should be; and those ideas are made by our needs, our education, our background or perhaps our ideas of our background. Because we read, really, to find our what we already know. . . .[66]

What Naipaul seems reluctant to acknowledge is that in traveling, as in reading, one can set out so well-wadded with received expectations that, in purportedly venturing into the "heart" of Africa, one proceeds instead to plunge, once again, deeper and deeper into the imagined heart of Conrad's fiction.

5

The Terms of Dismissal: 'Barbarism,' 'Primitivism,' and 'Simple Societies'

These people [in Trinidad] live purely physical lives, which I find contemptible. It makes them interesting only to chaps in universities who want to do compassionate studies about brutes.

V. S. NAIPAUL, "Naipaul Reviews His Past From Afar"

[There is] a danger that we may underestimate the variety of African sculpture; as we are less able to appreciate the respects in which they differ from one another than the respects in which they differ from those to which we are used, we tend to see a certain resemblance between them, which lies, in point of fact, merely in their common differentness.

MICHEL LEIRIS, "The African Negroes and the Arts of Carving and Sculpture"

A few years back, during the course of a quarrelsome interview, Naipaul scolded Bharati Mukherjee for trying to discuss his work in terms he could not relate to. "You see," he explained, "from the very early days I've been very careful in my work not to use words that produce the wrong associations. I don't use the word 'imperialist' or 'colonialist,' for example."[1] In shunning such terms, Naipaul turns elsewhere for the mainstays of his idiom: to "barbarous", "primitive", "tribal", "static", and "simple" societies, "world civilization," the "bush," "philistine", the "colonial", the "whole man", "security", "sentimentality", "parasitic", "borrowed culture", and "mimicry". Reiteratively, and in combination, these terms of reference become a compressed expression of Naipaul's *Weltanschauung*. The reasoning behind Leiris's caveat, in the second epigraph, against lumping together the diverse styles of African sculpture can be profitably directed at Naipaul for, as his compact portmanteau of rhetoric indicates, he is apt to homogenize unfamiliar, dissimilar cultures under the rubric of their "common differentness."

The assumptions of Naipaul's limited idiom, no less than his elective affinities with Victorian travelers and Conrad, connect him with the discursive traditions of imperialism. This link is most apparent in his ranging of Third World cultures between the "primitive," at the one extreme, and the "mimic," at the other. As I discuss in the following two chapters, Naipaul reviles the 'pure natives' and the *évolués* with equal vehemence: the former are insufficiently improved, hopelessly backward, while the latter ape metropolitan values, rather than absorbing them, and so become living parodies of civilization. Naipaul thus couches primitivism and mimicry as antipodes that, between them, contain the spectrum of Third World cultural identities. By resorting to this imperial catch-22, Naipaul forecloses rhetorically all possibility of affirmative cultural identities, self-respect, and productive cultural interchange. In the process, he proves himself quite beyond placation.

I shall reserve a separate chapter for a discussion of mimicry: it is sufficiently central to Naipaul's vision of postcolonialism to require protracted analysis. But the implications of his fixation on mimicry cannot be fully understood without the backdrop of the other two terms—"primitive" and "simple societies"—on which he relies most heavily for his blanket dismissal of Third World societies. In analyzing the pivotal positions of these two terms, one has to probe, in particular, their role in advancing his perception of the former colonies as fatally static. For if his theory of mimicry seeks to expose the illusory progress that results from cultural imitation, his use of "primitive" and the "simple society" argues for a conception of postcolonial societies as stagnant due, in large part, to their isolation from history. One can tease out the logic of this argument by considering the cultural assumptions which the terms "primitive" and "simple society" bring in train. This entails questioning Naipaul's use of these terms to distinguish evaluatively between cultures that possess history and cultures that, in his view, have never acquired it.

Because these terms are so persistent in his work, my discussion necessarily ventures across the breadth of his nonfiction. However, I place special emphasis on two texts: *India: A Wounded Civilization* (the 1977 sequel to *An Area of Darkness*), where his arguments against the "primitive" past appear in their most concentrated form, and *The Loss of El Dorado,* published in 1969. The latter, which one can usefully view as the pivotal volume in a New World trilogy opened by *The Middle Passage* and closed by *A Turn in the South,* is a charismatic, eccentric history of Trinidad that admits unique insight into Naipaul's conception of "simple societies".

'Barbarism'/'Primitivism'

For a contemporary writer, Naipaul employs the related terms "barbarous" and "primitive" with unusual frequency and license. "Barbarous" is the less complex of the two. It generally appears in the rhetorical matrix of his work as a self-consciously divisive gesture that is calculated, through its blatant bigotry, to offend one constituency and delight another. One does not have to search far for examples. On the subject of South Asian immigration to Britain he observes:

> I feel there will be a lot of difficulty. I don't see how it can be avoided, especially with these immigrants who are not migrating to a new identity or a new kind of citizenship. They are migrating to allow their barbarism to flower so they can be more Islamic or more Sikhish than they can be with the comparative economic stagnation of their home societies.[2]

It is significant that he issued this attack in *The Illustrated Weekly of India* and that he specifically targets Islamic and Sikh immigrants. The result is an easy style of outrageousness against groups who have minority status in India and who have already been singled out as 'barbarians' by Western discourse on terrorism. So while his use of "barbarism" may seem riskily offensive in relation to other "serious literature," read in the context of a wider political discourse, it can be seen to reinforce widespread prejudices against specific ethnic or religious groups who are deemed to be, in their entirety, exempt from civilization. Uttered at a time of resurgent populist racism in Britain, Naipaul's insistence on the recalcitrant barbarism of black immigrants confirms the sense, widespread in white British culture, that such people take advantage of British "hospitality" while refusing to compromise on their difference. On this reading, white racism (which does not earn a mention in Naipaul's articulation of immigrant tensions) becomes not the root problem, but a reflex gesture of self-defense against uncompromising, unassimilable invaders. Thatcher herself gave clear voice to this sentiment:

> . . . people are really rather afraid that this country might be swamped by people with a different culture. And, you know, the British character has done so much for democracy, for law, and done so much throughout the world, that if there is a fear that it might be swamped, people are going to react rather hostile to those coming in.[3]

To recall Thatcher here is not, of course, to equate her and Naipaul's styles of bigotry; each follows a distinctive course. But it remains crucial that we recognize how Naipaul's insistence on immigrant "barbarism" and his simultaneous refusal to discuss white British prejudice becomes useful to the project of Thatcherism's racist, authoritarian populism. Here, his own status as an immigrant from the colonies becomes the critical factor: by posing as a living oxymoron, a civilized barbarian, he can draw on his own experience to call the black immigrants' bluff.

Because of his attraction to binary thinking, one can map much of Naipaul's thought off four points of reference: at the broadest level, he counterpoints "barbarous" and "civilized" and then subdivides the "barbarous" into the "primitive" and the "mimic".[4] But "primitive" assumes a more critical place than "barbarism" in the rhetorical texture of his account of intercultural relations. And although he may also invoke it for purposes of theatrical racism, the term carries a more complex set of associations. Through the course of his nonfiction, "primitive" takes on different shades of reference: sometimes it appears as a synonym for "barbarous", sometimes as a reference to preindustrial economic and cultural forms, and on occasion it refers, more loosely, to partially modernized societies.

The differences between "primitive" and "barbarism" are primarily twofold. First, if "barbarism" evokes a sense of people *without* culture, "primitive" resonates with the idea of people who *possess* culture, but whose culture is quarantined from change. The latter term is therefore more central to Naipaul's arguments about cultural stasis. Second, compared to the polemically pejorative "barbarous", "primitive" retains a residual social scientific aura. Hence, according to circumstance, Naipaul can manipulate the term's uncertain mixture of methodological distance and emotive evaluation. Significantly, the equivocal character of the term corresponds to the two distinct voices that Naipaul employs in his travelogues: the analytical, explanatory, semiethnographic voice of the Third World "expert" and the temperamental, autobiographical voice of the grumpy traveler. This correspondence makes it easier for him to slide between the tones of "expert" analysis and bigoted dismissals.

Naipaul's problematic deployment of "primitive" is exemplified by his condemnation of the

> romanticism [that] begins by sympathizing with the oppressed and ends by exalting their values. . . . It would civilize Africans simply by denying that they are primitive; it would remove untouchability in India simply by denying that untouchability has any rational basis. But we reject this

attitude when, in Kenya, we see naked young savages, chalked white after some ceremony of the forest, prancing beside the highway, as though the world were still all bush.

. . .

The oppressed have their responsibility which the statement "A man is a man" denies, but which "I do not want to be like them" might awaken. The humane corollary is: "I want them to be like me." To civilize Africa (if that must be attempted—the issue is debatable), you recognize the primitive and try to eradicate it.[5]

This outburst brings into focus several of the rhetorical methods and political purposes associated with Naipaul's attachment to the term "primitive". First, there are the Manichaean divisions between cultures: those that deserve to be perpetuated and those that need to be eradicated. The genocidal inflection to the final sentence is accentuated by the "it" that follows "eradicate"; the formulation implicates Naipaul in the long colonial tradition of establishing the "primitive" as an object of study, in a manner that has rationalized control and not infrequently legitimized decimation. The tone and implications resurface in his more recent remark: "I'm not concerned with perserving the backward races. I find them very boring. . . . I'm interested in people with interesting minds."[6]

In dismissing the Kenyan "primitives", Naipaul launches two different kinds of appeal, classificatory and emotional, that are symptomatic of the way the term has traditionally produced slippage between pseudo-scientific and gut racism. He first chastizes Westerners who side with the oppressed for refusing to recognize "that they are primitive." Then, to clinch his argument, he creates a scenario of prancing "savages" and watches his "sympathetic" Westerner recoiling from this exposure to extreme difference. But this second appeal—like his rejection of the "backward races" because he finds them boring—is couched purely in terms of personal distaste. Thus an emotional response to cultural difference becomes the basis for an assessment of cultural value.

The issue of value is pivotal. If, as he suggests, some romantics uncritically exalt the values of the oppressed, Naipaul himself goes to the other extreme. Dividing cultures with Manichaean rigidity, he assumes that there is virtually nothing of cultural worth outside the West. Behind this categorical rejection there are really two assumptions: first, that the values of the globally marginalized and the "primitive" are not even functionally valid in their own contexts and, second, that such cultures have nothing to offer the West.

His Kenyan example ironically highlights the problems with the first of these assumptions. Naipaul ignores the fact that certain "ceremonies of the forest" of the sort that he derides were absolutely central to the resolve of the "Mau Mau" resistance and thereby played an important part in securing an end to British colonialism in Kenya.[7] Whatever neo-colonial residue remains in Kenya, is the demise of formal colonialism not to be considered a gain?

Indeed, from the perspective of the rhetoric of primitivism, one of the fascinating consequences of the anticolonial struggles was their subversion of Western mythologies of cultural stasis. The incontrovertible evidence of supposedly "static" societies generating strategies for seizing control of their destinies helped erode the scope and validity of the category "primitive" in the postcolonial era. In the process, the dynamism of the anticolonial struggles contributed to the attenuation of the disciplinary authority of anthropology itself.

The withered credibility of the term 'primitive' can be linked to its status as a temporal concept premised on evaluative myths of progress.[8] Through the experience of anticolonial resistance, many cultures emerged, rhetorically, for the first time, as the West's contemporaries. The rhetoric of nationalism and the forced acknowledgment that such cultures possessed history helped secure this transition.

So when Naipaul describes Kenyans, Indians, Iranians, and Zairians as "primitive", he is trying to reassert the temporal idiom—to set back the rhetorical clock. Given his commitment to an uncomplicated dismissal of Third World societies as devoid of history, it is scarcely surprising that he finds the temporal metaphor seductive. And while it is centered on his use of the term "primitive", it is by my no means limited to it. As he muses in *The Enigma of Arrival:* "From London to Trinidad to St. Kitts and Anguilla, Guatemala City and Belize: the journey might have been planned by a man wishing to move backwards in time . . . ."[9]

Western Sentimentality Towards the "Primitive"

It is characteristic of Naipaul that his attack on Kenyan and Indian "primitivism" began with a jab at Westerners who romanticize such cultures. For he repeatedly introduces the term "primitive" as a way of articulating his profound intolerance at what he perceives as the congruent sentimentalities of the West and of cultures comparatively remote from Western influence. Specifically, he expresses impatience both with the idealistic seekers who travel from Europe and America in order to expose themselves to alternative cultural values and with the inhabitants of those societies who, in his view, are self-destructively indulgent of their ruinous cultural pasts. In other words, Naipaul strives to expose the spuriousness of the non-Western values sought after by disaffected Westerners as well as the futile myths that isolated "primitive" cultures tell themselves.

These twin sentimentalities are, then, premised on positive conceptions of "primitive" society. Naipaul's criticisms of the first form of indulgence occur most frequently in his Indian writings. In *An Area of Darkness* he expresses distaste for

> the new type of American whose privilege it was to go slumming about the world and sometimes scrounging, exacting a personal repayment for a national generosity. . . . India, the world's largest slum, had an added attraction: 'cultural' humility was sweet, but 'spiritual' humility was sweeter."[10]

The most memorable of these naive, imposing, and idealistic "seekers" is an American named Laraine who, visiting India for two weeks, decides to stay for six months, steep herself in Hindu philosophy, and join an ashram.[11] Naipaul's primary complaints about her type are twofold: first, he is convinced that if Western civilization falls short, nothing outside it can be expected to help remedy any of its deficiencies; second, he argues that seekers' material security compromises the seriousness of their quests:

> They, the rich countries, even manage to export their romantic doubts about industrial civilization. These are the doubts that attend every kind of great success; and they are romantic because they contain no wish to undo that success or to lose the fruits of that success.[12]

As the tone of this remark suggests, Naipaul's impatience with the seekers who venture eastward in search of alternative values is consistent with his critique of Greene and the Georgian travel writers, who never pondered the security that cushioned their risk taking.

If Greene's time-machine response to non-Western cultures simultaneously primitivizes and romanticizes them, Naipaul, by contrast, wishes to retain the idea of the 'primitive' as a temporal category while ditching the romanticism. The seekers of the sixties and seventies, however, generally departed from both these approaches by retaining the romanticism without seeing the alternative cultures they probed as categorically backward in time. Where Naipaul imposes a rhetoric of primitivism on cultures that he sees as having reneged on reason and succumbed to magic and religion, the seekers refracted those same societies through a rhetoric of transcendence.

Plainly, most of the seekers allegorized non-Western cultures in terms of their personal needs. As a consequence, their involvement with those societies was often reduced, as Naipaul charges, to narcissistic, sheltered displays of cultural dabbling. Yet despite the accuracy of these criticisms, Naipaul's overall rejection of Western efforts to engage with the values of non-Western cultures remains unsatisfactory. If the seekers' quests were sustained by an unacknowledged set of privileges and their cultural self-criticisms attended by an element of bad faith, in what sense is Naipaul's return-ticket cynicism less compromised than their return-ticket idealism? His interest in non-Western societies can be just as ephemeral, fashionable, and uncostly as that of any questing metropolitan wanderer.

But more is at stake here than Naipaul's own unexamined bad faith. It is peculiarly symptomatic of his vision of the postcolonial era that the *only* Westerners whom he consistently condemns are those who crave contact with alternative values. Such desires are always and only sentimental. This judgment applies equally to the idealists who explore what Naipaul would class as "primitive" cultures ("ruled by ritual and myth") and those who travel to the partially Westernized "simple societies" of the Caribbean and Latin America.[13] The seekers who are drawn to the Caribbean, like those described in his essays on Trinidadian Black Power and Grenada, are likely to venture there for political rather than for spiritual motives.[14] But either way, whether these Westerners inquire into the old religious values of Hinduism, Islam, and Africa or look forward to the political transformation of so-called Third World societies, their engagement with other people's cultural values is wholly misguided.[15]

Naipaul's dismissal of any positive response to cultures outside the West looks particularly tendentious when one juxtaposes it to his refusal to engage critically with the political morality of imperialism. His position is part of his wider determination to recognize nothing of value in non-Western cultures per se, while, in addition, condemning cultural mixing. Of course, confusion and chaotic misunderstandings often do issue from cultural eclecticism; the problem is that Naipaul refuses to track anything but the negative consequences. Must one assume that none of his "primitive" or "simple" societies has anything to offer the West? And, moreover, that Western cultures have not already productively incorporated and adapted aspects of those cultures?

My objection to Naipaul's account of the sentimental "primitive" can be clarified by situating his rhetoric in terms of the debates that arose over the 1984–85 Museum of Modern Art exhibition " 'Primitivism' in 20th Century Art." The MOMA controversy revolved around very similar issues to those under discussion: the implications of the term 'primitive', questions of cultural stasis, transculturation, and colonialism, and the dangers of sentimentality.[16] The exhibition announced itself as celebrating the affinities between 'primitive' artifacts and some of the dominant currents in modern art. As such, it acknowledged the positive possibilities that can take shape at the cultural interface. If the titular "primitivism" refers to an aesthetic movement, the scare quotes nonetheless suggest that the organizers wished to muffle the pejorative reverberations of 'primitive'. One discerns, then, an implicit rejection of the very associations that Naipaul keeps in place: the residual taxonomic authority, the sense of temporal backwardness and irrationality.

However, the MOMA's decision to provide historical contexts for the Western but not for the so-called tribal art was loaded. First, the MOMA thereby avoided confronting the colonial circumstances behind the amassing of other cultures' art. But as Clifford has noted in his incisive critique of the exhibition, the colonial overtones surface in the language of the catalogue and the labeling—in terms like "preserving," "collecting," "the specimen," "discovering," and "the authentic." The absence of a historical context for the 'tribal' works has a second consequence: it sets up an implicit opposition between the developing aesthetic traditions of the West and the cultural stasis of the 'primitive'. In the one instance, history matters; in the other, it either doesn't exist or is inconsequential. As a result, the exhibition reproduces a brittle ethnic distinction between culture as *process* and culture as *timeless function*.[17]

Clifford points up two other major failings of the exhibition: the way it elevates 'pure' over 'mixed' tribal art and, relatedly, the absence of Third World modernisms. Hence, the account of cultural interaction that emerges is very one-sided. The emotional focus is on Western artists inventively transforming 'primitive' material, thereby introducing it to history. There is scarcely a hint of the reverse process—of Western material being incorporated into other aesthetic histories.[18]

The connections to Naipaul's theory of the 'primitive' become explicit when one crosses from Clifford's critique of the exhibition to the diametrically opposed critique articulated by Hilton Kramer in *The New Criterion*. If Clifford searches for the missing histories of the 'tribal' and the colonial, Kramer laments another absent history: "[A]ny serious account of the way bourgeois culture responded to this primitivist assault on its values."[19] Like Naipaul, Kramer refuses to dress his 'primitives' in scare quotes. And he reads the terminological tentativeness at the MOMA as a mark of the West's wavering resolve in the battle to keep alien modes of consciousness at bay.

Kramer and Naipaul have almost identical conceptions of the 'primitive' as the enemy. Kramer suffers from nightmares of the avant-garde and the 'primitive' in league against the values of the West; Naipaul feels that his civilization is in danger before the joint forces of "the people of the bush" and those sentimental enough in the West to indulge them.[20] In railing against cultural syncretism, both writers overestimate how much cultural purity there is in the civilization they cherish and underestimate the often regenerative role of hybrid values. Moreover, for polemical thrust, both Naipaul and Kramer depend on an untenable distinction between a pure, liberated individualism of the West and a tyrannical collectivism of the Rest.

It is important to recognize the institutional dimension to the correspondence between Naipaul's and Kramer's attraction to the rhetoric of the 'primitive'. Joseph Epstein, Kramer's ideological henchman at *The New Criterion* (and editor of *American Scholar*) is one of Naipaul's most vociferous defenders in the United States. And it says a lot about Naipaul's constituency and role that Epstein delights in his work largely because it breathes new life into terms like *primitive* and *barbarous:*

> It may well be that among living writers only Naipaul is able to speak of "barbarian peoples"; only he can say things that, *though perfectly apparent,* in the mouths of others would straightaway be declared racism. (Emphasis added)[21]

Internal Sentimentality and the Idea of the Past

Naipaul, I have suggested, discerns two complementary styles of sentimentality towards the "primitive"—one coming from outside the culture and one from within. The external sentimentality entails, in his terms, the irresponsible indulgence of styles of cultural vacancy that should be recognized as having nothing to offer the West. As he has stressed on several occasions, the West's sole responsibility toward non-Western societies is to desist from romanticizing them.[22]

How, then, does he conceive of internal sentimentality? In what sense can "primitive" or "simple" societies be seen to romanticize themselves with damaging consequences? My approach to these questions entails an integrated response to a couple of Naipaul's key cultural assumptions.

First, he distinguishes between the past and history: the former is simple and associated with "primitive" or "half-made" societies; the latter is complex and a prerogative of the West. He reviles the past because he associates it with the regressive myths and fantasies that 'tribal' societies fabricate about themselves. The possession of history, on the other hand, is a precondition for and product of human achievement. The motifs of absent history and the debilitating presence of a phantasmagoric past repeat themselves across Naipaul's Indian, Caribbean, and Islamic writings, resurfacing in essays on Zaire, Egypt, the Ivory Coast, Mauritius, and Argentina.

But it is not only "primitive" societies—those he sees as dominated by ritual and magic—that are disqualified from history. He also excludes "simple societies", one of his fundamental groupings, but one that he keeps deliberately vague. "Simple" is a penumbral adjective that, in Naipaul's register of social description, shades into both "primitive" and "mimic": on occasion it refers to nonindustrial or peasant societies; at other times he employs it interchangeably with "mimic". So if the poles of the "primitive" and the "mimic" allow Naipaul to divide Third World cultures into those mired in the primordial and those ruined by pseudo-sophistication, "simple" serves as something of a bridge between the two.

It is important to bear in mind the historical context for his critique of simple societies' sentimental fantasies about their pasts. The postcolonial period has been an era in which scores of newly independent societies have had to reconceive their identities, defining themselves to themselves and to others in national terms. The efforts to achieve national cohesion have entailed that these societies affirm distinctive identities through, among other rhetorical gestures, invocations of the past.

Naipaul's impatience with national assertions of the past is well illustrated by his response to the Gandhianism of Jagan, the hero of R. K. Narayan's novel, *The Vendor of Sweets*. Arguing that Jagan's attitudes reek of futile sentimentality, Naipaul represents them as

> a retreat from civilization and creativity, from rebirth and growth, to magic and incantation, a retrogression to an almost African night, the enduring primitivism of a place like the Congo, where, even after the slave-trading Arabs and the Belgians, the past is yearned for as *le bon vieux temps de nos ancêtres*.[23]

Naipaul's admonition of India is categorical: "[T]he past has to be seen as dead, or the past will kill."[24]

In treating the Indian past as pure impediment, Naipaul discusses the bullock cart at length as an instance of a "primitive" technology that Indian politicians and scientists have attempted to redeem, through adaptation, for an altered future. Naipaul would persuade us that the very notion of improving the performance of the bullock cart is risible and squanderous. Yet, in his attempt to do so, he skips too quickly and condescendingly over a fundamental concern—"that Indian technology should match Indian resources and take into account the nature of Indian society."[25] If he rejects all plans for "intermediate technology" out of hand and denies India any capacity for cultural synthesis, what does he tender instead? His ultimatum to India—no future until the nation agrees to efface its past—is airier than any scheme to upgrade bullock carts. Given his own critical dismembering of projects to reinvent a purely Aryan India, one might have expected a greater skepticism towards the feasibility or even desirability of cultural tabula rasae. Cultural change proceeds in a more compromised, more contaminated fashion. The abstraction of his starting point—the attempt to will into being a secular India that spurns its past—serves only, in the end, as a measure of the determination of his pessimism.

By forcing the distinction between the "primitive" category of the past and the Western category of history, Naipaul is able to hold Third World societies in one of his classic double-binds: without a sense of history, they can achieve nothing, yet what they tender as their history is something utterly different, amounting to embellishents of the past that either do not evidence achievement or elude description in historical terms. So Caribbean efforts to reconnect themselves with Africa—imaginatively and emotionally—are brushed aside as nostalgic, as the "sentimental camaraderie of skin."[26] And in Argentina he discerns "legend and antiquarian romance, but no real history."[27]

Whether he is anatomizing Indian, Trinidadian, Argentinian, or Egyptian nationalism, Naipaul's position on the past as a sentimental category remains constant. Gazing at a work of art adorning the insides of the pyramids, he muses:

> Perhaps that had been the only pure time, at the beginning, when the ancient artist, knowing no other land, had learned to look at his own and had seen it as complete. But it was hard, travelling back to Cairo, looking with my stranger's eye at the fields and the people who worked in them, the dusty towns, the agitated peasant crowds at railway stations, it was hard to believe that there had been such innocence. Perhaps that vision of the land, in which the Nile was only water, a blue-green chevron, had always been a fabrication, a cause for yearning, something for the tomb.[28]

The tone, in this outpouring of lyrical skepticism, is less bitter than when he scoffs at the Indian past. But the sentiments repeat themselves.

For Naipaul, a prominent factor in ensuring that "simple societies" remain simple is their failure to admit that the only sane response to the past is urgent forgetfulness. Suffering from what one might call Lot's Wife's syndrome, "simple societies" permit themselves a backward glance and are thereby doomed to cultural stasis. Yet here, as elsewhere in his thought, Naipaul's arguments are inadequate because he neglects to consider the corresponding phenomenon in the West—in this case, the relationship between the rhetoric of nationalism and the language of the past. Is one to assume, from his accounts, that "fabrications" of the past are endemic to the so-called Third World and absent from the First? Certainly, his silence about Western nationalisms and his discrimination between history as a rational Western category and the past as an irrational, Third World one suggest, in combination, that he sees the sentimental fantasy as a failing peculiar to decolonizing nations.

Naipaul distributes reason and unreason too cleanly. When Thatcher urges a return to the Victorian values that once made Britain great, when Reagan recognizes the contras as the moral equals of the founding fathers, when a French politician invokes the spirit of the French Revolution, why are these historical utterances, while Third World references to the past remain self-indulgent fantasies? The rhetorical paraphernalia of the national past is not a fatal flaw of the "simple society"; it is constitutive of what Benedict Anderson terms the imagined community of the nation.[29] The West has its corresponding styles of sentimentality, which are entangled in the business of—to borrow Hobsbawm and Ranger's phrase—the invention of traditions.[30] Globally, this inventiveness is, in itself, neither good nor bad; it can become either according to circumstance. Politically rivalrous, strategic fabrication around the idea of a shared past is an inevitable feature of modern nationalism and should therefore not be represented as a style of irrationality definitive of "simple societies".

El Dorado: The 'Simple Society' and Historical Form

I have suggested that the force of Naipaul's term 'simple society' requires that he successfully exclude such a society from the discourse of history that, in his terms, is the rational record of national achievement. In his effort to fence off history as a uniquely Western preserve, his commonest argument is that nothing significant happens in "simple societies"—there is therefore nothing to tell. But on occasion, he makes a more subtle case for a fundamental incompatability between history as a Western genre and the kind of events that occur outside the West. In *India: A Wounded Civilization* he launches precisely this style of argument:

> India blindly swallows its past. To understand that past, it has had to borrow alien academic disciplines; and, as with the technology, their foreign origin shows. Much historical research has been done; but European methods of historical inquiry, arising out of one kind of civilization, with its own developing ideas of the human condition, cannot be applied to Indian civilization; they miss too much. Political or dynastic events, economic life, cultural trends: the European approach elucidates little, has the effect of an unsuccessful attempt to equate India with Europe, and makes nonsense of the stops and starts of Indian civilization, the brief flowerings, the long periods of sterility, men forever claimed by the instinctive life, continuity turning to barbarism.[31]

Here the strength of Naipaul's argument derives from his recognition that history as a genre, as a particular textual tradition, is of Western provenance. At the same time, the double-bind becomes too formulaic: On the one hand, he deems that particular Western textual tradition untransferable; on the other, he does not take seriously alternative traditions of arranging the past.[32] In the context of the protracted polemics of *India: A Wounded Civilization,* and even in the context of the above passage, which wends its way unerringly toward "barbarism," the remark that "European methods of historical inquiry" are inapposite because "they miss too much," smacks of disingenuousness. For throughout *India: A Wounded Civilization,* as in the body of his oeuvre, Naipaul concerns himself less with what such historical methods *elide* than with what they *fabricate* by flattering such cycles of "nonevents" with the title of "events."

Naipaul mounts his most sustained polemics on the interdependent issues of the 'simple society,' historical form, and nonachievement in his Caribbean writings. He first announced his basic position—cryptically and infamously—in *The Middle Passage:*

> How can the history of this West Indian futility be written? . . . The history of the islands can never be satisfactorily told. Brutality is not the only difficulty. History is built around achievement and creation; and nothing was created in the West Indies.[33]

Seven years after asserting this view, Naipaul produced an elaborate, book-length defense of it: *The Loss of El Dorado: A History*.[34] Its title notwithstanding, the 380-page volume emerges as an antihistory of the island, a vindication, through fractured form, of the impossibility of narrating nonevents. *The Loss of El Dorado* emerges, in short, as a history of the absence of history.

This quirky, multifaceted volume is more than Naipaul's rendition of the origins and destiny of a "simple society." It stands, too, as an exercise in archival autobiography, an attempt to explain his personal sense of the absurdity of his East Indian-West Indian beginnings by staging a historical argument for the ineluctable absurdity of Trinidad per se.[35] He turns to the colonial archives in order both to explain himself and to trace the origins of his lifelong sense of Trinidad as a naturally static society cut adrift from the real world of historical events.

Written between 1966 and 1968 and published the following year, *The Loss of El Dorado* was born of a commission for a conventional travel book but quickly metamorphosed into something quite different. It can be read as extending Naipaul's autobiographical fixation with that peculiar sense of loss that follows from dwelling in fantasies as if they offered the security and substance of reality. As a child, he had lost Trinidad by dreaming of England; the dream England of his books, in turn, evaporated on his arrival in London; then his first trip to the sub-continent destroyed his imaginary India.

The personal urgency of *The Loss of El Dorado* rings on almost every page; it is a book of exceptional stylistic attainments, splendidly imagined, that animates select episodes of Trinidad's past by means of almost novelistic characterization. In the process of writing it, as Naipaul was much later to articulate, he had given himself "a past, and a romance of the past."[36] But this passionate need to equip himself with a past required, paradoxically, that that past be counted an absence, too insubstantial to rank as history. Thus conceived, it could ratify his lifelong sense of being starved of a real society, of suffering from the permanent pangs of hunger left by the fruit of dreams.

El Dorado becomes, thereby, Naipaul's most extended explication of the concept of the "simple society," the kind of place that fails not only to generate history but also to produce 'whole' human beings.[37] The formal procedures he adopts are of fundamental importance to these interwoven arguments about history and social simplicity. Naipaul circumscribes Trinidad's history by narrating, at length, "two forgotten stories."[38] The first of these, which has traditionally been dominated by Sir Walter Ralegh's account of the events, begins with Ralegh's assault

London Calling

on Trinidad and South America in 1595 and ends with his return to the island in 1617, on parole from the Tower of London. The centerpiece of this story, however, is the emergence of Trinidad as a Spanish base for the obsessive pursuit (notably by Fernando Berrio and Ralegh) of the illusory El Dorado. Then quite consciously (indeed, polemically), Naipaul skips almost 200 years to arrive at his second story: the British attempt, at the outset of the nineteenth century, to use Port of Spain as a base for the stimulation of revolts against Spain in South America, the grander design being to "liberate" the continent for British mercantilism. Although the British disseminated lofty anti-imperial ideas in the hopes of fomenting revolt, their overall strategy included (apparently without qualms over the contradictions) the transformation of the island into an agricultural slave colony.

Through paradoxical assertions that are indissociable from his conception of the historical incapacities of "simple societies", Naipaul views his history of Trinidad's capital as simultaneously limited and comprehensive:

> The history of Port of Spain, a special New World adventure, is contained in these stories. A place like Port of Spain, in the uncluttered New World, has no independent life; it alters with the people who come to it.[39]

In the foreword to the volume, he remarks analogously:

> People who write about Ralegh usually have to hurry back with him to the Tower of London; they pay as little attention as Ralegh himself to what was left behind. An obscure part of the New World is momentarily touched by history; the darkness closes up again; the Chaguanes disappear in silence. *The disappearance is unimportant; it is part of nobody's story.* But this was how a colony was created in the New World. There were two moments when Trinidad was touched by 'history'. This book attempts to record those two moments. The story ends in 1813. (Emphasis added)[40]

The rhetoric of this passage displays, quite starkly, the political premises of the book. The repeated figure of Trinidad being "touched by 'history' " merits particular reflection. In these terms, a "simple society" can never generate its own history or even produce history interactively with other societies. Instead, history is the prerogative of the metropole to bestow or to withhold at will. Curiously, Naipaul represents his project as redressing the bias of the historians who rush back to Europe with Ralegh, yet his remedial account remains predicated on a Eurocentric notion of what constitutes a historical event.

Naipaul's view of history as something that reaches in from abroad allows him to make the perplexing assertion that the disappearance of Chaguanes "is unimportant; it is part of nobody's story."[41] The comment is shadowed by ambiguity. Does the "nobody" refer to the colonial historians or to the inhabitants of Chaguanes? Insofar as the disappearance of the settlement passed unrecorded in any of the colonial documents that Naipaul excavated in the British Museum, the Public Record Office, and the London Library, it is indeed part of no written story. But his remark also suggests that the people of Chaguanes were of negligible account. What is disturbing here is his decision to abide by the standards of importance and unimportance that he finds in his colonial sources.

The West Indian historian, A. C. Wade, has queried the assumptions underlying Naipaul's historiographic approach in *The Loss of El Dorado* as follows:

> Naipaul is attempting to show the failure of the Colonial Adventure and its disruption of the first West Indian traditions. Yet, as we have seen, it feels more like a metropolitan loss than ours because Naipaul never explores the lives of the Negroes and Amerindians who comprised the two largest racial groups in that area. The author's one-sidedness is a result of his preoccupation with the records which the colonizers left. This raises the question of how else the story of Amerindian and Negro disruption may be examined if not through the records of the European exploiters in these islands.[42]

In other words, the "two forgotten stories" that Naipaul seeks to revive remain tales of metropolitan intervention told from a metropolitan vantage point. What, then, of the forgotten stories within the forgotten stories? Naipaul's text recovers scarcely any details about the cultures of the colonized and enslaved peoples. His few observations concerning them are focused through a schema predicated on his conviction that the colonial fantasies above were met from below by the congruent fantasies of the black underworld. No other sense of indigenous culture is admitted.

Given that Naipaul has chosen to focus solely on periods at the end of the sixteenth and the beginning of the nineteenth century, the task of reconstructing the cultures of the colonized people from colonial documents is indeed formidable. What alternatives are there to the historiographic methods and political assumptions of the colonial chroniclers? In *The Black Jacobins,* C. L. R. James responded to this question in a manner that constrasts instructively with Naipaul's approach. Like *The Loss of El Dorado, The Black Jacobins* is an idiosyncratically personal, polemical, and eloquent Caribbean narrative, but the methods and ambitions of the two works diverge significantly in that James's history of the

San Domingo revolution directly confronts the dilemmas and responsibilities of the West Indian historian.[43] Through its titular and textual subversion of Eurocentric categories, *The Black Jacobins* works to redeem the San Domingo revolution from the margins of European history. In James's words: "In 1938 I wrote *The Black Jacobins* in which I showed the role that Blacks played in the creation of modern Europe."[44]

Manifestly, no uprising in Trinidad compared in scale or duration to the revolution of 1791–1803, which brought Haiti its independence, but the very difference between Naipaul's and James's choice of focus is revealing. James reinscribes a Caribbean event into the global dynamics of history, so that Haiti does not appear *solely* as a product of European desires and actions. By contrast, Naipaul's commitment to the idea of the "simple society"s' historical stasis bars him from presenting blacks and Amerindians as in any sense agents in history, even in the emergence of their own society.

Because Naipaul has contoured his history to two primary motifs (the "simple society's" predilection for fantasy and its static history), *The Loss of El Dorado* acquires quite specific structural limitations. First, in his effort to convey the society's "sense of the missing real world" Naipaul quarantines events on the island from developments elsewhere.[45] John Updike describes the effect with precision:

> The richly detailed episodes of West Indian history hover, however, in a virtual vacuum; the matrix of world circumstances—not only the power struggles on the Continent but even the events on nearby islands—is so lightly limned that the machinations on Trinidad appear as eerie as the motions of a sleepwalker.[46]

By situating Trinidad in a geographical and historical vacuum, Naipaul accentuates the sense of the society as a natural site of unreal, irrational, simple, futile, chimerical causes.

If the autobiographical strains give the book a contemporary relevance, the timing of its publication suggests that the arguments were meant to carry a future force as well. What are we to make of the fact that in 1969, just a few years after Trinidad has achieved its formal independence from colonialism, Naipaul produces a theory that the island's fate was sealed by 1813—the last time anything happened there? In other words, how are we to interpret the appearance, at a moment of maximal historical change, of a deterministic argument that asserts that "Trinidad is exempt from history?"[47]

I would argue that Naipaul's book-long demonstration that myth habitually substitutes for history in Trinidad and, moreover, that the specific myth of El Dorado *defines* Trinidad's identity, took on a reactionary role at the time of its appearance. It did so for two reasons. First, in the years immediately following decolonization, there was a particularly strong need for a society like Trinidad to confront the future by reconceiving the past through the language of nationalism. That is, for any shared sense of purpose to emerge, it was necessary to *own* the past as history. This point can be illustrated by contrasting Naipaul's representation of the society's identity as one of constitutional stasis with Eric Williams's view, in his *History of the People of Trinidad and Tobago,* that it would be "a great mistake in respect of international affairs and domestic relations, if Trinidad and Tobago were to enter on its career of Independence without a history of its own, without some adequate and informed knowledge of its past. . . ."[48] Williams's book, no less than Naipaul's, is autobiographically inflected; when it appeared, in 1962, he was the new nation's first premier. Where Naipaul uses *El Dorado* to put Trinidad behind him, vindicating his rejection of it, Williams is committed to the possibility and the necessity of narrating change through historical form. For him, history is a strategy of hope.

There is a further, related reason why, in the postcolonial climate of the late sixties, *El Dorado* took on a reactionary aspect. At issue here is the question of agency. By charging that his two "lost stories" of imposed foreign fantasies *constitute* Trinidad's past, Naipaul denies the very process of decolonization including the active role of Trinidadians in securing their independence. *History of the People of Trinidad and Tobago,* by contrast, allocates only 39 of its 282 pages to what Naipaul asserts to be the definitive periods. Williams's account incorporates much more of the experience of the colonized peoples and presents those experiences as including substantial uprisings and a mushrooming movement for self-rule.[49] Bridget Brereton's *A History of Modern Trinidad 1783–1962* distributes its attention across a similar range of historical events.[50] Relative to Naipaul, both Williams and Brereton admit a more generous spectrum of experience as qualifying as historical event and, moreover, as lending itself to productive narration.

The Loss of El Dorado depends quite considerably for its coherence on Naipaul's scripting of Trinidad, in advance, as a "simple society". Indeed, as one critic observes, the term *simple* recurs in the text "as if recoined with a more sinister meaning."[51] Through the course of *El Dorado,* the word becomes overdetermined: it is an emanation of place; it depends on and accounts for the absence of history; it is the island's narrative premise and its narrative conclusion, applicable to colonizer and colonized alike, and to the 1960s no less than the 1590s.

Upon completing *El Dorado,* Naipaul promptly traveled back to Trinidad with the aim of returning the island to his newly acquired understanding of its past. By a quirk of history, he arrived in the midst of the Black Power uprising of 1970, an event that threw his theories of the island's static simplicity quite tangibly into disarray:

> I found an island full of racial tensions and close to revolution. So, as soon as I had arrived at a new idea about the place, it had ceased to be mine. . . .
>
> . . .
>
> Twenty years later the Negroes of Trinidad, following those of the United States, were asserting their separateness. They simplified and sentimentalized the past; they did not, like me, wish to possess it for its romance. They wore their hair in a new way. The hair that had with them been a source of embarrassment and shame, a servile badge, they now wore as a symbol of aggression.[52]

Naipaul's response to what he calls this "communal festering" is complex and confused.[53] Because his theory of the "simple society" does not admit such manifest historical agency, his account begins to appear more like a private vision—a romance, to use his term—and less like an authoritative explanation. The tone of his remarks about the arrival of dreadlocks is especially peculiar, as if he begrudges the passing of black servility. And even in recognizing the limits of his romance, he still locates the "simplified and sentimentalized" version of the past only on the other side.

Establishing the absence of history has long been a first move toward disqualifying cultures from the ranks of civilization. One discerns continuities between Hegel's slim pages on the place of Africa in world history, which conclude, "[A]t this point we leave Africa, not to mention it again. For it is not historical part of the World; it has no movement or development to exhibit," and Hugh Trevor-Roper's opinion, expressed 130 years later, that "perhaps in the future there will be some African history to teach. But at present there is none. There is only the history of Europeans in Africa. The rest is darkness. . . ."[54] For Naipaul, I have argued, there is only the history of Europeans in Trinidad. It is an attitude that participates in those imperial traditions that have used the rhetorical banishment of African and Caribbean societies from history to rationalize their domination while foreclosing serious consideration of their cultural complexities. By bestowing on the terms "primitive" and "simple society" a sovereign, global explanatory power, Naipaul appends himself to this lineage. His writing thereby comes to exemplify the "static binary between tradition and modernity" that V. Y. Mudimbe has critiqued so powerfully in his work on the invention of Africa. As Mudimbe points out, "[I]t is the *episteme* of the nineteenth and early twentieth centuries that invented the concept of a static and prehistoric tradition."[55]

So far from rendering him an oddity, Naipaul's preferred locutions link him securely to one of the West's most entrenched traditions of thought and action. If, as *El Dorado* testifies, the charisma of his prose often enhances the seductiveness of his arguments, Naipaul's high standing as an interpreter of the postcolonial era nonetheless relies centrally on his clearcut segregation of the static, irrational cultures left outside the orbits of history from the dynamic, rational, modern ones, which set and occupy those historical circuits. Were Naipaul to replace this inherited colonial division with less predictable, more differentiated readings of cultural identity and change, his nonfiction would risk losing—at least in Britain and the United States—much of its reflex intelligibility.

6

'Mimicry,' 'Parasitism,' and Resistance

Indian attempts at the novel further reveal the Indian confusion. The novel is of the West. It is part of the mimicry of the West, the Indian self-violation.

V. S. NAIPAUL *An Area of Darkness*

Naipaul blames us as much for being only Indians as for not being wholly Indian.

C. D. NARASIMHAIAH

The incident was tiny, but its resonances have rippled through his oeuvre. In 1961 Naipaul was standing on a veranda in British Guiana chatting to an elderly Indian lady. As the daylight vanished with tropical speed, his senses became focused on a floral perfume that wafted up from her garden. When he asked the name of the flower, she replied, "We call it jasmine." The answer took him aback, for he knew the word well from foreign books but had never associated it with anything in the unlabeled, everyday vegetation around him. Walking back to the hotel with a fragrant sprig in his buttonhole, he sought to establish the deferred association: "Jasmine, jasmine. But the word and the flower had been separate in my mind for too long. They did not come together."[1]

As a schoolboy reader, Naipaul turned to books for fantasy and became so habituated to the rift between metropolitan writing and his native locale that what began as an experience of disjunction developed into an expectation of the same. For that reason, the word *jasmine,* departing the book-world and settling onto a customary flower, had the power to disarm him.

Given the educational system that prevailed in Trinidad in the 1940s, the paucity of indigenous literature, and the centralized character of international publishing, it is unsurprising that from an early age Naipaul divided his globe into the far-off, alluring world of producers and the immediate, insubstantial, nondescript world of borrowers and copiers.

130

Paradoxically, "abroad" was both the source of fantasy and the center of his reality.

Yet Naipaul did not limit this division between real and unreal to the world of literature: he projected it as a political expectation, too. In his political commentaries, he fixates, as openly as in his writerly reflections on region and idiom, on the way language that travels to the periphery seems to skid, to lose its traction. Emerging in different, grander circumstances, such language becomes hazardous when taken up by "colonial" types who manifest an overdeveloped propensity for imitation and an underdeveloped sense of how "half-made" their societies are. The social consequences of the slippage between metropolitan idiom and "colonial" realities are, in this view, inherently disastrous.

Naipaul discerns signs of imitative dependency in all the postcolonial societies he visits. Indeed, *mimic* is the term he invokes most frequently to define the world he ranges; mutations of mimicry are worked through all his nonfiction prior to *The Enigma of Arrival* and permeate his fiction, too, most comprehensively the 1967 novel *The Mimic Men*.[2] If, for Naipaul, "primitives" experience the false security of living in relatively closed cultures, the "mimics" who inhabit the partly Westernized societies of the Third World have learned the security of living off the creativeness of others. By languishing in the idleness of that dependency, they dehumanize themselves. The complementary relationship between the rhetoric of "primitivism" and the rhetoric of mimicry is therefore fundamental to Naipaul's attempts to demonstrate one of his principal convictions: that the problems of the former colonies stem primarily from internalized habits of self-violation. As he once put it: "I'm the only one who has attempted to analyze these countries in my own way, without trying to say that there is an external enemy."[3] The remark is rhetorically typical of Niapaul's penchant for presenting himself as an intrepid minority of one at precisely the moment when he is performing most conventionally.

Mimicry, in Naipaul's usage, wavers between an explanation and an accusation. Through its protean appearances in his writing, the term has accrued some elaborate associations. Naipaul employs the word primarily to characterize a condition of insecurity that he considers endemic to Third World societies, especially but not only those that have recently won self-rule. On this account, the fundamental insecurity of such societies derives from a weak sense of history, the shock of partial modernization, habits of dependent idleness inculcated during the colonial era, and grandiose dreams. The bewilderment and lack of resources in such societies prompt them to plunder the Western nations for cultural and material values, political languages, and social institutions, all of which are appropriated in incongruous, denatured, and therefore damaging forms.

In tracing the destructive influence of metropolitan values on societies too weak either to resist or fully to absorb them, Naipaul takes only a slender, subsidiary interest in the persistence of imperialism and the forms of economic coercion that perpetuate and, conversely, are perpetuated by cultural hegemony. Where other prominent postcolonial writers, from Ngugi, Ousmane, and Achebe to Fanon, Lamming, and Braithwaite, have anatomized the workings of neocolonialism, Naipaul's contrasting concern is to characterize fragile Third World societies as witlessly derivative and given to grandiloquent, self-delusory, and ultimately self-destructive fantasies. At times, moreover, Naipaul writes of mimicry as if it were a form of colonialism from below, that is, as if the peripheral nations were imposing upon, and parasitically bleeding the global core.

In what follows, I investigate the ideological underpinnings of Naipaul's rhetorical obsession with mimic dependency. How, for instance, does his account of the gravitation of Third World middle classes toward the West differ from the explanations advanced by theorists of neocolonialism? In an unusual move, Naipaul portrays Third World revolt as an inverted manifestation of mimicry rather than as mimicry's antithesis. He argues that, as the former colonies derive their languages of resistance from the West, even their rejection of Western values is ultimately dependent and imitative. What are the implications of this theory for the way we perceive resistance in the former colonies? How productive is Naipaul's analysis, for example, as he applies it to the "technological parasitism" of Islamic societies, which he sees as simultaneously rejecting and relying on the West?

Colonial 'Mimicry'

Naipaul's longstanding concern with "mimicry" can be read as a variant of his autobiographical preoccupation with transplanted people, commodities, and ideologies, and especially with the cultural hybrids that may result. In a sense, he writes of exile and mimicry as inverse responses to the fated, foreshortened possibilities of life in the former colonies. Those who can, flee to a metropolitan land; those who cannot, flee in imagination, taking refuge in scattered fantasies of metropolitan provenance.

Naipaul perceived his own emigration from Trinidad as a bid for a level of self-sufficiency unattainable in that or any other "mimic" society. In his early conception of the mortifying threat of dependency lie the roots of his later insistence that he has never been anybody's hireling or imitator.[4] One recognizes, then, a personal and rhetorical affinity between his representation of the inhabitants of former colonies as unimaginative mimics and his conception of his own imagination as autonomous and self-defined. It is as if his image of himself as a writer has become predicated on a contempt for those whom he feels have capitulated to a parasitic or imitative life of the sort that he is confident he has eluded. Yet ironically, the special animus that he reserves for cultural and racial hybrids, far from securing his literary autonomy, binds him to a tradition of pathological colonial anxiety toward the *évolué* that marks writers from Froude, Haggard, and Kipling to Conrad and Cary. Naipaul's response to a lecturer at Uganda's Makerere University reeks of precisely that attitude: "Those are the ones that frighten me. . . . He's carrying a book. The ones that carry books scare the hell out of me, man."[5]

Naipaul's account of "colonial mimicry" is consistent with his general tendency to be less incensed by the imperiousness of the powerful than by the ideals and self-delusions of the largely disempowered. He directs his ire primarily at the misguided efforts of the formerly colonized peoples to emulate the values and institutions of "whole", substantive nations like the United States, England, and France in territories where such values and institutions can be unwittingly parodied but not meaningfully transplanted.[6]

As Naipaul invokes it, "colonial" is a potentially confusing term, as he extends its customary frame of reference. A "colonial," in his sense, is any inhabitant of any colony or erstwhile colony (with the notable exception of the United States). The term thus becomes historically and geographically inclusive: a British settler in eighteenth-century century Trinidad is a "colonial", as is any citizen of Argentina, Jamaica, or India in the 1970s. This has the effect of collapsing distinctions between the colonial and postcolonial periods, as well as effacing differences between colonizers and colonized. By viewing the beneficiaries and casualties of colonialism in the same terms, he establishes "colonial mimicry" as a function of place, not a function of power.[7] I referred in an earlier chapter to Naipaul's professed avoidance of the terms *colonialism* and *imperialism;* his quirkily broad usage of "colonial" confirms this, for it neutralizes the sense of *colonial* as a synonym for *colonist.*

Naipaul's failure to make these distinctions is polemical rather than

casual. For instance, his definition of the West Indies as static is implicit
in his conception of mimicry as historically constant. That much is apparent from the opening epigraph of *The Middle Passage,* where he cites
Froude's conviction: "There are no people there [in the West Indies] in
the true sense of the word, with a character and purpose of their own."[8]
Naipaul uses Froude as a springboard for his contention that the region
is populated with mutilated mimics and that its imitative orientation
toward Europe prevents it from sustaining "whole," self-motivated individuals, in the 1960s no less than in the 1880s.

Naipaul's theory of "colonial mimicry" surfaces initially in his Caribbean writings. *The Middle Passage* is the first in a line of texts that draw
a moral distinction between creative metropolitan people and the
uncreative inhabitants of the colonies and former colonies who live in-
criminating lives of idle dependency. Contending that Argentina, after
more than 160 years of independence, remains crippled by the nation's
colonial beginnings, Naipaul dismisses its citizens through the familiar
formula that "they were in fact living on a borrowed culture; they had
created nothing."[9] In these terms, Argentina can never aspire to self-
definition because, no less than Caribbean nations, it is a society
founded on colonial fantasies and so severed from the checks of the
"real" world that fantasy has become a national pastime. What Naipaul
sees, in short, is a hollow imitation of Europe, a pretense of a nation that
does not recognize the self-destructive character of what he terms its
philistinism.

Naipaul draws an analogy between fantasy and mimicry in his treatment of early nineteenth-century Trinidad, which he perceives as
scarred by "the absence of the real world," by a legacy of dreams of El
Dorado and airy British schemes to foment South American revolu-
tions.[10] Furthermore:

> The colonial society, that could refer only to race and money, whose
> stored wisdom was only about cacao, tobacco, sugar and the management
> of Negroes, was as deformed as Governor Hislop had sensed in Trinidad
> and Miranda in his early life in Caracas and during his recent adventure at
> Coro. It wasn't only that the wines, the manners, and the graces, the
> books and the art and the ideas of a living culture came from outside. The
> simple society bred simple people.[11]

The two points of reference in this inert territory, race and money, are
also the touchstones for Naipaul's theory of the modes of mimicry that
generally characterize colonial societies. The obsession with race fuels
forms of "racial assertion" that are dependent on rhetorical styles of

protest imported from the metropole, and the overriding materialism of the colonials blunts their capacity to generate their own values and, concomitantly, to create a complete, coherent culture. However, beyond that, the above passage from *The Loss of El Dorado* dramatizes Naipaul's more orthodox designation of "colonial" as a term that includes European settlers, but, as he makes explicit elsewhere, is not restricted to them.

Naipaul's enthusiasm for the concept "colonial" is best explained biographically. His theory derived initially from his recognition of the "colonial" in himself and from his attempts to transcend that psychological condition:

> When I came to England in 1950 I was a thorough colonial. Now, to be a colonial is, in a way, to know a total kind of security. It is to have all decisions about major issues taken out of one's hands. It is to feel that one's political status has been settled so finally that there is very little one can do in the world.[12]

Naipaul proceeds to remark how, by 1971, he had become less of a "colonial" by acknowledging his insecurities.[13] From allied pronouncements one deduces that he despises the "colonial" mentality because it renders people self-satisfied and resigned and hedges them about with a false security, the security of impotence. He focuses, rather idiosyncratically, less on the disruptive impact of colonialism and neocolonialism than on how these processes shield people from responsibility by encouraging them to depend on the ideas and labor of others. The more one reads Naipaul on this score, the more he appears to reinvent the myth of the lazy native. He condemns the "colonials" for their handout mentality; they come to sound like shirkers and freeloaders, not people whose labor and territorial resources have been and often continue to be plundered for the purposes of metropolitan ease. As he reasons in an interview:

> One of the terrible things about being a colonial, as I have said, is that you must accept so many things as coming from a great wonderful source outside yourself and outside the people you know, outside the society you've grown up in. That can only be repaired by a sense of responsibility, which is what the colonial doesn't have. Responsibility for the other man.[14]

That "great wonderful source outside" makes the metropolitan West sound like Santa Claus. Naipaul ignores the possibility that the philanthropic metropole might have been implicated in actively underdeveloping the periphery. His suggestion that the "colonial" "repair" himself by developing a sense of responsibility typically stresses individual, autonomous volition as opposed to collective efforts to redress historical wrongs.

A tendency to see parasitism where others might see a legacy of domination extends to Naipaul's readings of immigration. Thus he describes the passage of Indians to England as "a flight to the familiar security of second-class citizenship, with all its opportunities for complaints, which implies protection, the other man's responsibilities, the other man's ideas."[15] Here Naipaul uses his thesis of the "colonial"s' congenital abdication of responsibility to produce a picture of whiners and spongers flooding in from the so-called New Commonwealth, the kind of image of black immigrants that ratifies the stereotypes disseminated by Enoch Powell and the National Front.[16]

Naipaul's accounts of the "colonial mentality" vary in emphasis; he may stress political indifference or excessive individuality or the mutual distrust between colonial and metropolitan societies.[17] One critic discerns simplicity to be the term's defining characteristic, while Angrosino, writing from a strongly Caribbean perspective, is more specific: for Naipaul, "to be a 'colonial' implies that the psychological loss of identity which is the result of oppression has occurred within a context of spatial displacement."[18] On this view, the West Indian remains a deracinated drifter who, as "a complete invention of empire," can never psychologically surmount the disturbance of his or her ancestral uprooting. Thus the crisis of identity experienced by members of West Indian migrant communities is what Naipaul means by the term "colonial"; it does not obtain to Africans or Indians.

Certainly, this accords with Naipaul's commonest usage of the term, as when, for instance, he visits India in the hopes of recuperating a sense of home and repairing his identity but discovers his separateness from that land and has to remain "content to be a colonial, without a past, without ancestors."[19] Yet ultimately this definition of Naipaul's conception of the "colonial" remains inadequate for two reasons. First, Angrosino's definition does not take into account Naipaul's application of the term, in *The Middle Passage* and *The Loss of El Dorado,* to *all* Caribbeans (not just "the oppressed"). Second, Naipaul's travels in India prompted him to rethink his association of the term "colonial" with displacement:

A colonial, in the double sense of one who had grown up in a Crown colony and one who had been cut off from the metropolis, be it either England or India, I came to India expecting to find metropolitan attitudes.

I had imagined that in some ways the largeness of the land would be reflected in the attitudes of the people. I have found, as I have said, the psychology of the cell and the hive. And I have been surprised by similarities. In India, as in tiny Trinidad, I have found the feeling that the metropolis is elsewhere, in Europe or America. Where I had expected largeness, rootedness and confidence, I have found all the colonial attitudes of self-distrust.[20]

Middle-Class 'Mimicry' and Neocolonialism

Naipaul is not alone in favoring 'mimic' as a term for diagnosing the ills of Third World societies. In 1961, one year before Naipaul expounded on his notion of mimicry in *The Middle Passage,* Frantz Fanon railed against the "nauseating mimicry" of the underdeveloped national bourgeousie, in *The Wretched of the Earth*.[21] In his celebrated chapter "The Pitfalls of National Consciousness," Fanon opined:

> In underdeveloped countries, we have seen that no true bourgeoisie exists; there is only a sort of little greedy caste, avid and voracious, with the mind of a huckster, only too glad to accept the dividends that the former colonial power hands out to it. This get-rich-quick middle class shows itself incapable of great ideas or of inventiveness. It remembers what it has read in European textbooks and imperceptibly it becomes not even the replica of Europe, but its caricature.[22]

Fanon paints the national bourgeoisie as a bogus middle class, bankrupt of ideas, uninventive, unproductive, and derivative. With its "wave lengths tuned in to Europe," it "has adopted unreservedly and with enthusiasm the ways of thinking characteristic of the mother country, has become wonderfully detached from its own thought and has based its consciousness upon foundations which are typically foreign. . . ."[23]

While such passages resonate with a motif of mimicry that anticipates Naipaul's idiom, the impulses behind the two writers' exasperation are quite remote from each other, as are their consequent analyses. Where Naipaul sees "colonial" derivativeness as a travesty of the eminent cultural life of the West, Fanon sees it less as philistinism than as a betrayal, marking the elite's failure to come to terms with the cultural forms of its own nation. That is, he views the middle class's derivativeness as symptomatic of its alienation from the majority of the population, not of its distance from the "real world" of the metropolitan West.

Naipaul either overlooks or derides the indigenous, less imitative cultural practices of classes who are more obliquely subject to Western hegemony. His instinct, in the case of India, is to dismiss them as anachronistic, "primitive" hindrances to the land's entry into the modern world of nations, while at the same time dismissing the 'modernizers' as mimics. And in the Caribbean, he either scorns or ignores the rich range of popular cultural forms: from calypso, steel bands, ska, reggae, and oral traditions to street theater.[24] Persuaded by his theory of mimicry that ex-colonies cannot sustain popularly rooted cultures of their own or generate inventive syntheses, he misreads a class-based dimension of the national condition for the state of the nation en masse. So he portrays the members of a spread of classes as manifesting a monolithic "colonial" psychology that parrots metropolitan cultural values.

The differences between the two writers' conceptions of mimicry follow partly from Fanon's determination to fuse his understanding of the psychological dynamics of neo-colonialism to an economic understanding of the same process, while Naipaul is reluctant to do so. Fanon's treatment of the limitations of a peripheral national bourgeoisie evidences the strengths of his integrative ambitions. If the elite imitates Western norms and becomes a primary conduit for metropolitan values that often jar with local necessities, these inclinations are inseparable from the dominant class's external economic orientation and severely dependent power. As a deformed middle class, a pseudobourgeoisie, it is primarily administrative and managerial, deficient in industrial magnates and financiers, and possesses only a frail base in the nation's productive structure. Its authority derives primarily from its ability to help the metropolitan-based transnationals maintain a bridgehead on the periphery, so that its relative privilege and dependency become mutually reinforcing.[25]

In parts of Africa, the members of this sepoyist class are sometimes spoken of as WaBenzi, people of the Mercedes Benz; in Pakistan, as *chamche,* spoons; in India, as box-wallahs.[26] Indeed, this false bourgeoisie is better equipped to mime the material trappings of the metropolitan middle classes than to emulate their power or inventiveness. When the prototypical bourgeoisies emerged in Europe, Fanon points out, they were creative as well as expropriative. They helped develop the forces of production, were more organically related to the population as a whole than has been the case in neocolonial circumstances, and also contributed to the creation of distinctive national identities (however selectively defined) and national cultures. By contrast, most peripheral bourgeoisies have proved sterile in their dependent, middleman status and incapable of directing the development of their nations' productive forces.[27]

As the direct beneficiaries of metropolitan patronage, the peripheral middle classes cannot be seen as representative of the nation at large. For this reason Naipaul stands on firmest ground when writing about the derivative values of the golf-playing, English-educated business class in Calcutta and of what, in a fine phrase, he has called "the philistinism of the renonçant."[28] But his attachment to "mimicry" and "colonial" as classless terms prompts him to conflate the cultural mentality of the middle classes and those of other more populous strata of Third World nations. It is, however, unsurprising that Naipaul should project his sense of the middle-class "colonial"s' psychology onto the population at large, whether in Calcutta, Buenos Aires, Yamoussoukro, Kinshasa, Port of Spain, Mauritius, or Karachi. For the majority of his recorded exchanges are with the most cosmopolitan classes. The reasons for this are varied: access, often influenced by language, and the fact that he is a foreign visitor spending much of his time in international hotels and airports. But it is also a question of choice. As he remarks in his essay on the Ivory Coast, he seeks out the company of people who are attached to more than one culture for, however critical he may be of them, he can identify with their more international perspectives and complex affiliations.[29]

Unlike many Third World writers and politicians who have been skeptical of the capacity of formal independence to inaugurate substantial progress, Naipaul does not conceive of the problem as one provoked, at least initially, by neocolonialism. On a superficial reading, his emphasis on the continuities between the colonial condition before and after formal independence might appear to support the theories of neocolonialism advanced by Fanon, Kwame Nkrumah, and Julius Nyerere, among others, in the 1960s. But examined more closely, Naipaul's "colonial" comes back to look more like neocolonial's antonym.

Naipaul points repeatedly to the "colonial's" abdication of responsibility as a fundamental cause for the ailing condition of many Third World societies. Theorists of neocolonialism, by contrast, have tended to center their analyses on economic factors, viz. Europe and North America's continued economic domination of the former colonies. In these terms, direct colonialism cedes to indirect modes of domination sustained largely through the application of economic pressures that thwart Third World nations' attempts both to enhance their development and to maintain political authority over that process. However reductive theories of neocolonialism often became, there was some validity, particularly during the 1960s and 1970s, to Nkrumah's cryptic definition of the process:

> The essence of neo-colonialism is that the state which is subject to it is, in theory, independent and has all the outward trappings of international

sovereignty. In reality its economic system and thus its political policy is directed from outside.[30]

Hence, in Nkrumah's aphorism, "for those who practise [neocolonialism], it means power without responsibility, and for those who suffer from it, it means exploitation without redress."[31]

Nowhere, for example, does Naipaul refer to the persistence of lopsided terms of trade between the West and the former colonies. And his interest in issues of class is too fitful for him to consider in any depth the political effects of intersecting economic interests between locally dominant classes and the metropolitan bourgeoisies. Here one encounters a further disjunction in Naipaul's thinking around the term "colonial." He insists that after independence the inhabitants of the periphery remain stuck in a "colonial" frame of mind but, on the other hand, has no problem assuming that the metropolitans have advanced to a postcolonial, postimperial mentality. Such an intellectual posture is classically orientalist.

Any account of neocolonialism should acknowledge the considerably varied conditions faced by the former colonies: Each has its own relations of national production, class and ethnic configurations, and in each instance the ascendant classes locally and in the metropole will intersect distinctively. The measures for perpetuating peripheral dependency on the metropolitan powers are no less varied. These range from International Monetary Fund "austerity programs," the debt treadmill, the "revolving credit" of aid packages, the reluctance of transnationals to invest in creating national infrastructures beyond those enhancing their profits, capital flight, anticommunism as a pretext for military or economic intervention, deteriorating terms of trade resulting in unequal exchange of exported raw materials for imported manufactured goods, the blocking of Third World attempts to reverse the declining value of raw materials relative to manufactured goods, to the frustration of attempts to draw up an international code for regulating the conduct of multinationals.[32]

If the notion of neocolonialism on its own can never wholly explain the widespread malaise in the Third World, by the same token, no adequate account of that malaise can be formulated without recourse to it. In discussing Conrad and Naipaul, I alluded to the neocolonial circumstances of Zaire in the 1960s and 1970s, circumstances that pass unmentioned in Naipaul's essay on that nation. Similarly, while Naipaul has written extensively about the Caribbean, stressing the psychological legacy of colonialism and the persistence of mimicry, he has never documented (far less protested) the United States' economic and military subordination of the region. Naipaul seems untroubled by the political morality of a situation where most Caribbean countries are dependent on exporting just two or three commodities (supplemented by tourism) for their foreign exchange and where the value of those commodities is externally controlled.[33]

Of the countries Naipaul visits, one thinks of Zaire's reliance on copper, Jamaica's and Guyana's on bauxite, Grenada's on nutmeg, and the dependence of Mauritius and many of the Caribbean countries on revenues from sugar. Such countries are unduly vulnerable to the unequal trading relations that persist between core and satellite economies. The latter possess little bargaining power and have proved unable to reverse the devaluation in the price of raw materials relative to manufactured products, a critical feature of the world economy since the early 1950s. The situation has been exacerbated by inadequate international controls on the conduct of transnationals.

There is, however, one anomalous moment in Naipaul's travel writing where his thinking moves into the conceptual vicinity of the theorists of neocolonialism. It occurs in a prefatory note added to *The Middle Passage* in 1969, seven years after the book's initial publication. The amendment reads as follows:

> A New Zealand writer, reviewing another book of mine, said that I was writing about the problems of a client culture and a client economy. I wish those precise words had occurred to me when I was writing *The Middle Passage*. They would have made many things more clear. The book might have had more shape; and it might have been less romantic about the healing power, in such a culture, of political or racial assertion.[34]

Aside from the fact that no critic other than Naipaul himself has construed *The Middle Passage* to err in the direction of romantic optimism, the prefatory note remains a curious statement. The mention of client economies and cultures is unexampled in Naipaul's nonfiction and is at variance with his usual portrait of dependent mimicry as imitation from below. The wording makes clear his obliviousness to the derivation of the terms *client economy* and *client culture;* they were not coined by the New Zealander but emerged as part of the basic idiom employed by theorists of neocolonialism who had adapted anthropological theorizing on clientage to the field of international relations.[35] Nkrumah, for example, describes neocolonialism as "clientele sovereignty, or fake independence: namely, the practice of granting a sort of independence by the metropolitan power, with the concealed intention of making the liberated country a client-state. . . ."[36] In such contexts, the metropolitan powers are taken to task for the distance between their rhetoric and actions, for announcing independence while hypocritically retaining undue political and economic control.

A major theoretical assumption underlying the language of clientship is thus traditionally one of metropolitan implication in peripheral dependency. The idiom is related, moreover, to attempts to exercise the "healing power" of political assertion, which Naipaul, in his pessimism, considers nullified by the client condition. It is therefore incongruous to find a writer who persistently repudiates the former colonies for their idle dependency drawing on terms from a body of thought fundamentally critical of metropolitan-induced dependency. The political freight a term carries can, of course, alter with circumstance and time. Nonetheless, the language of clientship makes little sense, when applied to international relations, if it is divorced from notions of imperialism or neocolonialism. The two sets of terms are causally intertwined. Yet as we have seen from Naipaul's *Salmagundi* interview, he is adamant in his refusal to bring the concepts of imperialism and neocolonialism to bear on postindependence societies as, to his mind, they draw a false set of connotations in train.

Were Naipaul more alert to the workings of neocolonialism, he might have begun to redress the imbalance between his preoccupation with the psychology of mimicry and his comparative indifference to the economics of dependency. In other words, he conceives of mimicry as a function of geographical psychology—how people behave when they feel marginal—rather than addressing psychological questions in tandem with economic ones. By playing down the continuities between the mostly defunct strategies of direct colonialism and the less direct styles of domination (what Harry Magdoff calls "imperialism without colonies"[37]), Naipaul writes as if the metropole's underdevelopment of the periphery were a thing of the past.

Writers as varied as Gunder Frank, Immanuel Wallerstein, Samir Amin, and Walter Rodney, among others, have generated a radically different set of responses to the economic relationship between the West and the Third World.[38] Despite their diversity, these figures were united, at the most rudimentary level, in rejecting modernization theorists' vision of the newly independent nations as "traditional societies" that had been insufficiently exposed to capitalism but could move toward parity with the metropolitan nations by reenacting the stages of capitalist development those nations had undergone. To the contrary, dependency theorists tended to view the new nations (and the periphery in general) as having been actively underdeveloped through their incorporation into international capitalism. Indeed, such theorists invariably insisted that core development required peripheral underdevelopment.

In their world system models, dependency theorists have too often advocated an anticolonialism that, paradoxically, remains Eurocentric. The hubris of their global vision has frequently had the effect of disqualifying or derogating local resistance, as well as underestimating the exploitative complicity of comprador classes on the periphery.[39] However, dependency theorists did help reconceive underdevelopment as a largely induced condition, rather than an original "backwardness." Underdevelopment has entailed a transfer of capital from the periphery to the core industrialized capitalist countries. Under such circumstances, local investment of "surplus" has often been minimal or remained substantially controlled by the transnationals and, as a consequence, has helped reproduce dependency by inhibiting the development of productive forces on the periphery.

The persistence of structural underdevelopment on the economic front is precisely what Naipaul is most oblivious to. Indeed, his indifference to questions raised by the international division of labor becomes a central deficiency in his work. His blindness to such questions would be less critical—and less symptomatic—were he not himself such an international writer in terms of the range of Third World societies he visits and anatomizes.

If Naipaul's one-sided emphasis on the psychological issue of mimicry distances him from theorists who emphasize questions of economic dependency, it draws him, by the same token, toward a tradition of thought about colonial dependency that includes the psychologists Albert Memmi and Dominique Mannoni.[40] In Mannoni's words, "[W]herever Europeans have founded colonies of the type we are considering, it can safely be said that their coming was unconsciously expected—even desired—by the future subject peoples."[41] Fanon and Aimé Césaire have both challenged Mannoni on this score, arguing that to portray a state of colonial dependency as inevitable and psychologically attractive is to erase the economic motives behind colonial conquest and to allow colonialism a backdoor absolution.[42] Naipaul lays himself open to to allied criticisms when he, too, blames the victim by intimating that colonized peoples courted their subjection. "I always try to understand," he once remarked, "why certain countries have invited conquest."[43] This utterance is, moreover, of a piece with Naipaul's vision of colonial dependency as a self-subverting condition.

'Parasitism' and Islam

No discussion of Naipaul's vision of "mimicry" is complete without a
consideration of the allied concept, "parasitism." Together, the two
terms dramatize one of the high themes of his oeuvre: that Third World
societies are held back principally by habits of self-destructive dependency. Naipaul expresses this sentiment tersely in an essay on Trinidad,
where he pronounces against "the new politics, the curious reliance of
men on institutions they [are] yet working to undermine. . . ."[44]

Naipaul holds the figure of the parasite in great affection and applies it
widely, descrying parasitic Mauritians, parasitic Guianans, parasitic
Trinidadians, parasitic Argentinians, parasitic Uruguayans, parasitic Indians, parasitic Iranians, and parasitic Pakistanis.[45] But the image appears with unique persistence in *Among the Believers,* the record of his
1979 journey through four non-Arabic Islamic countries: Iran, Pakistan,
Malaysia, and Indonesia. In describing the manifestations of "parasitism", Naipaul, as usual, extrapolates from individuals to nations, and
vice versa. Of the Uruguayans he observes:

> [They] say that they are a European nation, that they have always had
> their back to the rest of South America. It was their great error, and is part
> of their failure. Their habits of wealth made them, profoundly, a colonial
> people, educated but intellectually null, consumers, parasitic on the cul-
> ture and technology of others.[46]

The lineaments of "parasitism" begin to show: It is pervasive in "colonial" societies, is linked to "mimicry" through its association with uninventive cultures lulled by dependency, and is most perceptible in the
form of technological "parasitism".

If "parasitism" can be a national trait and an international process,
Naipaul also writes, on a more personal level, of the discomfiting sensation of playing host to human parasites. The occasion is a dance per-
formed by Amerindian women: the location, the hinterland of British
Guiana:

> I did not find them attractive. I had tried hard to feel interest in the
> Amerindians as a whole, but had failed. I couldn't read their faces; I
> couldn't understand their language, and could never gauge at what level
> communication was possible. Among more complex peoples there are
> certain individuals who have the power to transmit to you their sense of
> defeat and purposelessness: emotional parasites who flourish by draining
> you of the vitality you preserve with difficulty. The Amerindians had this
> effect on me.[47]

Naipaul's record of this encounter clarifies his sense of "parasitism" as a process associated with yet partly distinguishable from "mimicry". On the interpersonal as on the international front, the parasite constitutes a drain on the host individual's or nation's resources, whereas the mimic, though void of initiative and understanding, does not constitute a threat to the integrity of the party mimicked. It is the difference, if you will, between a leech and a parrot.

The Guianan incident is noteworthy for two further reasons. This scene, where a male traveler projects his own enervation and bewilderment onto indigenous people, particularly women, is a standard topos in narratives of colonial exploration and serves to link Naipaul to that tradition.[48] Moreover, it is significant that Naipaul experiences a sensation of being bled of his vitality when confronted by a group from whom he is maximally alienated; he does not command their language and finds their culture incomprehensible and unenticing. It is perhaps not coincidental, therefore, that Naipaul feels freest in applying the term *parasite* to Islamic individuals and cultures. For of all his major journeys, the trip through Iran, Indonesia, Malaysia and Pakistan finds him most stranded linguistically and most blatantly out of sympathy with the people he encounters. Whatever his partialities in writing about the Caribbean and India, he could claim a measure of connection to those societies. In *Among the Believers* the sense of disconnection becomes acute. As Naipaul spoke none of the languages, his interlocutors had to convey their ideas and their personalities through English or, at times, through the mediations of an interpreter.[49] In the most literal sense, Naipaul found the cultures indecipherable, for he could not transliterate the Arabic alphabet.

If his outrage at Islamic "parasitism" bears the imprint of his distance from such cultures, it is marked, too, by a suspicion of Islamic communities that dates from his childhood:

> Muslims were part of the small Indian community of Trinidad into which I was born; it could be said that I had known Muslims all my life. I knew little of their religion. My own background was Hindu, and I grew up with the knowledge that Muslims, though ancestrally of India and therefore like ourselves in many ways, were different. . . . The difference was more a matter of group feeling, and mysterious: the animosities our Hindu and Muslim grandfathers had brought from India had softened into a kind of folk-wisdom about the unreliability and treachery of the other side.[50]

Naipaul had written about these formative animosities before. Some two decades earlier he had described, in *An Area of Darkness,* his childhood education in the need to be mistrustful of Muslims, telling how a particular graybeard Muslim came to embody "every sort of threat."[51]

As Sudhai Rai has observed, there is, in *An Area of Darkness,* a diametrical difference between Naipaul's empathy for Brahmanical Hindus and his experience of Muslims as opaque. Naipaul recounts how a ritualistic meal with a Brahman family "dislodge[d] a childhood memory" and pleasantly "awakened a superseded consciousness"; so, conversely, his encounters with Muslims on the Indian and the Islamic journies are suffused with the sense of youthful bigotries stirring.[52] For the six months of Naipaul's first sojourn in India, he employed a Muslim, Aziz, as his personal servant, but he never grew to trust or like the man. His relationships with Muslims in Iran had a similarly inauspicious beginning: on the first page of *Among the Believers,* we are introduced to his first interpreter, Sadeq, who is full of the "sneering pride" and the apolitical "resentments" that, for Naipaul, characterize the revolution.[53]

When he writes and talks about Islam, *parasitic* and *barbarous* are among his routine epithets. To a query about how much Islamic literature he had read before setting off, Naipaul responded:

> Not too much. I wanted an open mind. There's an awful lot of missionary stuff being passed off as scholarship by people who lie, who won't call a parasite a parasite, a barbarian a barbarian. Who say, "Poor little wog, poor little cannibal, he hasn't had his fresh meat today."[54]

Here one perceives the confluence of Naipaul's conceptions of open-mindedness and prejudgment. This perception is strengthened by the fact that he carries with him the same portmanteau of adjectives he has taken on his earlier travels: *"resentful," "enraged," "vengeful," "simple," "mimic," "uncreative," "emotional," "irrational," "frenzied," "intoxicated."* However, this time, one concern is driven through the book with unusual force: the double-think of the parasite.

That preoccupation was there from the outset of the voyage. The idea for the trip came to Naipaul one evening while watching television in Connecticut. An Iranian was vaunting the revolution, yet he seemed, in his tweed jacket, intent on projecting a sophisticated image of himself at odds with his utterances. From this and similar incidents Naipaul determined that the revolutionaries felt an unadmitted attraction to the West, an attraction that manifested itself as a concoction of "dandyism, mimicry, boasting, and rejection."[55] The trip ensued, and the book it produced brought his obsession with the various styles of Third World hypocrisy to a head.

But the Islamic form of hypocrisy, as he formulates it, differs in its specifics from "mimicry". If Third World socialists and advocates of Black Power denounce the West but depend on the West for the phrasing of their denunciations, Islamic revivalists exhibit an inverse "mimicry"—they possess an endemic language of revolt but remain reliant on Western technologies and goods to a degree that compromises their principled hostility. Hence, the *mauvaise foi* of the parasites: they take, but they do not give, and they pretend, all the while, that they are above taking. Naipaul explains:

> The West, or the universal civilization it leads, is emotionally rejected. It undermines; it threatens. But at the same time it is needed, for its machines, goods, medicines, warplanes, the remittances from the emigrants, the hospitals that might have a cure for calcium deficiency, the universities that will provide master's degrees in mass media. All the rejection of the West is contained within the assumption that there will always exist out there a living, creative civilization, oddly neutral, open to all to appeal to. Rejection, therefore, is not absolute rejection. It is also, for the community as a whole, a way of ceasing to strive intellectually. It is to be parasitic; parasitism is one of the unacknowledged fruits of fundamentalism.[56]

Naipaul discerns this particular style of bad faith in all four of the nations he visits; it is perhaps most noticeable in Pakistan, where (at the time of his trip) the attempt to install an Islamic state had proceeded furthest and the limits to that ambition were therefore most exposed.

Naipual does succeed in exposing the worthlessness of quests for purity in their more rarified form. He rightly debunks the myth of the precise return, the dream of restoring an Islamic order scoured of inauthenticities.[57] The conundrum he poses is this: how does a faith remain firm—ideologically unaccommodating—yet devise institutions and technologies adequate to the modern world? Time and again, Naipaul impales his (almost uniformly middle-class) interlocutors on the horns of this dilemma by stressing the gap between their ideological rigor and their continued reliance on appropriated or at best renovated Western products. And so, in the course of his travels, he develops a bloodhound's nose for the telephone, the electric typewriter, the air-conditioning unit, the photocopying machine, and the Western degree.

Yet there remains something too clean, too zealous about Naipaul's Manichaeanism. On the side he places the creative, living, generous "universal civilization"; on the other, the destructive, inert, resentful cultures of Islam. Islam shares that far side with all sterile cultures—with those of Zaire, for instance, where, as we have seen, "the visitor" introduced ideas of "responsibility, the state and creativity."[58]

When discussing the "universal civilization," Naipaul is fond of making smug allusions to "the visitor," and the "living, creative civilization"; in so doing he soft pedals any suggestion that such universality might often be imperial in its expansiveness. Seen against this backdrop, his quarrel with Muslims (of all persuasions) is straightforward: their relationship to the West will remain contradictory and self-destructive as long as they continue to utilize the visitor's technologies while denouncing Western ideologies, that is, as long as they refuse to recognize those technologies as the fruit of the disparaged ideologies. Naipaul leaves no doubt that this dissociation is widespread and, in many instances, damaging. Yet in choosing Islamic bad faith as the high theme of his book, he assumes, without question, the good faith of the West in its dealings with his four Islamic societies. The West is consistently portrayed as exploited by lesser societies resentful of its benign, or at worst, neutral, creativity. Indeed, Naipaul is so decided in his distribution of moral and cultural worth between the cultures of anarchic rage and the "universal civilization" that he ends up demonizing Islam almost as routinely as the most brittle-minded of his Islamic interlocutors demonize the West. At one point, he castigates a Malaysian acquaintance (introduced simply as Shafti): "I think that because you travelled to America with a fixed idea, you might have missed some things."[59] The tone of this rebuke discloses Naipaul's considerable lack of self-awareness, as if his own responses on his Islamic travels were untouched by fixed preconceptions.

Some of the critical responses to *Among the Believers* suggest how the author's unmodulated binary thinking promotes racism and encourages the drawing of self-satisfied equations between technological inventiveness and human worth. Hugh Trevor-Roper, writing in *The New York Review of Books,* describes Naipaul as having encountered "complacent parasitism on the material achievements of the West and on the unearned wealth which Western technology has bestowed upon its passive critics."[60] Here one observes how, once the image of the ungrateful parasite is in place, a quick figurative crossing can be made to assumptions about the unappreciated host's forbearance and philanthropy. Indeed, that "unearned wealth" captures precisely the underlying sense in Naipaul's book that Islamic "parasitism" is a form of theft.

Eugene Goodheart, glossing a remark by Naipaul to the effect that only select societies sustain the concept of human quality (Trinidad and Pakistan, for instance, do not), judges that "the societies in which the quality of people is held to be important are advanced technological societies. If technology does not humanize, it creates the conditions for a society in which the quality of people is valued."[61] This raises interesting questions. Is South Africa, by far the most technologically advanced society in Africa, a nation where conditions have been generated most suitable for the respect of human worth? Goodheart asks none of the necessary questions. Who controls the technology? Is it disproportionately military? What percentages of the extracted surplus are invested internally and in the metropolitan nations? Internally, is wealth concentrated within a narrow elite or broadly distributed? Does the advent of technology tighten or loosen the knots of dependency? Many Third World nations favor a redistribution of technological resources, but many of them are also alert to the workings of the "global assembly line," whereby industrial misery is concentrated in so-called offshore installations situated in peripheral nations.

One can be broadly in favor of technology without assuming, like Goodheart and Naipaul, that it will perforce generate an increased respect for human quality. Goodheart makes the familiar error (à la modernization theory) of assuming that underdevelopment is an original rather than a substantially induced condition. He makes the accompanying mistake of assuming that technology (stripped of political trappings) will automatically play a redemptive role. Though Goodheart's approach may seem extraordinary, it is easy, in returning to the figurative matrix of *Among the Believers* to see how the book encouraged his conclusions.

An insistent literary figure is more than decorative, more than the tinsel of ideas; rather, it is symptomatic and constitutive of the patterns of thought. There are in *Among the Believers* two primary figures expressive of Naipaul's paradoxical poles of the exploitative yet weaker societies and the exploited powerful ones. If the central figure for the former is the parasite, for the latter it is the ironic image of the bazaar. Naipaul's Muslims covet modern goods but fail to recognize them as products of Western creativity and industry, treating them instead "as the stock of some great universal bazaar."[62] Migrant workers are described returning to Pakistan laden with modern effects, "names of the new universal bazaar, where goods were not associated with a particular kind of learning, effort, or civilization, but were just goods, part of the world's natural bounty."[63] What Naipaul has done is to take an image descriptive of a precapitalist institution and apply it to the workings of international capitalism in its monopoly phase. Clearly, he himself does not see Western products as bazaar goods; the choice of image represents an attempt to see those commodities through Islamic eyes, that is, to capture the kind of "simple" vision that overlooks the effort behind Western production and thereby does the West an injustice. Yet even if one accepted this as a pervasive Muslim view of Western products, Naipaul would remain guilty of counter-simplifying, for his perception of the postcolonial West as pure, unappreciated creativity is as limited as his imagined Islamic perception of it as an open bazaar.

Naipaul uses the figure of the bazaar to expose Islamic naïveté or bad faith, but the figure is also inapposite for reasons that he does not wish to bring into play. Specifically, the difference in scale between the local bazaar and international capitalist operations is also a difference in a peripheral society's vulnerability to outside domination through the inculcation of foreign tastes for foreign advantage—economic as well as political. Prolix on the subject of Western inventiveness, Naipaul has little to say on questions of hegemony and intervention.

The consequences of this silence are felt most directly in his treatment of Iran, the nation that serves as the centerpiece of his narrative. The timing of *Among the Believers* to coincide with the height of American–Iranian tensions boosted its success and propelled Naipaul onto the cover of *Newsweek*. And it was in Iran that the relation between Islamic revivalism and a recent history of Western domination ought to have been most transparent.

In the late seventies, not long before Naipaul was to undertake his Islamic journey, Reza Baraheni, an Iranian poet who had been incarcerated by the shah and tortured by the secret police, published a book entitled *The Crowned Cannibals: Writings on Repression in Iran*. In describing the consequences of the shah's notions of Westernization, Baraheni invokes an updated version of Naipaul's figure of the bazaar to point up some of the drawbacks of that ambiguous category 'modernity', at least as it manifests itself in a client culture:

> This Woolworth mentality has been aptly summed up by one of the great intellectuals of the country, Jalal Al-ahmad, as "Westomania." The worst taste in architecture is complemented by a sickening dosage of cheap Western goods and commodities. . . . To witness the collective dispossession of the nurtured tradition and way of life in an entire nation, travel to Iran. The people of the country are being alienated from their cultural and ethnic roots and thus from their identity. The have been denied all that is of merit in the West while their own values are corroded.[64]

Baraheni outlines the creation of an American client regime: how in 1953 a democratically elected regime was terminated by a CIA-sponsored coup that installed the shah; how SAVAK, his secret police, was trained and equipped by the CIA and so routinely tortured political prisoners (numbering at times between 25,000 and 100,000) that, in the late seventies, the secretary-general of Amnesty International declared Iran to have the worst record of human rights in the world.[65]

The shah is alluded to twice in *Among the Believers*: once when the author skims a magazine in Qom that "raged about the Shah," and again when he recalls having seen graffiti in London and other Western cities "about the torture by the Shah's secret police; about the 'fascism' of the Shah."[66] Otherwise on that score, Naipaul maintains a studied silence. (His brother, Shiva, who traveled to Iran as the shah's reign was ending, goes further, justifying his ambitions and trivializing his atrocities.[67]) V. S. neither accuses nor excuses the shah. Instead, he simply declines him a presence in the narrative, knowing, perhaps, that to do so would jeopardize his Manichaean analysis. What the brothers share is a perception of the Islamic revivals as breaking with the rational tradition where rationality, and hence comprehensibility, are proportionate to Westernization. When V. S. declares categorically that "political Islam is rage, anarchy," one realizes that his experience of Islamic cultures as opaque has been mutated so that a *relationship* between a foreign observer and the observed cultures resurfaces as a defining set of *attributes*—irrationality, anarchy, incomprehensibility, impenetrability—of those same cultures. This kind of transference—a stock in trade of travel writers—might have been obviated had Naipaul shown more interest in internal accounts (such as Baraheni's) of Islamic societies' recent experiences with the West.

'Modernity,' 'civilization,' 'technology': when read in the context of America's hegemony over Iran during the two-and-a-half decades prior to Naipaul's visit, the terms begin to blur, losing the precise, wholly positive connotations that Naipaul and, following him, Goodheart assume for them. Can one separate 'modernity' from the tawdry tyranny of a kept kleptocracy? Or 'civilization' from the shah's rhetoric about delivering his country to the portals of "The Great Civilization?"[68] Or 'technology' from the rift between the advanced technologies of torture and repression and the technological impoverishment of other sectors of the nation? To pose these questions is not to vindicate, for an instant, the Khomeini regime's even more egregious record on human rights. One needs, however, to ask for a more complex account than Naipaul's tale of Muslim passion, rage, anarchy, resentment, idleness, and parasitism. And one needs, as well, to label as amnesiac his affirmation that "The life that had come to Islam had not come from within. It had come from outside events and circumstances, the spread of the universal civilization."[69] By holding his hand over the recent history of 'modernity's' entanglements with imperialism, he is unable to perceive the quandaries of people who wish to maintain selective access to 'modernity' without being thrust more deeply into clientship. Naipaul has a quick eye for the excesses of renunciation and the attendant hypocrisies. But he might have rendered them less inscrutable and been less pious about the universal civilization had he acknowledged those excesses as, in large part, responses to the excesses of imperial imposition.

Eqbal Ahmed has written insightfully into the importance—and difficulty—of integrating a critique of Western orientalist discourse with a critique of the forms of authoritarianism that are currently widespread in the Islamic world.[70] Reflecting on the continuing crises in many Islamic societies, he argues for the necessity of recognizing the joint roles of colonialism and modernization in bringing about "the erosion of economic, social, and political relationships which had been the bases of traditional Muslim order for more than a thousand years."[71]

Among the Believers is a classic instance of how not to undertake the difficult endeavor that Ahmed has urged. Naipaul's Manichaean oppositions—between a parasitic Islam and an open, generous universal civilization, between idle dependence and industrious productivity, between irrationality and rationality—foreclose the whole question of how a crisis of modernization intersects with traumatic memories (both age-old and raw, recent ones) of Western colonialism and the imperial subjugation of Islamic societies.

We have seen the erasure of that history repeat itself in American media analyses of the 1990–91 Gulf Crisis. In the quest for underlying factors contributing to Saddam's decision to invade Kuwait, how seldom did the media include the collusion of Western powers in inventing and sustaining the mini-Gulf States. There was almost no mention of Britain's historic role, while carving up the region, in ensuring that Iraqi power would be contained by denying it a port. Instead, the media preferred to explain the invasion by resurrecting the specter of the Islamic madman as sole cause.

There is a coda to all this. It is unsurprising to find, in the midst of the Gulf Crisis, Naipaul rehashing his theory of the showdown between Islamic irrationality and "Our Universal Civilization" (as the piece is entitled), on the Op-Ed page of *The New York Times,* where it keeps company with a perfectly supplementary William Safire essay on "Stopping the Saddam bomb."[72] A decade back, during the Iran hostage crisis, Naipaul had first perfected his orientalist opposition between a generous "civilization" and a parasitic "barbarism". In 1990, we find recurring in a depressingly unadjusted mode, both his terms for explicating a Western–Islamic crisis and the public appeal to Naipaul as an expert on Islam.

Resistance as Mimicry

A resigned pessimism is one of the seals of Naipaul's thought, and he has always doubted the capacity of a Trinidadian, a Grenadian, an Indian, a Uruguayan, or a Zairean to slough off his or her colonial mentality and become a "whole person." In Naipaul's terms, if this transformation is to be achieved at all, it will be through self-decolonization, that is, by a subject consciously breaking with the idleness and irresponsibility of dependency. Nowhere in his work does he envisage collective action as a possible remedy for the colonial condition.

Against this backdrop, large sections of Naipaul's travel writing can be read as fatalistic denials of Fanon's insistence that "the very forms of organization of the struggle will suggest a different vocabulary."[73] Repeatedly, Naipaul rebuts any suggestion that the language of resistance is indeed that different; in his view, it remains borrowed, a form of concealed "mimicry" that masquerades as "mimicry's" opposite. His distaste for all forms of resistance—whether launched from planks of race, socialism, religion, gender, class, or sexual preference—encourage him to bar the exits from quietism by announcing that collective opposition to dependency is itself a species of dependency. It is to the strange logic behind this equation, and to its consequences, that I now turn.

Naipaul's conception of resistance as "mimicry" crested in his writings on Black Power and, above all, in an essay on Grenada. In 1984 Naipaul published a scalding attack on the Grenadian revolution, based upon a visit he made seventeen days after the U.S. Marines invaded the island.[74] The essay, published on both sides of the Atlantic—in the London *Sunday Times* and in *Harpers*—constitutes one of his fullest statements on the workings of the "mimicry" of resistance, placing special emphasis on its linguistic manifestations. It also constitutes one of the pieces where the term "mimicry" is obviously overextended. Anyone familiar with the body of Naipaul's work could be forgiven for assuming that "An Island Betrayed" was indexed prior to being written. The essay brims with set pieces of Naipauliana: the myth of racial redemption; revolution as theater; the cycles of futility; the stress of self-wounding behavior and the indifferences to imperial factors; the portrait of progressive Americans and other "internationalists" as misguided and sentimental; the governance of fantasy; the disjunction between posh imported words and scraggy local realities; and above all the persistence of "mimicry".

Naipaul's fixation with the Caribbean "colonial"s' predilection for self-damaging mimicry bars him from including an imperial dimension in his account of the devastation of Grenadian socialism. Despite the fact that Naipaul arrived in Grenada two-and-a-half weeks after the invasion, with signs of American violations of the island's national sovereignty all about him, the betrayal in the essay's title refers only to the New Jewel Movement's self-betrayal. "An Island Betrayed" contains not a murmur against the invading forces, against the United States as the region's "parvenu predator" perpetuating the Caribbean tradition of the imperial prerogative.[75]

The essay seeks to create an ironic tension between the revolutionaries' perception of their actions as alleviating the island's dependency and Naipaul's understanding of these actions as mimic measures that leave the Grenadians even more cravenly dependent. That is to say, he contends that a nation of Grenada's proportions can get caught up in the cyclical game of exchanging one style of dependency for another but cannot advance toward greater self-sufficiency. To stand, his argument has to be braced by the term *mimicry,* frequently applied in the rigid sense of an exact replication whose exactness is the mark of its insanity. Naipaul lays much of the blame for the alleged influx of derivative idealism on the internationalist workers:

> [They] were anxious for the socialist mimicry to be as complete, as pure, as possible. . . . As the mimicry was perfected, so the excitement grew among the faithful in many countries; and the Grenadian revolution had a good press abroad. Little Grenada, agricultural, backward, and black, had not only had the revolution; it had also had an eruption of all the correct socialist forms. The mimicry was like proof of the naturalness and rightness of the cause.[76]

Naipaul tries insidiously to blunt any sense of the New Jewel Movement as a flexible Grenadian-based order responsive to internal dissatisfactions and capable of generating its own successes. He prefers to see it as an international experimental hothouse for socialist dogma, the ideas seeded exclusively from outside.

Chris Searle has contested Naipaul's line of argument in one of the finest of the few closely argued rebuttals of any of Naipaul's nonfiction.[77] As someone who worked for several years in Grenada in a national teacher education program and has written extensively about the cultural dimensions of the revolution, Searle is well placed to offer a sophisticated contrary opinion. Like most other scholars acquainted with Grenada between 1979 and 1983, Searle disputes the existence of any socialist blueprint for the island. He writes not of a political system brittle with the purity of what Naipaul calls "the imported system of socialist rule," but of a system that was unusually ductile because of its responsiveness to grassroots demands.[78] A nation of 110,000 inhabitants inevitably labored under many disadvantages, but one positive consequence of its miniature size was that it proved possible to narrow the gap between the general population and the ruling party. The evidence weighs against Naipaul's retrospective speculation, in response to the national emphasis on production, that "in the peasant setting it [production] seemed a very big word, a strange word. It could never have had its proclaimed meaning; it must always have stood for the power of those who ruled."[79] In fact, for most of the four-and-a-half years of its tenure, the New Jewel Movement was distinguished by its success in generating productive institutions, that is, in fleshing out, at a local level, the meaning of production.

After the revolution had collapsed, through a combination of imperial pressures and bloody factionalism within the leadership, and after the island's fate had been sealed by the American invasion, Naipaul paid his visit and concluded that the revolution had all along been cosmetic in its "imported" radicalism and had generated no deeper gains. "For four and a half years the People's Revolutionary Government did nothing": only a steadfast commitment to a theory of Caribbean stasis, mimic cycles, and idleness could have elicited such a judgment. Moreover, Naipaul keeps mum about the impressive advances in literacy and health care and a per capita growth high enough to ensure the begrudging praise of even the World Bank, a body at ideological loggerheads with the policies of the New Jewel Movement.[80]

Grenadian dependency was most strikingly attenuated through the regeneration of cultural resources, with democratic, grassroots institutions ensuring an organic interchange—a far cry from an official culture imported intact and imposed from above. But Naipaul records only the residual slogans. It is understandable that a writer might look for a failure of language as a primary indicator and, indeed, as a significant cause of what he considers to be a society's self-betrayal. Not surprisingly, then, Naipaul seeks to clinch his arguments by closing with some thoughts on Grenadian rhetoric:

> The revolution depended on language. At one level it used big, blurring words; at another, it misused the language of the people. . . . The revolution was a revolution of words. The words had appeared as an illumination, a short-cut to dignity, to newly educated men who had nothing in the community to measure themselves against and who, finally, valued little in their own community. But the words were mimicry. They were too big; they didn't fit; they remained words. The revolution blew away; and what was left in Grenada was a murder story.[81]

Naipaul cites two different kinds of words that have been abused: those arriving from above and afar and those surfacing from below and nearby. In the first instance, he uses "mimicry" preemptively (in a manner by now familiar) to deny the islanders their right to dignity on the grounds that their ambitions are "theatrical, out of scale." But Naipaul does not consider the more subtle alternative to this view of words as the inalienable possessions of the metropolitan societies they derive from. Words may recur on the periphery in appropriately adapted forms, polymorphously reoriented rather than monotonously replicated.[82]

If Naipaul's theory of "mimicry" precludes the imported word from assuming local significance, it also inhibits the recognition that local words and, more broadly, local cultural forms can attain stature. Yet a reading of almost any detailed account of the revolution's cultural innovations would be sufficient to refute Naipaul's assertion that the "newly educated men, [*sic*] finally, valued little in their own community." Such a reading would also refute his implication that Maurice Bishop slyly adopted small people's rhetorical styles only to turn those styles autocratically against the people. Here, as elsewhere, Naipaul demonstrates a blindness to the value and power of popular cultural forms, particularly the calypso and performance poetry that flourished symbiotically with the New Jewel Movement. His neglect of these processes allows him to perfect his catch-22: the imported language can never take root, and the rooted language is not worth tending.

Mimicry as Resistance

The shortcomings in Naipaul's efforts to reduce resistance to "mimicry" can best be highlighted by contrasting it with Homi Bhabha's insistence that mimicry may itself contain ambiguous expressions of resistance. In his astute and resonant essay "Of Mimicry and Man," Bhabha conceives of mimicry as a facet of both colonial dominion and colonial resistance. He interprets mimicry, first, as expressing the overlords' desire for "a reformed, recognizable Other, as a subject of a difference that is almost the same, but not quite."[83] Underlying such an ambition is the sense that an utterly alien "Other," out of reach of recognition and comparison, is more threatening to the colonizer than one who has been brought within the ambit of colonial values, measured by them, and found lacking. Thus colonial institutions served to generate sepoyist classes whose necessarily flawed mimicry of their rulers made visible, through comparison, their ostensible ethical and cultural deficiencies. For Bhabha—and here he differs decisively from Naipaul—mimicry is nonetheless an ambiguous process. It is a mark of subjugation but also, paradoxically, of potential empowerment, as in seeking to resemble the colonizers, the colonized can translate mimicry into a style of subversive mockery.

Unlike Naipaul, Bhabha focuses on the constitution of colonized subjects in the heyday of colonialism, an era of direct control rather than one of indirect imperial hegemony as often exercized postindependence. However, many of his insights remain pertinent to the era of Naipaul's prominence. Bhabha is far more willing that Naipaul to view mimicry as the consequence of external institutional domination. By the same token, unlike Naipaul, he keeps alive the possibility of radical, resistant styles of imitation that, in their impurity, may challenge or redirect a prevailing hegemony. Naipaul's account of "mimicry" leaves no room for retaliatory, knowing, partial appropriations. His mimics are inane and self-aggrandizing. They exhibit inflated capacities for fantasy, their indebtedness to the "real" world serving as a measure of their distance from achieving a firm local reality. The passion of their incongruous ambitions only throws into relief the depths of their uncomprehending dependency. Mimicry becomes a catch-all, a notion elastic enough to accommodate, on the one hand, imported ideologies "mangled in transmission" and, on the other, rigidly introduced technologies that have been insufficiently adjusted to fit local needs. The notion is expansive enough to accommodate the Calypso players who perform for tourists and the protestors who would rid the islands of tourism.[84] Thus Naipaul ensures that both resistance and capitulations to neocolonial dependency are reduced to the same rhetorical terms.

According to Jack Beatty, Naipaul's "great subject is the imperialism of Western moral styles and jargons in the 'poor countries.' "[85] That is to misstate the case by inverting it. Naipaul's grand theme is the Third World's capacity for parroting the West, for botched and illicit borrowings; he scarcely considers the imperial imposition of Western values and rhetoric, whether through coercion or hegemony.

John Lukacs once portrayed Naipaul as a writer concerned less with questions of justice than with a loyalty to the truth. Elaborating, he remarked:

> . . . there hangs over our world a filthy, polluting cloud of untruth. And in this respect, a person like Naipaul should really merit all of our respect, because he is consumed by the easy acceptance of lies in our society, by the propagation of catchwords and formulas.[86]

Naipaul, in this view, succeeds in reaching the truth by holding to an exemplary commitment to interrogate what Lukacs calls "the ethics of rhetoric." As we have seen, among Naipaul's British and American followers, this is quite a customary stance: he is lauded for his probity, for his even-handed exposure of lies per se. He is treated, in short, as if he wrote out of a rhetoric-free zone. I have sought, in the preceding pages, to trouble that assumption by exploring the ideological implications of his idiom. For perhaps by bringing a different set of interests and an alternative mode of attention to bear on his catchwords and formulas, one can assist in keeping alive such questions as "whose ethics?" and "whose rhetoric?"

How, ultimately, are we to situate Naipaul's theory of "mimicry" in relation to the recent wave of writers and intellectuals—figures as varied as Homi Bhabha, Audre Lorde, and Salman Rushdie—who have reflected on the resourcefulness of difference? Bhabha, for one, has suggested that a "split-space of enunciation may open the way to conceptualising an international culture, based not on the exoticism of multi-culturalism or the diversity of cultures, but on the inscription and articulation of culture's hybridity."[87] Lorde writes of inhabiting "the very house of difference rather than the security of any one particular difference."[88] And Rushdie has extolled the virtues of

> hybridity, impurity, intermingling, the transformation that comes of new and unexpected combinations of human beings, cultures, ideas, politics, movies, songs. It rejoices in mongrelisation and fears the absolutism of the Pure. Mélange, hotch-potch, a bit of this and a bit of that is how newness enters the world.[89]

Too often, by contrast, Naipaul assumes a jealous, proprietary attitude toward his difference. He tends to perceive himself as standing, a solitary homeless figure, in the pure space of authorial autonomy aloof from the domain of politics. And thus his early, hyperbolic sense of his autonomy and homelessness come to underlie the deficiencies in his attitude to cultural syncretism. That much is apparent when he claims for himself the desire "to be free to be *anything,* to take anything I want from anybody or any place culturally"; however, when others act on similarly eclectic ambitions, he repudiates them for "mimicry" and "parasitism".[90]

Conclusion:
A Kinder, Gentler Naipaul?

With the passing of each decade, Naipaul has invested more and more of his energy in travel writing, producing less and less fiction. During the ten years that followed the appearance of his first novel, *The Mystic Masseur* (1957), he published nine titles, seven of them novels or collections of short stories. Between 1968 and 1975 his industry was split equally between fiction and nonfiction, generating two books of each. But in the sixteen years since *Guerillas* (1975), he has produced only one full novel, *A Bend in the River* (1979), while his travel and autobiographical writings have grown ever more prolific. In addition to *The Enigma of Arrival* (1987), a hybrid work of autobiography and fiction, the period since 1975 has seen seven works of nonfiction: *India: A Wounded Civilization* (1977), *The Return of Eva Peron* (1980), *A Congo Diary* (1980), *Among the Believers* (1981), *Finding the Center* (1984), *A Turn in the South* (1989), and *India: A Million Mutinies Now* (1990).

While it is crucial to observe Naipaul's increasing commitment to travel writing, it remains paradoxically equally important to recognize his impassioned efforts during the late 1980s to terminate his travels. His writing during the early part of the decade (*Among the Believers* and the Grenadian essay, "An Island Betrayed") was cast in Naipaul's standard, brittle categories—"mimicry", "barbarism", "world civilization", "parasitism", and "simple societies". But the split title of *Finding the Center: Two Narratives* indicated a threshold text: the long travel essay on the Ivory Coast was vintage, predictable Naipaulia, while the book's other half, "A Prologue to an Autobiography," pulled in a contrary direction, anticipating the new developments that would ensue in *The Enigma of Arrival, A Turn in the South*, and *India: A Million Mutinies Now.*

Each of his three latest books marks an attempt to make his peace with one of the three cultures that have contributed most to his identity—England, Trinidad, and India. In the process, each includes an element of muted self-criticism. *The Enigma of Arrival,* as the title intimates, is suffused with a sense of an ending. In the central section of the book, Naipaul reviews his life and ponders, among other things, the distortions of his identity that prompted him to ignore the rich lode of immigrant experience in London during the 1950s and 1960s. Naipaul's condensed, revisionist rewriting of his collective travels in *The Enigma of Arrival* was meant to be a kind of terminus. He would, he insisted, write travel no more.

Yet he went on to produce *A Turn in the South.* His first American travel book, it brought him unexpectedly face to face with his Trinidadian ancestry and childhood. The bonds he discovered between the South and Trinidad—bonds of slavery, racial conflict, and plantation society—stirred in him a mixture of anguish and serendipity. A powerful strand of the book traces his attempt to review, from the paradoxical distance and proximity of the South, the roots of his old rage at Trinidad. As in *The Enigma of Arrival,* we observe a cautious homecoming, this time as he becomes (at least in spirit) more accommodating of the society that he fled in bitter shame and toward which he has been so vindictive ever since. His newfound conciliatory mood toward Trinidad does not prevent him, however, from reanimating his bigotries toward the black cultures of the New World.

A Turn in the South, too, was announced as his last travel book. But, having faced, first, England, then Trinidad, he returned to India to resolve his differences there. The prevailing restraint, even tenderness, of *India: A Million Mutinies Now* makes for an astonishing contrast with his earlier writings about the subcontinent. Significantly, Naipaul closes *India: A Million Mutinies Now* by reviewing his first Indian travelogue, *An Area of Darkness,* anatomizing, in the process, the youthful rawness that contributed to its limitations.

To the Manor Borne: *The Enigma of Arrival*

For three decades, Britain and the United States, the sites of Naipaul's residence and his principal audiences, had been constitutively absent from his travel writing.[1] So when, in quick succession during the late

1980s, he finally swung round to face these two societies, the decision marked a major departure. *The Enigma of Arrival* and *A Turn in the South* abut postcolonial travel writing somewhat tangentially: the British book because it is a lightly fictionalized autobiography in which arrival serves more as metaphor than event, the American book because it admits only ambiguous continuities with Naipaul's postcolonial preoccupations. But significantly, these experiments with a change in locale, from Third World to First, have produced sharp shifts in temper and focus. Naipaul admits a less curbed range of emotions, breaking away from his customary disdain and irritability into tolerance, empathy, tearfulness, deferential curiosity, even naked delight.

The new tack really began with *Finding the Center,* the 1984 volume that fell into two parts: "Prologue to an Autobiography" and the travel essay on the Ivory Coast. The latter piece, as well as his especially cynical article on Grenada (which surfaced that year in *Harpers* and the *London Sunday Times*) displayed Naipaul in his familiar, hatchet-jobbing self. But "Prologue to an Autobiography" introduced a different impulse. It returned him, in memory, to the Trinidad he had retreated from with the intent of becoming a writer, after having watched his father's creative talents get dashed by that unsupportive environment. In pursuit of his own literary origins, Naipaul embarked on a quest for Bogart, the man who once inspired his first callow, literary sentence.

Despite being marketed as fiction, *The Enigma of Arrival,* which appeared three years later, comes closer to the autobiography forecast by that prologue. The book mulls over journeying as metaphor and event. Naipaul revisits and reconceives his 1950 passage to England while musing, in addition, on the unstable sensation of having "arrived" as a writer, of possessing a career to survey. As, in close succession, his brother, his sister, and Indira Gandhi (whom he deeply esteemed) all pass away, the writing becomes shadowed by an alertness to death as the terminal arrival. Above all, *Enigma* depicts a homecoming of sorts to the Wiltshire estate of Waldenshaw, where Naipaul takes up residence.

In composing *The Enigma of Arrival,* Naipaul invents postcolonial pastoral. There is decidedly no other British writer of Caribbean or South Asian ancestry who would have chosen a tucked away Wiltshire perspective from which to reflect on the themes of immigration and postcolonial decay. It is a place where Naipaul stands alone as an oddity, and the result is a self-engrossed, deeply solitary, almost evacuated, though powerful work. Having deferred confronting, in autobiographical terms, his own presence in England, the version of England Naipaul ultimately faces is a garden county suffused by an ambience of Constable, Ruskin, Goldsmith, Gray's *Elegy,* and Hardy; of chalk downs, brookside strolls, footbridges, bridle paths, Stonehenge, and delicate beds of peonies. Naipaul stations himself in a cottage on the fringe of an estate from which he observes, with half respectful, half erotic voyeurism, the withering of his aristocratic landlord's hold on his property and health alike.

Enigma stages Naipaul's transformation into an English writer, in the old and new senses of the phrase. He elects himself to the great pastoral tradition of English literature, but his racial presence there ensures that he both continues and disrupts the lineage. A temperamental fascination with decay

> had been given me as a child in Trinidad partly by our family circumstances: the half-ruined or broken-down houses we lived in, our many moves, our general uncertainty. Possibly, too, this mode of feeling went deeper and was an ancestral inheritance, something that came with the history that had made me; not only India, with its ideas of a world outside men's control, but also the colonial plantations or estates of Trinidad, to which my impoverished Indian ancestors had been transported in the last century—estates of which this Wiltshire estate, where I now lived, had been the apotheosis. Fifty years ago there would have been no room for me on the estate; even now my presence was a little unlikely.[2]

Naipaul savors the irony of his liminal, postcolonial presence between the two estates—the colonial plantation that had been his grandparents' destiny and the English manorial grounds long sustained by the wealth drawn from such foreign properties. He detects a hint of historical justice that the waning of Waldenshaw should satisfy his enduring fascination with "a sense of glory dead," a fascination instilled in him by empire in the first place.[3] The effect is profoundly ambiguous. By inserting himself into a diorama of faded grandeur, Naipaul is able to disturb a certain notion of Englishness while warming his hands over the embers of the "real" England he inhabited in childhood fantasy, the England that never was that nonetheless existed, as we have seen, as a lifelong rebuke to Trinidad and the Third World for all they could never be.

In mulling over the construction of Naipaul's authorial identity, *The Enigma of Arrival,* more generously than any of his previous work, accommodates self-criticism. And the stylistic amplitude that pervades Naipaul's work begins to be matched by a munificence of spirit. Yet contradictions remain, for this self-interrogation repeats a late romantic ideology of the isolated, self-made author who dwells apart from the corrupting ideologies of the world. To achieve that elevated solitude—to survey his own presence in that pastoral scene—requires that he compose his isolation, not least through the textual extinction of his wife, Patricia, whose sustaining companionship in the manorial cottage is held from view. Her acknowledged presence would have jeopardized the uninterrupted "I" who is wedded to the Wiltshire landscape and, through it, gains entry into the lineage of romantic English pastoral.

Naipaul's focus on the crumbling of a select England allows him to rein in his anger. (Although even here a viciousness may break loose to reveal the pleasure he gains from the vicarious class fantasy of admission to the gentry. On certain employees of the manor: "They were servants, all four. Within that condition (which should have neutered them) all their passions were played out.")[4] The absent England becomes as thematic as the one he chooses to represent. Behind the tender elegy to the manageable decline of Wiltshire stand the unmentioned circumstances of Brixton, Notting Hill, Tottenham, Southall, Bristol, Bradford, and Handsworth, communities of displaced minorities rife with the forms of racial and religous tensions and social dereliction Naipaul would have hounded down in the societies to which he ordinarily travels. Naipaul's angle, ingenious yet perverse, screens out the violent decrepitude of London and Birmingham's inner cities as well as the monumental industrial collapse of the rusting north, all regions where he could not have nurtured the sensation of his "oddity" or mused with delicate melancholy on the England of Roman conquerors and Camelot. Ruin, in its unpopulated, bucolic English mode, becomes a ruminative, poetic affair, where in the Third World it made him irascible and accusatory.

A Turn in the South

Just two years after *The Enigma of Arrival,* Naipaul emerged with his first American book, the record of a journey through seven southeastern states undertaken over a period of four months. In his ventures through the South we see the flowering of a whole new approach toward the sensation of travel:

> Driving back one stormy afternoon in Mississippi from the Delta to Jackson, and excited by the dark sky, the rain, the lightning, the lights of cars and trucks, the spray that rose window-high from heavy wheels, I began to be aware of the great pleasure I had taken in traveling in the South. Romance, a glow of hopefulness and freedom, had already begun to touch

the earlier stages of the journey: my arrival at Atlanta, the drive from there to Charleston.[5]

In every Third World country he visited, traveling had been a necessary burden in order that he might write; for the first time, outside Jackson, this gets reversed, and Naipaul wishes he could simply savor the delights of the trip itself, liberated from the anxiety of working it into words.

But more than that has changed. Remarkably, over half of *A Turn of the South* falls between quotation marks. The implications are clear: southerners deserve to be heard, and Naipaul is quick to listen, tardy in judgment. This approach rewards him richly. Had he adopted his customary intrusive, spiky manner, a man called Campbell would never have waxed lyrical about redneck culture, revealing to Naipaul (at a distance) a style of life that would emerge as the obsession and chief delight of the trip. Nor would Naipaul have come around to admiring civil rights leader Hosea Williams, after initially dismissing him as a glib performer on the protest circuit. And through steady listening and restrained questioning he draws on poet Jim Applewhite's considerable insight into tobacco curing, the wellsprings of his art, and what Naipaul calls—in a perfect phrase—"the religion of the past."[6]

Naipaul's newfound tolerance and his almost reverential curiosity give *A Turn in the South* a novelistic edge. He clears sufficient space for his white characters to expand in rather than populating his narrative with ciphers of the particular national or cultural essence he is committed to indicting. For the kind of characterization absent from the southern book, one has only to turn back to his meeting with Sadeq, which, on the first page, sets the tone for *Among the Believers*. Sadeq gets expeditiously dismissed as simple-minded and sneering, only to be replaced by a slew of figures (Pakistani, Indonesian, Malaysian, and Iranian) embodying Islamic resentment.

The Naipaul of *A Turn in the South* finds himself once more an atheist among the believers. Indeed, some of his finest insights reveal the versatility of religion in the South and the improbable alliances it sustains. But his stance toward both religious fundamentalism and racial tension becomes indulgent to a degree quite unlike his attitude to related phenomena in, say, Trinidad, Pakistan, and Malaysia. This discrepancy becomes especially stark in his writing about white southern evangelists and racists, of both the genteel and redneck varieties.

Among these fundamentalists Naipaul exercises remarkable self-government, coming to accept southern Christianity as a necessary irrational compensation for the anguish and fractured order of the past. His preferred tone is generous and reflective rather than snappish, pusillanimous, and unforgiving. The contrast with his earlier Indian and Islamic writings—where he condemns all forms of religion as stifling, sentimentally seduced by the past, irrational, and antiquated—could scarcely be more pointed. Naipaul's lopsided secularism calls to mind the furor, stirred up by the Rushdie affair, over the British decrees that define blasphemy as an offense, not against religion, but against Christianity.

A Turn in the South is the only one of Naipaul's travel books to be principally about white culture. It is also the only one of which any reviewer could say, as did Thomas D'Evelyn in the *Christian Science Monitor,* that "Naipaul tries so hard not to offend that it's hard not to be offended."[7] Yet that statement is only selectively accurate; Naipaul's new-found tact retains a racial slant. As Arnold Rampersad first observed in an acute essay on *A Turn in the South,* the book betrays an imbalance in the distribution of Naipaul's sympathies and attention to the point of bigotry.[8] Transfixed by country-and-western music's inventiveness, he remains silent about blues and jazz. White writers get a full billing as artists; black writers are scaled down to representatives of racial frenzy or despair. In encounters with southern churchfolk and political leaders, too, Naipaul manages to uncover the noble pathos of a vanishing past amidst white southern communities, but among black communities, he unearths self-violation and back-to-back dereliction. Predictably, Naipaul finds himself drawn to Booker T. Washington while recoiling in irritation from the more radical W. E. B. DuBois. Naipaul's general disdain toward southern black culture contains dim echos of his more violent dismissals of the Caribbean, such as his scoffing account of Trinidadian Carnival "as a version of the lunacy that kept the slave alive."[9]

Naipaul's writing about Wiltshire admitted, for the first time, a note of wistful reverence into his prose, a tone so evidently tied to his new-found capacity for dwelling—in the deep, affirmative sense of that word—in a cordial landscape. That harmoniousness is matched by the sensation, during his southern turn, that he has completed the most congenial journey of his life. By the end one feels that it was a voyage he had always half-knowingly sought although unable to anticipate its shape or location. Especially in the final third of the book, a sustained meditation on the pathos of redneck culture, the elegiac tone of *The Enigma of Arrival* returns. Again, the normally disputatious Naipaul is reduced to whispered devotion by his immersion in a beleaguered culture of white, agrarian ruin. If he views both black and redneck worlds as tragic, pained by the knowledge of "the past as a wound," only the rednecks get embraced with all the emotion of a cause.[10] Here Naipaul's enchantment with country-and-western music becomes symptomatic of the turn to elegy: it is the cultural form that expresses, most consummately, white melancholy and loss.

For the first time in his lifelong travels, Naipaul agrees to recognize a culture's transcendental, mythologized past as a visible consolation rather simply a debilitating prop:

> The past transformed, lifted above the actual history, and given an almost religious symbolism: political faith and religious faith running into one. I had been told that the conservatives of North Carolina spoke in code. The code could sometimes be transparent: "Tobacco Is a Way of Life" being the small farmer's plea for government money. But in this flat land of small fields and small ruins there were also certain emotions that were too deep for words.[11]

This passage paves the way for the book's resolution, not the enervated, exasperated departure scene that recurs across Naipaul's Third World travelogues, but a scene of a quite contrary emotional intensity that has Naipaul and the southern poet James Applewhite bonding in an almost sacramental moment. As Applewhite cradles memories of his rich yet depleted past, Naipaul enters a condition of quasi-religious transport and recovers, rapturously, a childhood rendered dormant by denial.

In Applewhite's phrase, the South tends to "cherish the unreasonable, the unreasoning."[12] These irrational strains in the culture—religious fervor, overzealous community loyalties, and ritual attachments to myths of the past—are exactly what Naipaul finds most moving about the South, even when they manifest themselves in a hidebound disciple of Jesse Helms. Naipaul finds, stirring in himself, a special affinity for an ethos that melds fierce frontier individualism with fidelity to a closeknit community. Above all, he identifies with the South's obsessive toying with history. This version of the South helps him salvage affecting memories from his own Trinidadian childhood, a past he once so forcibly rejected. Time and again, as he stumbles on an unimagined bridge between the southern and the West Indian past, serendipity breaks through and his reflections acquire an edge of self-affirmation.

A Turn of the South should ultimately be read, not just as Naipaul's solitary experiment in First World travel writing, but as the consummation of his New World ventures. As such it can be recognized—despite the new tone—as the final volume of his slave society trilogy, a book that strikes a truce with the Trinidadian past he had written off with such bewildered rancor in *The Middle Passage* and later in *The Loss of El Dorado*.

Applewhite, in a memoir about his encounter with Naipaul, speaks of their shared desire to cherish

> the illusion of being co-originators of a narrative that solaced both our hurts from early ignorance and cultural dispossession, creating out of the harsh sun and weedlike leaf and sight of its harvesting a culture-story with both a before and an after, antecedent and consciousness: a story out of an ignorance and a folly which explained.[13]

One may read in Applewhite's words more than simply a recollection of a moment of high union. For they convey something larger about the shift in Naipaul's perspective begun by "Prologue to an Autobiography" and carried forward by *The Enigma of Arrival, A Turn in the South,* and *India: A Million Mutinies.* His determined disowning of a past that had injured him resulted in a lifelong sensation of severance that he dubiously portrayed as "homelessness." It is only in these later works that he finds the forms of forgiveness—both literary and emotional—that would allow him to reintegrate the perpetual present of elected abandonment into unbroken narrative. This restitution of the past lies at the very heart of his late-middle-aged inquiry into the enigma of arrival.

One feels gratified to see Naipaul's writing recover a generosity not seen since *A House for Mr. Biswas.* He seems, once more, capable of an emotion that borders, at times, on something like hope. Several factors lie behind this altered mood: his growing awareness of death, his reacquaintance with family grief, his return (and that is surely part of age) with fresh passion to the painful tensions of his youth. All of these seem to me crucial, yet on their own, insufficient explanations. It remains too grim an irony that this new self should first emerge from under its carapace when England and the United States shift from being merely his audiences to becoming the subjects of his prose. One observes an insidious correspondence between a change of heart and a change of location. By Naipaul's standards of affront, even his diminution of the achievements of black American culture falls short of his customary abuse. To say as much is not to detract from the force of the injustice, but merely to suggest that in writing about America for Americans he comes under pressure to curb some of his more splenetic prejudices. He evidently felt no such pressure in "The Crocodiles of Yamoussoukro," for instance, when giving credence to expatriate rumors that cannibalism flourishes in the Ivory Coast.

Naipaul remarks how, in writing up his American travels, he had to adjust his approach to the genre because the United States is "not open to casual inspection, unlike Africa."[14] That vague "Africa," he intimates, has the transparency of a simple society. Yet his altered approach to travel ought to be seen less as a response to the differences between an opaque complex society and a transparent "simple" one than as a consequence of different kind of answerability. Had he inspected the United States with the casualness with which he skimmed the Ivory Coast and Zaire, the American reviewers and readers on whom he depends would have dragged *A Turn in the South* to the slaughterhouse.

How are we now to read the harsh polemics in his Third World travel writings, where much of his energy went into excoriating precisely those tendencies that, in *The Enigma of Arrival* and *A Turn in the South,* receive sympathetic, even heroic treatment? For the first time, fixations with the past—his own and others'—are not dismissed as self-destructive or escapist but found to be brimming with poetic pathos. In *The Middle Passage,* Afro-Caribbean efforts to reconnect themselves with Africa—imaginatively and emotionally—got brushed aside as nostalgic, as the "sentimental camaraderie of skin." And in the Argentina of *The Return of Eva Peron* Naipaul discerned "legend and antiquarian romance, but no real history." Yet what finer definition could one imagine of the white plantation tales that so engage Naipaul than "antiquarian romance"?

Naipaul might feasibly have called his American book *The South: A Wounded Civilization.* But that would have defeated the redemptive dimension best suggested by the chapter titles: "The Truce with Irrationality," "The Religion of the Past," "Sanctities." Yet in *India: A Wounded Civilization* his stance toward any show of devotion to the past was scoured of fascination and indulgence. His admonition to India was categorical: "[T]he past has to be seen as dead, or the past will kill."

India: A Million Mutinies Now

A Turn in the South had been billed as Naipaul's final venture in travel. But he found, in writing it, such revived spirits and such a fresh conception of the form's possibilities that, far from heralding his retirement, the American book spurred him to embark on the journey that would produce his most ambitious and epic work. Undertaken in 1989, the trip took him to Bombay, Goa, Chandigarh, Bangalore, and Madras, then up to Calcutta, Lucknow, and Punjab, ending in Kashmir at the Hotel Liward for a rendezvous with the former self who resided and wrote there at the close of his first Indian voyage in 1962.

India: A Million Mutinies Now marks the most decisive new departure in Naipaul's career since he exchanged the profound social commentary of *A House for Mr. Biswas* (1961) for the uncontrolled, skidding invective of *The Middle Passage* a year later. To get a measure of his latest shift in orientation and tone, one has only to contrast his lacerating indictment of Gandhi in *India: A Wounded Civilization* (the section is entitled "Not Ideas, but Obsessions") with his positive buoyancy when asked, in 1990, his opinion of the mahatma: "I adore him. . . . He's a fabulous man. . . . He is a man whose life, when I contemplate it, makes me cry; I am moved to tears."[15]

The Indian edition of *A Million Mutinies Now* carries, on the back cover, a delightfully uncharacteristic photo of the newly animated Naipaul in action. It departs radically from the standard dust jacket shot of him gazing at the camera year after year, book after book, with marmoreal impassivity. Normally, so little does his posture change that the gradual aging of his portraits seems virtually computer simulated. Hence the shock of the new photo: it catches him in profile outdoors, complete with sunglasses and a colored handkerchief draped over his head, while making jottings on a little pad. The snap has a positively jaunty, unbuttoned feel to it. Above all, that hanky, which seems to signal, "I'm in thick with the locals."

The photo conveys with instinctive precision the difference in approach between this and every other work in which Naipaul has faced an Asian, African, Caribbean, Latin American, or Middle Eastern society. The least polemical of his travel books, it is also the one where he breaks loose from the straitjacketing idiom of his paradigm—"primitivism," "barbarism," "mimicry," "parasitism," and "self-violation"—that had given the bulk of his work such a reiterative character. He had, of course, first moved beyond such terms in *The Enigma of Arrival* and *A Turn in the South,* but as those departures had coincided with his arrival as a literary voyager on British and American soil, they confirmed rather than eased one's sense of his resolute prejudices.

The change in tenor is inseparable from a change in form. One can perhaps best depict *A Million Mutinies Now* as a halfway house between oral history and travel writing. Long swathes of the book, particularly during the first half, have the texture of a work like *Blood of Spain,* Ronald Fraser's oral history of the Spanish Civil War. The analogy is partial, but it conveys the sense of a roving, literary-minded professional listener, someone restrained in his interference and whose restraint becomes a measure of his enthusiastic investment.

In an interview, Naipaul explains the lure of this altered approach:

> The idea of letting people talk in the book on the South was really quite
> new to me. And so in this book I thought it was better to let India be
> defined by the experience of the people, rather than writing one's personal
> reaction to one's feeling about being an Indian and going back—as in the
> first book [*An Area of Darkness*]—or trying to be analytical, as in the
> second book [*India: A Wounded Civilization*].[16]

Even the most generous interviewing is never disinterested, and Naipaul's remark that he holds "no views, no philosophy—just a bundle of
reactions," is as silly as it ever was.[17] Just as, in *A Turn in the South,*
black southerners were more likely than white to be spoken for, so in *A
Million Mutinies Now,* even when women's experience is the subject,
Naipaul's interlocutors are unremittingly male. They also emerge as
mostly urban, middle aged, and middle class.

Nonetheless, the scores of life stories, all told in the first person, make
for such an utterly different effect from what one has come to expect
from Naipaul. How unlike his method in *Among the Believers,* where his
slash-and-burn orientalism laid interviews waste in advance. And how
unlike *An Area of Darkness,* where, as Naipaul himself intimates in the
closing moments of *A Million Mutinies Now,* he was, fresh off the boat
from England, too nervy, too introverted to intuit what questions to ask.
Indeed, although he still defends *An Area of Darkness* as belonging to
its moment, we can read *A Million Mutinies Now* as a compensatory
sequel twenty-seven years deferred.

Naipaul's oft-reiterated claim that he looks and sees where others
blindly obsess has, over the course of his oeuvre, accrued the force of a
controlling metaphor. Now finally, in the realm of the senses, his ear has
dethroned his imperious eye. Naipaul's decision to give the locals more
air-time is a gesture of great formal cunning. For the centrifugal scatter-
ing of voices stages his overriding concern with the dispersion of India,
the dismembering of the nation's body politic under pressure from a
myriad mutinies.

Like the term "Mau Mau" in Kenya, "mutiny" in India is a colonial
word that implies a colonial vantage point. Naipaul polemically dismisses the 1857 uprising as warranting the alternative appellation, "First
War of Indian Independence"; he finds it too aggrandizing.[18] Instead, he
stays with "mutiny" and finds in that historically charged word the presid-
ing trope for his book.

In tracking a myriad mutineers across India, Naipaul may ultimately
overtax the term: it covers everything from regional secessionist movements to religious and caste chauvinisms—ex-Naxalite, Dalit, Shiv

Sena, Dravidians Aryan, Muslim, and Sikh—to middle-class individuals (stockbrokers, filmmakers) tinkering with the edges of caste rituals in order, say, to make a commuter life in Bombay more manageable. Naipaul's perception of all these as mutinies becomes crucial for the book's central paradox: India has entered a state of regenerative disintegration. As Naipaul remarks: "[S]trange irony—the mutinies were not to be wished away. They were part of the beginning of a new way for many millions, part of India's growth, part of its restoration."[19] An even stranger irony: some reviewers have charged Naipaul—surely for the first time—with gratuitous, irresponsible, willful optimism.[20]

So once more, Naipaul stirs controversy, though of an unfamiliar kind. In the book's most contentious formulation, he writes of

> A million mutinies supported by twenty kinds of group excess, sectarian excess, religious excess, regional excess; beginnings of self-awareness, a central will, a central intellect, a national idea. The Indian Union as greater than the sum of its parts.[21]

This is probably a minority view, especially since Rajiv Gandhi's assassination, although not a unique one. Amitav Ghosh, for instance, has recently seen some glimmerings of possibility in the emergence of new Indian coalitions and new conceptions of identity. Amidst the spiraling violence, he argues:

> What is really at issue is the question of finding a political structure in which diverse groups of people can voice their grievances through democratic means. It seems to me that India is indeed lurching in fits and starts toward finding such a structure. . . . In many ways, the turmoil is a sign of the astonishing energy that India has generated over the last couple of decades.[22]

But there remains a distinctively autobiographical dimension to Naipaul's political conclusions. The book could not have been written at any other point in his career. It is as if, in projecting mutiny as a prelude to healing, he envisages Indian history as mirroring and thereby ratifying his personal passage from a sensibility of ruin toward late restoration. Amidst his swirling interviewees, many of them bewildered or panicked, the lasting image of Naipaul is of a man becalmed in the eye of a storm. Newly whole, in the sense of having made peace with the places of his past, he no longer cultivates and wields against others his wounded sense of having inherited—to invoke a keenly subcontinental word—a partitioned life. Where once he would have clasped Rashid, a Lucknow

Muslim, with the dead hand of cynicism, now he responds with an empathy reminiscent of the intense fellow feeling he achieved with Jim Applewhite. Nowhere more so than when Rashid laments:

> I also know that I can never be a complete person now. I can't ignore partition. It's a part of me. I feel rudderless. . . . The creation and existence of Pakistan has damaged a part of my psyche. I simply cannot pretend it doesn't exist.[23]

Despite its startling freshness, *India: A Million Mutinies* is far from being a tabula rasa. The book bears the traces of many of Naipaul's lasting themes, such as his vision of extended family life as an analogue for the corruption of collective political endeavor. Listening to Kala, a woman of Tamil brahman origins, articulate her experience of familial confinement, Naipaul is suddenly thrust back on his own memories:

> The clan that gave protection and identity, and saved people from the void, was itself a little state, and it could be a hard place, full of politics, full of hatreds and changing alliances and moral denunciations. It was the kind of family life I had known for much of my childhood: an early introduction to the ways of the world, and to the nature of cruelty. It had given me, as I suspected it had given Kala, a taste for the other kind of life, the solitary or less crowded life, where one had space around oneself.[24]

Naipaul has stressed this analogy frequently enough over his forty-year career for it to become central to any psychological explanation of his hostility toward mobilization for political change.[25] He invariably perceives community or collective endeavor of any kind as a noose, strangling all hope of solitude and individuality. Manifestly, community contains equivocal possibilities—it can be stifling or sustaining. But Naipaul almost never acknowledges the latter as a possibility. And so prior to the recent emergence of his understated, forgiving (if still intermittently bigoted) self, his standard impulse was to demonstrate that in Third World societies, to engage in collective political resistance or cultural self-assertion was to become implicated in pointless, compromised, misguided, ignoble endeavors. Naipaul thus ended up—at times openly, at times by default—sanctioning the status quo. Trademarked Naipaul phrases like the "congruent corruptions of colonizer and colonized," and "the negative colonial politics of protest," along with his skepticism about the "healing power" of "political and racial assertion" convey, in capsule form, his tenacious preference for inertia over resistance.[26]

In an interview, Naipaul once came to reflect self-critically on this personal and political predilection, characterizing himself as "unable to take decisive action on behalf of anything: it is very hard to be against.

I am aware that I have probably been rather feeble and non-involved."[27] Yet strictly speaking, only the latter part of the statement is accurate, for he has long found it easy to be against againstness—in Eugene Goodheart's words, "if Naipaul moralizes against anything, it is against resentment."[28] Goodheart's phrasing is precisely Naipaulian in reducing political action to an expression of temperament. The image of Naipaul lecturing against "resentment" is also in accord with his loathing for "causes."[29] Yet collective action requires binding causes, requires what Naipaul would call obsessions and what others might call commitments. Without causes to galvanize them, without grievances, the struggles for decolonization could never have been launched, nor could formal independence (however inadequate the achievements) have been attained. Indeed, the colonizers frequently dismissed such struggles as irruptions of "native resentment," the ingratitude of the disempowered.

In *The Enigma of Arrival,* Naipaul surveys the trajectory of his career and concludes: "[T]o see the possibility, the certainty, of ruin, even at the moment of creation: it was my temperament."[30] One would be hard-pressed to word more succinctly what, prior to his latest work, became one of the great continuities of his sensibility. That same eye for ruin prompted him to embrace Conrad's assertion that "something inherent in the necessities of successful action. . . carried with it the moral degradation of the idea" and to deem the shortfall between idea and act so severe in Third World societies as to render action self-defeating.[31]

Naipaul's fascination with ruin—he once described himself as an ironist rather than a satirist, because satire presumes a modicum of optimism—long rendered him an incompetent observer of regeneration and resistance.[32] His attitude toward imperialism has been, moreover, contradictory: Disliking the effects of imperialism, he has tended to find imperial ideas more compelling than those bracing anticolonial and antiimperial struggles. His affection for the high style of that "sense of glory lost" has only sharpened this tendency.[33] His position is further complicated in that his criticisms of the effects of imperialism are readily metamorphosed into anger at those who bear the scars of that legacy. What, for instance, is one to make of his remark that "my sympathy for the defeated, the futile, the abject, the idle and the parasitic gets less and less as I grow older"?[34] The cluster of nominal epithets illustrates his incorrigible weakness for that imperial tradition of thought that brackets subjugation with idleness.

Naipaul's obsession with ruin has long been yoked to his indifference to action, just as his moralizing about "resentment" has been coupled to

NOTES

Introduction

1. Derek Walcott, "The Garden Path," *New Republic,* 13 Apr. 1987, p. 28.

2. Like postcolonial itself, the term *Third World* retains an imperfect, ambiguous, yet seemingly unavoidable presence in contemporary postcolonial debate. As Kumkum Sangari suggests, the term "both signifies and blurs the functioning of an economic, political and imaginary geography able to unite vast and vastly differentiated areas of the world into a single underdeveloped terrain." "The Politics of the Possible," *Cultural Critique* (Fall 1987), 158.

I agree with Trinh T. Minh-ha that "To survive, "Third World" must necessarily have negative *and* positive connotations: negative when viewed in a vertical ranking system—"underdeveloped" compared to over-industrialized, "underprivileged" within the already second sex—and positive when understood sociopolitically as a subversive, "non-aligned" force. Whether "Third World" sounds negative or positive also depends on *who* uses it. . . . Thus, if "Third World" is often rejected for its judged-to-be derogative connotations, it is not so much because of the hierarchical, first-second-third order implied, as some invariably repeat, but because of the growing threat "Third World" consistently presents to the Western bloc the last few decades." (*Woman, Native, Other: Writing Postcoloniality and Feminism* (Bloomington: Indiana University Press, 1989), pp. 97–98). For two examples of precisely the kind of rejection that Trinh speaks of, one can turn to Pascal Bruckner, *The Tears of the White Man,* trans. William R. Beer (1983; New York: Free Press, 1986), p. x, and Shiva Naipaul, "The Illusion of the Third World," *An Unfinished Journey* (New York: viking, 1987), pp. 31–41.

As critics like Aijaz Ahmad and Timothy Brennan have pointed out in their different ways, Third World retains a political and polemical force that ought not to be miscontrued as implying a homogeneous referent free of contradictions. Ahmad's unpublished paper, " 'Third World Literature': Conditions of Emergence, Terms of Negation," offers profound insight into the dangers of extrapolating from Three Worlds Theory to a notion of three discrete, self-contained entities.

For some qualified uses of the term, see Brennan, *Salman Rushdie and the Third World: Myths of the Nation* (London: MacMillan, 1989), pp. xiii–xiv; Ahmad, "Third World Literature," p. 58; Kwame Anthony Appiah, "Out of Africa: Topologies of Nativism," *Yale Journal of Criticism* 2 (Fall 1988), p. 155; Homi K. Bhabha, "The Commitment to Theory," *New Formations* 5 (Summer 1988), p. 6; Wilson Harris, "In the Name of Liberty," *Third Text* 11 (Summer 1990), p. 15; Rukmini Bhaya Nair and Rimli Bhattacharya, "Salman Rushdie: The Migrant in the Metropolis," *Third Text* 11 (Summer 1990), p. 19; Henry

Louis Gates, Jr., "Critical Fanonism," *Critical Inquiry* 17 (Spring 1991), pp. 457, 465; Gayatri Chakravorty Spivak, *The Post-Colonial Critic,* ed. Sarah Harasym (New York: Routledge, 1990), pp. 64, 65, 96–7, 163.

3. Anon, "Naipaul Gets Eliot Award," *New York Times,* Sept. 16, 1986, p. C20.

4. Anon, New Yorker, May 19, 1980, p. 158; Joseph Epstein, "A Cottage for Mr. Naipaul," *New Criterion,* October 1987, p. 15; Jane Kramer, "From the Third World," *New York Times Book Review,* April 13, 1980, p. 11; Phyllis Rose in Peter Webb, "The Master of the Novel," *Newsweek,* Aug. 18, 1980, p. 37.

5. H. B. Singh, "V. S. Naipaul: A Spokesman for Neo-Colonialism," *Literature and Ideology* 2 (Summer 1969), p. 85; Eric Roach, *Trinidad Guardian,* May 17 1967, p. 5; Chinua Achebe, "Viewpoint," *Times Literary Supplement,* Feb. 1, 1980, p. 113; Michael Thelwell, "Contra Naipaul," *Duties, Pleasures, and Conflicts: Essays in Struggle* (Amherst: University of Massachusetts Press, 1987), p. 201.

6. Bharati Mukherjee and C. J. Wallia, both quoted in Scott Winokur, "The Unsparing Vision of V. S. Naipaul," *Image,* May 5, 1991, p. 11.

7. Ibid, pp. 10. The author of this comment is quoted anonymously. Ishmael Reed interprets the vogue for Naipaul among American liberals and conservatives as symptomatic of a lastditch effort to check the rising tide of multiculturalism (ibid, p. 11).

8. See Bernth Lindfors, "The West Indian Conference on Commonwealth Literature," *World Literature Written in English,* 19 (1971), 10.

9. Louis Heren, quoted on the cover of *India. A Wounded Civilization* (1977; rpt. Harmondsworth, England: Penguin, 1979).

10. *Newsweek,* Nov. 16, 1981.

11. V. S. Naipaul, "Our Universal Civilization," *New York Times,* 5 Nov. 1990, p. A21.

12. Conor Cruise O'Brien, Edward Said, and John Lukacs, "The Post-Colonial Intellectual: A Discussion with Conor Cruise O'Brien, Edward Said and John Lukas," *Salmagundi* 70–71 (Spring–Summer 1986), 65–81.

13. David Hare, *A Map of the World* (London: Faber and Faber, 1982).

14. Bharati Mukherjee and Robert Boyers, "A Conversation with V. S. Naipaul," *Salmagundi* 54 (Fall 1981), 11.

15. John Updike, *Hugging the Shore: Essays and Criticism* (New York: Alfred A. Knopf, 1983).

16. V. S. Naipaul, "Conrad's Darkness," in *The Return of Eva Peron, with The Killings in Trinidad* (New York: Vintage, 1981), p. 233.

17. Ronald Bryden, "The Novelist V. S. Naipaul Talks about His Work to Ronald Bryden," *The Listener,* 22 Mar. 1973, p. 367.

18. Charles Michener, "The Dark Visions of V. S. Naipaul," *Newsweek,* 16 Nov. 1981, 104.

19. Remarks like this one prompt me to disagree with Sara Suleri when she seeks to temper criticisms of Naipaul by pointing to "a western audience pre-

pared to credit Naipaul with more authority than he asks for." It strikes me that Naipaul claims at least as much authority for his work as do his followers. Similarly, Naipaul's repeated foregrounding of his special difference runs contrary to Suleri's reading of his work as a quest for "an idiom in which to address his perception of himself as a postcolonial cliché." See Sara Suleri, "Naipaul's Arrival," *Yale Journal of Criticism,* 2 (Fall 1988), 33.

20. The first six of these publications boast circulations between 100,000 and upward of a million. In the case of his brother, Shiva, we witness the same phenomenon, though on a smaller scale. *The Spectator,* the primary British patron of his nonfiction, has a circulation in the region of 23,000. *The New Republic,* where some of the *Spectator* essays have been reprinted for an American readership, has a current circulation of around 90,000.

21. V. S. Naipaul, Foreword to Seepersad Naipaul, *The Adventures of Gurudeva and Other Stories* (London: Andre Deutsch, 1976), p. 11.

22. Ibid., p. 12. Cf. Naipaul's related judgment that his father's commitment to writing was "a version of the pundit's vocation." "Prologue to an Autobiography," in *Finding the Centre: Two Narratives* (New York: Knopf, 1984), p. 67.

23. Foreword to *The Adventures of Gurudeva,* p. 7.

24. Ibid., p. 10.

25. Ibid., p. 22.

26. *Finding the Centre,* pp. 18–20.

27. V. S. Naipaul, *A Turn in the South* (New York: Knopf, 1989).

28. Foreword to *The Adventures of Gurudeva,* p. 19.

29. Arnold Rampersad, "V. S. Naipaul: Turning in the South," *Raritan,* 10 (Summer 1990), 45–46.

30. Curt Suplee, "Voyager with the Dark and Comic Vision—through the World of Islam and Beyond, V. S. Naipaul," *Washington Post,* 19 Nov. 1981, p. C-1.

31. *The Enigma of Arrival* (New York: Alfred A. Knopf, 1987), pp. 152–53.

32. *Finding the Center,* p. 45.

33. Ibid., p. 83.

34. Michener, "The Dark Visions of V. S. Naipaul," p. 108.

35. *Finding the Center,* p. 76; Michener, p. 108.

36. Naipaul's emphasis. "Jasmine," in *The Overcrowded Barracoon* (1972; rpt. New York: Vintage, 1984), p. 25.

37. Salman Rushdie, "Imaginary Homelands," *London Review of Books,* Oct. 1982, p. 18.

38. *The Overcrowded Barracoon,* p. 25.

39. To date, Naipaul has published ten volumes of travel writing and journalism, one diary, and numerous uncollected nonfictional essays. Of his eleven volumes ordinarily listed as fiction, one, *The Enigma of Arrival,* contains a long section that makes no pretense at being anything other than autobiography. Another collection, *In a Free State* (Harmondsworth, England: Penguin, 1980), while containing mainly fiction, includes a couple of travel essays.

40. *The Enigma of Arrival*, p. 146.

41. V. S. Naipaul, *The Middle Passage: Impressions of Five Societies—British, French and Dutch—in the West Indies and South America* (1962; rpt. London: Andre Deutsch, 1981).

42. Since *The Middle Passage* appeared in 1962, the proportion of his work that is nonfictional has increased steadily. Only one of the six books that he had published by 1963 was nonfictional. Of the following six books (up to 1972), three were nonfictional. But nonfiction comprises seven-and-a-half of his ten most recent volumes, the ones appearing since 1973.

43. *The Middle Passage*, p. 5.

44. 1983 Foreword to *A House for Mr. Biswas* (1961; rpt. New York: Vintage, 1984), p. 6.

45. V. S. Naipaul, "Conrad's Darkness," in *The Return of Eva Peron, with The Killings in Trinidad* (New York: Alfred A. Knopf, 1980), p. 233.

Chapter 1

1. Charles Michener, "The Dark Visions of V. S. Naipaul," *Newsweek*, 16 Nov. 1981, p. 105.

2. Leon Gottfried, "Preface: The Face of V. S. Naipaul," *Modern Fiction Studies*, 30 (Autumn 1984), 443.

3. Adrian Rowe-Evans, "V. S. Naipaul" [interview], *Transition*, 40 (1971), 59.

4. John King, " 'A Curiously Colonial Performance': The Eccentric Vision of V. S. Naipaul and J. L. Borges," *The Yearbook of English Studies*, 13 (1983), 232.

5. Evelyn Waugh, *Labels: A Mediterranean Journal* (1930; rpt. London: Penguin, 1985), pp. 205–206.

6. Derek Walcott, "What the Twilight Says: An Overture," in *Dream on Monkey Mountain and Other Plays* (New York: Farrar, Straus and Giroux, 1970), p. 17.

7. George Lamming, *The Pleasures of Exile* (1960; rpt. London: Allison & Busby, 1984), p. 13.

8. In this, his orientation contrasts even with that of the novelist Sam Selvon, another displaced Trinidadian of Indian stock, for Selvon's Creolized peasant background made him more assimilable to mainstream Trinidadian society.

9. Rowe-Evans, "V. S. Naipaul," p. 59.

10. "Without a Place: V. S. Naipaul Interviewed by Ian Hamilton," *Savacou*, 9–10 (1974); rpt. in Robert D. Hamner, ed., *Critical Perspectives on V. S. Naipaul* (London: Heinemann, 1979), p. 41.

11. Mary McCarthy, "Exiles, Expatriates and Internal Émigrés," *The Listener*, 25 Nov. 1971, p. 705.

12. Edward Said, "Reflections on Exile," *Granta*, 13 (1984), pp. 157–72. Along with the forceful, succinct essays by McCarthy and Said, Hannah

Arendt's *Origins of Totalitarianism* (1951; rpt. New York: Harcourt Brace Jovanovich, 1968), esp. pp. 266–98, is replete with insight into the creation and status of refugees and exiles in the twentieth century. Other substantial reflections on the subject include: George Steiner, "Extraterritorial," in *Extraterritorial: Papers on Literature and the Language Revolution* (Harmondsworth, England: Penguin, 1972), pp. 14–21; Halvard Dahlie and Ian Adam, "Editorial," *Ariel: A Review of International English Literature,* 13, 4 (1982), 3–6 [a special issue on exile]; Andrew Gurr, *Writers in Exile: The Creative Use of Home in Modern Literature* (Atlantic Highlands, N.J.: Humanities Press, 1981); and Bruce Robbins, "Homelessness and Worldliness," *Diacritics,* 13 (Fall 1983), 69–77. Benedict Anderson's *Imagined Communities: Reflections on the Origin and Spread of Nationalism* (London: Verso and New Left Books, 1983) provides an important reverse angle on the issue of exile; his analysis of the development of the national community as a hegemonic concept contributes directly to an understanding of the conditions under which people have been cast out from such communities.

13. Cf. Arendt: "A much less reliable and much more difficult way to rise from an unrecognized anomaly to the status of recognized exception would be to become a genius. . . . Only fame will eventually answer the repeated complaint of refugees of all social strata that 'nobody here knows who I am. . . .' " *The Origins of Totalitarianism,* p. 285.

14. Quoted by Anthony Heilbut, *Exiled in Paradise: German Refugee Artists and Intellectuals in America from the 1930s to the Present* (New York: Viking, 1983), p. 431.

15. Sudha Rai, *V. S. Naipaul: A Study in Expatriate Sensibility* (New Delhi: Arnold–Heinemann, 1982).

16. Rowe-Evans "V. S. Naipaul," p. 59.

17. Quoted in Edward Said, *The World, the Text, and the Critic* (Cambridge, Mass.: Harvard University Press, 1983), p. 7.

18. Eileen Dzik, "Words of Revolt" [interview with Breyten Breytenbach], *Passion* (June–July 1986), p. 11. Breytenbach expresses similar opinions about exile in an interview with Vivienne Walt, "Elbow Room in Hell," *Village Voice,* 2 Apr. 1985, p. 30.

19. Paul Theroux, *V. S. Naipaul: An Introduction to His Work* (New York: Africana, 1972), p. 7.

20. "Conrad's Darkness," in *The Return of Eva Peron, with the Killings in Trinidad* (1980; rpt. New York: Vintage, 1981), p. 236.

21. Ibid., p. 244.

22. Shiva Naipaul, "Writer Without a Society," in *Commonwealth,* ed. A. Rutherford, pp. 114–23; Israel Shenker, "V. S. Naipaul, Man Without a Society," *New York Times Book Review,* 17 Oct. 1971, pp. 4, 22–24; Ian Hamilton, "Without a Place," *Times Literary Supplement,* 30 July 1971, pp. 897–98; Mel Gussow, "Writer Without Roots," *New York Times Magazine,* 26 Dec. 1976; Jesse Noel, "Historicity and Homelessness in Naipaul," *Caribbean Studies,* 11, 3

(1972), 83–87; Martin Seymour-Smith, "Exile's Story," *The Spectator*, 5 May 1967, p. 528; Keith Garebian, "V. S. Naipaul's Negative Sense of Place," *Journal of Commonwealth Literature*, 10 (1975), 23–35; Nana Wilson Tagoe, "No Place: V. S. Naipaul's Vision of Home in the Caribbean," *Caribbean Review*, 10 (1980), 37–41; Anon., "Nowhere to Go," *Times Literary Supplement*, 8 Oct. 1971, p. 1199. The convention of describing Naipaul's life-history in wholeheartedly negative terms is made to seem all the more credible by the ambience of negativity encircling his personality. His friend Paul Theroux remarks: "Doubt, disbelief, skepticism, instinctive mistrust; I had never found these qualities so powerful in a person, and they were allied to a fiercely independent spirit. . . ." "V. S. Naipaul," *Modern Fiction Studies*, 30 (Autumn 1984), 449.

23. The phrase is Theodor Adorno's imaginative, embroidered synopsis of a sentiment expressed in Walter Benjamin's "Theses on the Philosophy of History." *Minima Moralia. Reflections from Damaged Life*, trans. E. F. N. Jephcott (1951; rpt. London: Verso, 1984), p. 151. Cf. Walter Benjamin, *Illuminations* (New York: Schocken, 1969), pp. 258–59.

24. William Walsh, *V. S. Naipaul* (Edinburgh: Oliver & Boyd, 1973), pp. 72–73; Martin Greene, *Dreams of Adventure, Deeds of Empire* (New York: Basic Books, 1979), p. 336.

25. Theroux, *V. S. Naipaul: An Introduction*, p. 76.

26. *Ibid.*, p. 91.

27. Rowe-Evans, "V. S. Naipaul," 59.

28. "The Novelist V. S. Naipaul Talks About His Work to Ronald Bryden," *The Listener*, 22 Mar. 1973, p. 367.

29. Gussow, "Writer Without Roots," p. 18, 8.

30. Ibid., pp. 9, 19. So, too, Larry David Nachman declares: "What place may he call home? What place may he take for granted and where may he be taken for granted? Wherever he goes, Naipaul is a visitor, and he sees. . . . He has somehow gained the intellectual freedom to perceive the world undistorted by the reigning ideologies and the current sentimentalities." "The Worlds of V. S. Naipaul," *Salmagundi*, 54 (Fall 1981), 620.

31. Alfred Kazin, "V. S. Napaul, Novelist as Thinker," *New York Times Book Review*, 1 May 1977, p. 7.

32. Michener, "The Dark Visions of V. S. Naipaul," p. 110. The opposition between observation and obsession surfaces most insistently in Naipaul's Indian writings.

33. Irving Howe, "A Dark Vision," *New York Times Book Review*, 13 May 1979, p. 1. Cf. Leon Gottfried's excited defense of Naipaul against critics who "overlook the deep pain of a human being who insists on seeing—those eyes again!—what is actually before him, not as it wishes to be, or to be seen, but as it is, and who will report the truth of what he sees and what he feels without fearing either the subject or himself." "Preface: The Face of V. S. Naipaul," p. 441. Jane Kramer makes the link between Naipaul's purported exile and his purported clearsightedness just as bluntly as Howe: "It is as if his foreignness,

his status as 'one of them,' gives him a license to see, as if our hypocrisies translated into his ethnic privilege. Naipaul's exile is not really a matter of displacement or dispossession. It has to do with a bitter, almost fanatic clarity. . . ." "From the Third World," *New York Times Book Review,* 13 Apr. 1980, p. 1. Kramer's "fanatic" is drawn with daring directness from Naipaul's own rhetoric of contempt. But where Third World "fanatics" are blinded by their obsessions, Naipaul's exile is interpreted as safely metamorphosing his particular fanaticism into clear-sightedness.

34. Walsh, *V. S. Naipaul,* p. 15.

35. Ibid., p. 25.

36. Mary Louise Pratt, "Scratches on the Face of the Country; or, What Mr. Barrow Saw in the Land of the Bushmen," *Critical Inquiry* 12, 1 (1985), 119–43; and Pratt, "Field Work in Common Places," in *Writing Culture. The Poetics and Politics of Ethnography,* ed. James Clifford and George E. Marcus (Berkeley: University of California Press, 1986), p. 32.

37. Conor Cruise O'Brien, Edward Said, and John Lukacs, "The Intellectual in the Post-Colonial World: A Discussion," *Salmagundi,* 70–71 (Spring–Summer 1986), 79. Lukacs and O'Brien both seek to defend Naipaul against Said's charges of partisanship by designating him, quite straightforwardly, a "truth-seeker." Lukacs further declares that "contrary to what Mr. Said has said, he does not write for or pander to Western intellectuals. . . . Unlike most other intellectuals, particularly those from ex-colonial countries, Naipaul is not a strident collector of injustices. In fact, he castigates some of the post-colonial countries themselves" (p. 68). That last expression of amazement—the "in fact"—illustrates how, as late in Naipaul's career as 1985, critics could still conceive of arguing for his impartiality by remarking that he is *even* prepared to assail Third World nations. Lukacs's style of reasoning, both here and in the passage quoted in the body of my text, is characteristic of the way attention is diverted away from any admission of Naipaul's strong, well-established position in England and the effect that might have on his "neutrality."

38. Eugene Goodheart, "V. S. Naipaul's Mandarin Sensibility," *Partisan Review,* 50 (1983), 244, 252. This essay follows the convention of isolating displacement as the primary fact of Naipaul's life and binding it to a distinguishing clear-sightedness. At one point Goodheart tempers his general admiration for Naipaul's observational powers by introducing the notion of "prejudiced clear-sightedness" (p. 246). But this is a straightforward attempt to cleanse Naipaul's prejudgments of opprobrium by denying that they impair his vision. Goodheart believes, moreover, that Naipaul eludes all ideologies.

39. Kenneth Ramchand, *The West Indian Novel and Its Background* (London: Faber & Faber, 1970), p. 202.

40. Robert D. Hamner, "Conversation with Derek Walcott," *World Literature Written in English,* 16 (1977), 415.

41. V. S. Naipaul, *The Overcrowded Barracoon* (1972; rpt. New York: Vintage, 1984), pp. 9–16; "What's Wrong with Being a Snob?" in Hamner, *Critical*

Perspectives, pp. 34–38. Naipaul articulates his attitudes toward the United States even more sparingly. Prior to *A Turn in the South,* his only piece of nonfiction set in America was an account of a visit to the 1984 Republican convention in Texas ("Among the Republicans," *New York Review of Books,* 25 Oct. 1984, pp. 5, 8, 10, 12, 14–17). Otherwise his most sustained reflections about the United States appear in the *Salmagundi* interview, where he passes some dispirited remarks about his year of teaching as Wesleyan and the decline of America's youth. See Mukherjee and Boyers, "A Conversation with V. S. Naipaul," pp. 4–22.

42. V. S. Naipaul *The Enigma of Arrival* (New York: Alfred A. Knopf, 1987).

43. Michener, "The Dark Visions of V. S. Naipaul," p. 104. Naipaul's penchant for backhanded swipes at Africa while ostensibly slapping England on the wrist resurfaces in "What's Wrong with Being a Snob?": "To civilize Africa (if that must be attempted—the issue is debatable), you recognize the primitive and try to eradicate it. To create the classless society [in England] you do not deny class differences. You ceaselessly wage class war." Hamner, *Critical Perspectives,* p. 37).

44. Naipaul, "What's Wrong with Being a Snob?" p. 36.

45. V. S. Naipaul, "Did You Hear That?" *The Listener,* 15 Mar. 1962, p. 197. For a related encomium to "that mid-Victorian certainty" so manifest in Trollope's writing, see V. S. Naipaul, "The Little More," *The Times* (London), 13 July 1961; rpt. in Hamner, *Critical Perspectives,* p. 13.

46. Naipaul, "Did You Hear That?" p. 197.

47. Quoted in Jeremy Seabrook and Trevor Blackwell, "Mrs. Thatcher's Religious Pilgrimage," *Granta,* 6 (1983), p. 44.

48. Derek Walcott, "The Spoiler's Return," in *The Fortunate Traveller* (New York: Farrar, Straus, and Giroux, 1981), p. 54.

49. Howe, "A Dark Vision," p. 1.

50. Naipaul, *The Enigma of Arrival,* p. 40. See also his remark in an adjoining passage that "the London I knew or imaginatively possessed was the London I had got from Dickens. It was Dickens—and his illustrators—who gave me the illusion of knowing the city" (p. 41).

51. "The Novelist V. S. Naipaul Talks About His Work," p. 367.

52. Hamilton, "Without a Place," p. 897.

53. Elizabeth Hardwick, "Meeting V. S. Naipaul," *New York Times Book Review,* 13 May 1979, p. 1.

54. "The Novelist V. S. Naipaul Talks About His Work," p. 367.

55. Shiva Naipaul, "Living in Earl's Court," in *Beyond the Dragon's Mouth: Stories and Pieces* (1984; rpt. New York: Viking, 1985), p. 210.

56. V. S. Naipaul, "Cricket," *Encounter,* Sept. 1963; rpt. *The Overcrowded Barracoon,* 1972; rpt. New York: Vintage, 1984, p. 17. Naipaul's metaphoric evocation of the cultures of the colonized recoiling upon the cultures of the colonizers anticipates the similarly modulated title of Hazel Carby and Stuart Hall's *The Empire Strikes Back: Race and Racism in 70s Britain* (London: Hutchinson, 1982).

57. Naipaul, *The Enigma of Arrival,* pp. 142–43.

58. Michiko Kakutani, "Naipaul Reviews His Past from Afar," *New York Times,* Dec. 1, 1980, p. C15. "Bush" is simply Naipaul's buzzword for barbarism; it has nothing to do with vegetation. Deserts can be Bush.

59. Shiva Naipaul, "Two Colonies," in *Beyond the Dragon's Mouth,* p. 394.

60. Perry Anderson, "Components of the National Culture," *New Left Review,* 50 (1968), 3–56; Raymond Williams, "Beyond Cambridge English," in *Writing in Society* (London: Verso, 1983), pp. 177–91; Paul Gilroy, *There Ain't No Black in the Union Jack* (London: Hutchinson, 1987).

61. Williams, p. 223.

Chapter 2

1. Martin Amis, "Books of the Year," *Observer Review,* 6 Dec. 1981, p. 25.

2. On this score, see Naipaul's remarks in Bharati Mukherjee and Robert Boyers, "A Conversation with V. S. Naipaul," *Salmagundi,* 54 (Fall 1981), 19.

3. Paul Fussell, *Abroad: British Literary Traveling Between the Wars* (New York: Oxford University Press, 1980).

4. V. S. Naipaul, *The Middle Passage. Impressions of Five Societies—British, French, and Dutch—in the West Indies and South America* (1962; rpt. London: Andre Deutsch, 1981), pp. 71–73.

5. Ibid., p. 26.

6. Ibid, p. 255. Naipaul prizes this quote sufficiently to repeat it on p. 27.

7. In tone, *A House for Mr. Biswas* belongs with the earlier fiction and marks the end of that distinctive phase of his career. It was published in 1961, after Naipaul had traveled through the Caribbean but before the record of that voyage had appeared as *The Middle Passage.*

8. See the 1984 foreword to *A House for Mr. Biswas* (1961; New York: Vintage, 1984), pp. 5–6.

9. Anon., "V. S. Naipaul Discusses How Writing Changes the Writer," *Ndaanan,* 4 (1974), 62.

10. Ibid., p. 62.

11. Naipaul, *The Middle Passage,* p. 7.

12. C. L. R. James, *The Black Jacobins* (1938; rpt. New York: Vintage, 1963).

13. Considering that the British empire had proved the most generous patron of explorers and travel writers, it is sadly ironic that Eric Williams's Third World, postcolonial patronage of Naipaul should have generated a text with such imperial overtones. The irony is redoubled in that two years after *The Middle Passage,* the first book-length rebuttal of Victorian accounts of the Caribbean appeared under the title *British Historians and the West Indies.* The author? None other than Williams himself. The ideological tenor of the two books could scarcely be more distinct.

14. V. S. Naipaul, "The Little More," *The Times* (London), 13 July 1961, p. 7.

15. Even in quoting Tacitus to press the analogy between the Roman and British empires, Naipaul strikes a common Victorian pose. See *The Middle Passage,* p. 42.

16. V. S. Naipaul, "Did You Hear That?" *The Listener,* 15 Mar. 1962, p. 197.

17. See Roger Abrahams and John Szwed, *After Africa: Extracts from British Travel Accounts and Journals of the Seventeenth, Eighteenth, and Nineteenth Centuries Concerning the Slaves, Their Manners, and Customs in the British West Indies* (New Haven: Yale University Press, 1983), p. 20.

18. Naipaul, *The Middle Passage,* p. 87. Cf. Naipaul's remark on another occasion: "I can't see a Monkey—you can use a capital M, that's an affectionate word for the generality—reading my work. No, my books aren't read in Trinidad now—drumbeating is a higher activity, a more satisfying activity." Michiko Kakutani, "Naipaul Reviews His Past from Afar," *New York Times,* 1 Dec. 1980, p. C15.

19. Naipaul, *The Middle Passage,* p. 39.

20. V. S. Naipaul, *The Enigma of Arrival* (New York: Knopf, 1987), p. 153.

21. Mukherjee and Boyers, "A Conversation with V. S. Naipaul," p. 6.

22. Peter Webb, "The Master of the Novel," *Newsweek,* 18 Aug. 1980, p. 35.

23. V. S. Naipaul, Introduction to *East Indians in the Caribbean: Colonialism and the Struggle for Identity,* Proceedings of a Symposium on East Indians in the Caribbean, The University of the West Indies, June 1975, (Millwood, N.Y.: Kraus International, 1982), p. 9.

24. Paul Theroux, "V. S. Naipaul," *Modern Fiction Studies,* 30 (Autumn 1984), 448.

25. V. S. Naipaul, "Where the Rum Comes From," *New Statesman,* 4 (1958), 21.

26. Charles Michener, "The Dark Visions of V. S. Naipaul," *Newsweek,* 16 Nov. 1981, p. 104.

27. Conor Cruise O'Brien, Edward Said, and John Lukacs, "The Intellectual in the Post-Colonial World: A Discussion with Conor Cruise O'Brien, Edward Said and John Lukacs," *Salmagundi* 70–71 (Spring–Summer 1986), 79.

28. V. S. Naipaul, "Graham Greene," *The Daily Telegraph Magazine,* 8 March, 1968, p. 28.

29. V. S. Naipaul Interviewed by Ian Hamilton," *Savacou,* 9–10 (1974); rpt. Robert D. Hamner, ed., *Critical Perspectives on V. S. Naipaul* (London: Heinemann, 1979), p. 43.

30. Quoted in M. Banning Eyre, "Naipaul at Wesleyan," *South Carolina Review,* 14 (1982), 37.

31. Samuel Hynes, *The Auden Generation: Literature and Politics in England in the 1930s* (London: The Bodley Head, 1976), p. 228.

32. Fussell, *Abroad,* p. 58.

33. Ibid., pp. 209–10.

34. Fussell's invocation of Empson is symptomatic of his participation in the tradition of pastoral effacement that Raymond Williams traces so persuasively.

Where Fussell hears the harmonies of benign paternalism, Williams hears discordant social injustice muffled by Golden Age motifs. Williams once remarked sardonically of relations between city and country, "The loved places are the 'unspoiled' places, and no group agrees with this more readily than those who live in the spoiled." His insight could apply equally to the global adventures of the interwar travelers: Arcady is no place to inhabit, but it is a fine place for empire's progeny to take their excursions. See Raymond Williams, *The Country and the City* (New York: Oxford University Press, 1973), p. 253.

35. V. S. Naipaul, "Epilogue, from a Journal: The Circus of Luxor," in *In a Free State* (1971; rpt. London: Penguin, 1973), p. 246.

36. Naipaul, *The Middle Passage*, p. 5.

37. Ibid., p. 42.

38. V. S. Naipaul, *An Area of Darkness* (1964; rpt. New York: Vintage, 1981), p. 16.

39. Ibid., p. 46.

40. Anon., "Angry Young Indian," *Newsweek,* 19 Apr. 1965, p. 103.

41. Naipaul, *East Indians in the Caribbean,* p. 7.

42. Michener, "The Dark Visions of V. S. Naipaul," p. 109.

43. See also Mukherjee and Boyers, "A Conversation with V. S. Naipaul," p. 8. This is a position Naipaul has asserted on other occasions, as when an interviewer expressed perturbation at her guest's "dismissal of the passions of people in these far-off places." No, Naipaul responded, he did not dismiss their passions; he wrote about such people out of concern, not contempt. Ibid., p. 19. He expresses similar sentiments in the interview with Curt Suplee, "Voyager with the Dark and Common Vision—Through the World of Islam and Beyond, with V. S. Naipaul," *Washington Post,* 19. Nov. 1981, p. C-1.

44. Ham Mukasa, *Sir Apolo Kagwa Discovers Britain* (1904; rpt. London: Heinemann, 1975); John Pepper Clark, *America, Their America* (1964; rpt. New York: Africana, 1971); Ibrahim Abu-Lughod, *Arab Rediscovery of Europe: A Study in Cultural Encounters* (Princeton: Princeton University Press, 1963).

45. Evelyn Waugh, *When the Going Was Good* (1946; rpt. Boston: Little, Brown, 1984), pp. 6–7.

46. Gazing back from the perspective of the mid-eighties, Naipaul has described how he overlooked the literary potential and historic momentousness of the great movement of people toward London in the forties and fifties of which he was a part. Waugh's "displaced persons," whom Naipaul portrays as "the flotsam of Europe after the war" mingled with the likes of Naipaul, the products of the unraveling of empire. As if to make amends for this omission, Naipaul recalls affectingly in the autobiographical section of *The Enigma of Arrival* how a mutual dependence developed between Angela, a displaced Italian, and him, a displaced Indian West Indian, both at sea in the newness of a postwar London that was redefining its identity and theirs. *The Enigma of Arrival,* p. 104.

47. Claude Lévi-Strauss, *Tristes Tropiques,* trans. John Russell (1955; New York: Atheneum, 1970), p. 17. One observes, incidentally, that in attempting to

pinpoint the age of *real* travel, Lévi-Strauss locates it centuries earlier than Fussell does.

48. V. S. Naipaul, "Dark Places," *New Statesman,* 18 Aug. 1961, p. 222.

49. Dean MacCannell, *The Tourist: A New Theory of the Leisure Class* (New York: Schocken Books, 1976). I cannot hope in this brief, selective synopsis to do justice to MacCannell's account in all its intriguing complexitites. Nor can I enter fully into reservations I have about aspects of the theory; my feeling, for instance, that he overstretches the analogy between the tourist and the social scientist, overstates the tourists' centrality to the condition of modernity, and is on occasion given to brittle structuralizing. For two instructive responses to MacCannell, see Georges Van Den Abbeele, "Sightseers: The Tourist as Theorist," *Diacritics,* 10 (Dec. 1980), 3–14, and Jean-Paul Dumont, "A Matter of Touristic 'indifférance'," *American Ethnologist,* 11 (1984), 139–51.

50. MacCannell, *The Tourist,* p. 45.

51. Hans Magnus Enzensberger, "Tourists of the Revolution," in *Critical Essays,* ed. Reinhold Grimm and Bruce Armstrong (New York: Continuum, 1982), pp. 159–85.

52. Ibid., pp. 160–61.

53. Naipaul, *The Middle Passage,* p. 253.

54. Ibid., p. 250.

55. Ibid., p. 70.

56. Ibid., p. 191.

57. Aimé Césaire, "Notebook of a Return to the Native Land," in *The Collected Poetry,* trans. Clayton Eshelman and Annette Smith (Berkeley: University of California Press, 1983), p. 83.

58. Naipaul, *The Enigma of Arrival,* p. 152.

Chapter 3

1. Edmund Leach, *Claude Lévi-Strauss* (New York: Viking, 1970), p. 4.

2. James Clifford, *The Predicament of Culture: Twentieth-Century Ethnography, Literature, and Art* (Cambridge, Mass.: Harvard University Press, 1988), p. 24.

3. S. P. Mohanty, "Us and Them: On the Philosophical Bases of Political Criticism," *Yale Journal of Criticism,* 2, 2 (1989), 31.

4. See, for example, Edward Said, "Bitter Dispatches from the Third World," *The Nation,* 3 May 1980, p. 25.

5. See V. S. Naipaul, *Finding the Centre: Two Narratives* (New York: Knopf, 1984), p. 103.

6. V. S. Naipaul, *The Middle Passage. Impressions of Five Societies—British, French and Dutch—in the West Indies and South America* (1962; rpt. London: Andre Deutsch, 1981), p. 210.

7. V. S. Naipaul, *India: A Wounded Civilization* (1977; rpt. Harmondsworth, England: Penguin, 1979), p. 102.

8. Quoted in Louis A. Sass, "Anthropology's Native Problems: Revisionism in the Field," *Harper's Magazine,* May 1986, p. 50.

9. James Clifford and George Marcus, eds., *Writing Culture: The Poetics and Politics of Ethnography* (Berkeley: University of California Press, 1986), p. 4; Edward Said, "Representing the Colonized: Anthropology's Interlocutors," *Critical Inquiry* 15 (Winter 1989), 209.

10. In keeping with these new currents in the discipline, one encounters studies on ethnographies as texts, on the generic conventions of ethnographic realism, on ethnographic naturalism, on modernity and postmodernity in ethnography, on ethnographic allegory, on ethnographic surrealism, on the rhetoric of ethnographies, on ethnographic defamiliarization, and on narrative point of view and polyphonic effects in ethnography. See especially James Clifford, "On Ethnographic Surrealism," in *The Predicament of Culture,* pp. 117–51; Steven Webster, "Realism and Reification in the Ethnographic Genre," *Critique of Anthropology,* 6 (1986), 39–62; George E. Marcus and Dick Cushman, "Ethnographies as Texts," *Annual Review of Anthropology,* 2 (1982), 25–69; George E. Marcus and Michael M. J. Fischer, *Anthropology as Cultural Critique: An Experimental Moment in the Human Sciences* (Chicago: University of Chicago Press, 1986), esp. pp. 7–44, 111–36; and Marc Manganaro, ed., *Modernist Anthropology: From Fieldwork to Text* (Princeton: Princeton University Press, 1990).

11. The most illuminating accounts of these developments are furnished by Clifford ("On Ethnographic Authority") and Webster ("The Historical Materialist Critique of Surrealism and Postmodernist Ethnography") in *The Predicament of Culture* and *Modernist Anthropology* respectively.

12. Webster, "The Historical Materialist Critique," pp. 266–99.

13. Paul Rabinow, *Reflections on Fieldwork in Morocco* (Berkeley: University of California Press, 1977), p. ix.

14. On the subject of ethnographic-autobiographical relations, see especially Johannes Fabian, *Time and the Other: How Anthropology Makes Its Object* (New York: Columbia University Press, 1983), pp. 87–97.

15. In a fine essay on these distinctions, Mary Louise Pratt observes the "well-established habit among ethnographers of defining ethnographic writing over and against older, less specialized genres, such as travel books, personal memoirs, journalism, and accounts by missionaries, settlers, colonial officials, and the like. . . . In almost any ethnography dull-looking figures called 'mere travelers' or 'casual observers' show up from time to time, only to have their superficial perceptions either corrected or corroborated by the serious scientist." "Field Work in Common Places," in Clifford and Marcus, *Writing Culture,* p. 27.

16. Webster, "Realism and Reification," p. 49.

17. Elenore Smith Bowen, *Return to Laughter* (New York: Harper & Row, 1954); Michel Leiris, *L'Afrique fantôme* (1934; rpt. Paris: Gallimard, 1950).

18. Vincent Crapanzano, *Tuhami: Portrait of a Moroccan* (Chicago: Univer-

sity of Chicago Press, 1980); Jean-Paul Dumont, *The Headman and I* (Austin: University of Texas Press, 1978); Manda Cesara [Karla Poewe, pseud.], *Reflections of a Woman Anthropologist: No Hiding Place* (New York: Academic Press, 1982).

19. On this score, I concur with Webster's cautionary note against the tendency to view ethnography's dilemmas in overly formal terms that mask its material context. See "The Historical Materialist Critique," pp. 266–99.

20. C. D. Narasimhaiah, "Somewhere Something Has Snapped," *The Literary Criterion,* Summer 1965, p. 87; Said, "Bitter Dispatches from the Third World," p. 24; Benedict Anderson, "James Fenton's Slideshow," *New Left Review,* 158 (1986), 86.

21. D. J. Enright, "Who Is India?" *Encounter,* Dec. 1964, p. 60.

22. Naipaul, *India: A Wounded Civilization,* p. 7.

23. Ibid., p. 9.

24. Enright, "Who Is India?" p. 60.

25. Cf. Fabian's critique of ethnographic methodology: "No provision seems to be made for the beat of drums or the blaring of bar music that keep you awake at night; none for the strange taste and texture of food, or the smells and the stench. How does *method* deal with the hours of waiting, with maladroitness and gaffes due to confusion or bad timing? Where does it put the frustrations caused by diffidence and intransigence, where the joys of purposeless chatter and conviviality? Often all this is written off as the 'human side' of our scientific activity. Method is expected to yield objective knowledge by filtering our experiential 'noise' thought to impinge on the quality of information." *Time and the Other,* p. 108.

26. Naipaul, *Finding the Centre,* p. 12.

27. V. S. Naipaul, *Among the Believers. An Islamic Journey* (1981; rpt. New York: Vintage, 1982), p. 3.

28. The first half of the volume is Naipaul's only protracted attempt at pure autobiography and even so would be better described as autobiography circumscribed by two journeys: his journey to England, which he repeatedly speaks of as a departure towards a vocation, and his travels in pursuit of a Port of Spain character named Bogart. Faced with the problem of centering this account of his literary beginnings, he chooses as his narrative hub the writing of his first story. His obsession with that earliest narrative generates a quest for Bogart, whose name inspired the tale. In 1977, twenty-seven years after leaving Trinidad, Naipaul unearths him in a Venezuelan village.

29. Ibid., p. 11.

30. Naipaul, Author's Foreword to *Finding the Centre,* pp. 12–13.

31. Naipaul, "The Crocodiles of Yamoussoukro," in *Finding the Centre,* p. 92.

32. Ibid., p. 149.

33. Ibid., p. 166. Because of his obsession with the purportedly ubiquitous subversion of reason by African magic, Naipaul has a vested interest in dramatiz-

ing the difficulty of getting unequivocal information, of presenting the unknown (that is, seldom reported) world as unknowable. A level of journalistic sloth inexcusable in the metropole is suddenly passable in reports from the global periphery—as when Naipaul feels at liberty to include, among his litany of Ivoirian inconsistencies, "How many students attended the university? Someone said six hundred, somebody else said sixty." Such banal bafflement could have been remedied by elementary leg-work.

34. Ibid., p. 10.

35. Ibid., p. 103.

36. On this score, see Clifford, *The Predicament of Culture,* pp. 34–54.

37. Fischer in Marcus and Fischer, *Anthropology as Cultural Critique,* p. 233. Ralph Bulmer and Ian Majnep experiment with this bifocal approach in *Birds of My Kalam Country,* a text in which the Western ethnographer becomes a partial subject of the narrative and the person who would formerly have been an object of anthropological inquiry rises to the status of coauthor.

38. Naipaul, *The Enigma of Arrival,* pp. 343–54.

39. Talal Asad, "A Comment on the Idea of Non-Western Anthropology," in *Indigenous Anthropology in Non-Western Countries,* ed. Hussein Fahim (Durham, N.C.: Carolina Academic Press, 1982), pp. 283–87.

40. Aijaz Ahmad, "Jameson's Rhetoric of Otherness and the "National Allegory," *Social Text,* 17 (1987), 5.

41. Quoted in ibid., p. 5

42. Naipaul, *The Enigma of Arrival,* p. 154.

43. V. S. Naipaul, *An Area of Darkness* (1964; rpt. New York: Vintage, 1981), p. 213.

44. Ibid., p. 32.

45. Ibid., p. 32. See also ibid., p. 44; "Prologue to an Autobiography," in *Finding the Centre,* p. 42; *The Enigma of Arrival,* pp. 153–54; and V. S. Naipaul, Foreword to Seepersad Naipaul, *The Adventures of Gurudeva and Other Stories* (London: Andre Deutsch, 1976), pp. 7–23.

46. "Prologue to an Autobiography," pp. 59, 45, 42.

47. Bertolt Brecht, quoted in Hans Magnus Enzensberger, "Tourists of the Revolution," in *Critical Essays,* ed. Reinhold Grimm and Bruce Armstrong (New York: Continuum, 1982), p. 175.

48. Naipaul, *An Area of Darkness,* p. 77.

49. Fouad Ajami, "In Search of Islam," *New York Times Book Review,* 25 Oct. 1981, p. 32.

50. Nissim Ezekiel, "Naipaul's India and Mine," in *New Writing in India,* Adil Jussawalla, ed. (Baltimore: Penguin, 1974), p. 83; H. H. Anniah Gowda, "Naipaul in India," *The Literary Half-Yearly,* 2 (1970), 163; Raja Rao, "Out of Step with Shiva," *Book Week,* 29 Aug. 1965, p. 4.

51. Ibid., p. 212.

52. Ibid., p. 176.

53. In the light of my earlier discussion of Naipaul's weakness for Victorian

imperialism, it is worth noting that the grandfather's role in equipping Naipaul with an imaginary India in advance should be seen alongside a second source of prefigurement: Kipling. Indeed, at one point Naipaul suggests that Kipling's portrait of India is so enduringly precise as to render his own voyage redundant: "It was all there in Kipling, barring the epilogue of the Indian inheritance. A journey was not really necessary. No writer was more honest and accurate. . . ." *An Area of Darkness,* p. 191. The dismissal of independence as an "epilogue" is consistent with Naipaul's determination to downplay the significance of both colonialism and decolonization in India.

54. Ibid., p. 46. He expresses a similar sentiment in Adrian Rowe-Evans, "Interview with V. S. Naipaul," *Transition,* 40 (1971), 59.

55. See Naipaul, *An Area of Darkness,* p. 281.

56. In Seepersad Naipaul, pp. 7–23; "Prologue to an Autobiography," pp. 17–48; *A House for Mr. Biswas* (1961; rpt. Harmondsworth, England: Penguin, 1969; New York: Vintage, 1984), pp. 1–6. Cf. his brother Shiva's description of the chaotic extended family gatherings as "the closest I have ever come to feeling I 'belonged' to an organism larger than myself, to having an 'identity' accepted by myself and recognised and reinforced by others: the closest I have ever come to a social existence." *Beyond the Dragon's Mouth: Stories and Pieces* (1984; rpt. New York: Viking, 1985), p. 27.

57. In Curt Suplee, "Voyager with the Dark and Comic Vision—Through the World of Islam and Beyond, with V. S. Naipaul," *Washington Post,* 19 Nov. 1981, p. C-17.

58. Ezekiel, "Naipaul's India and Mine," p. 74.

59. Gordon Rohlehr, "The Ironic Approach: The Novels of V. S. Naipaul," in *Critical Perspectives on V. S. Naipaul,* ed. Robert Hamner (Heinemann: London, 1979), p. 184.

60. Naipaul, *An Area of Darkness,* p. 198.

61. V. S. Naipaul, *The Overcrowded Barracoon* (1972; rpt. New York: Vintage, 1984), p. 81.

62. Naipaul, "Prologue to an Autobiography," p. 12.

Chapter 4

1. V. S. Naipaul, "Conrad's Darkness," in *The Return of Eva Peron, with the Killings in Trinidad* (1980; rpt. New York: Vintage, 1981), p. 203; "Michael X and the Black Power Killings in Trinidad," in ibid., pp. 74–76.

2. V. S. Naipaul, "A New King for the Congo: Mobutu and the Nihilism of Africa," in *The Return of Eva Peron,* pp. 185–219; V. S. Naipaul, *A Congo Diary* (Los Angeles: Sylvester and Orphanos, 1980); V. S. Naipaul, *A Bend in the River* (1979; rpt. New York: Vintage, 1980); Shiva Naipaul, *North of South: An African Journey* (1978; rpt. Harmondsworth, England: Penguin, 1980). For other sustained invocations of Conrad by V. S. Naipaul, see "The Killings in Trinidad," in *The Return of Eva Peron;* "A Note on a Borrowing from Conrad,"

New York Review of Books, 16 Dec. 1982, pp. 37–38; and "Our Universal Civilization," *New York Times,* 5 Nov. 1990, p. A21. For a discussion of the strong Conradian strains in *A Bend in the River,* see Lynda Prescott, "Past and Present Darkness: Sources for V. S. Naipaul's *A Bend in the River,*" *Modern Fiction Studies,* 30 (1984), 547–60.

3. Naipaul, "Conrad's Darkness," p. 223.

4. V. S. Naipaul, *Finding the Centre* (New York: Alfred A. Knopf, 1984), p. x.

5. Philip Caputo, *A Rumor of War* (New York: Rinehart and Winston, 1977); Joan Didion, *Salvador* (New York: Simon and Schuster, 1983).

6. Graham Greene, *Journey Without Maps* (1936; rpt. Harmondsworth, England: Penguin, 1978); André Gide, *Travels in the Congo;* trans. Dorothy Bussy (1929; rpt. New York: Modern Age Books, 1937); Hannah Arendt, *The Origins of Totalitarianism,* Part 2: *Imperialism* (1951; rpt. New York: Harcourt Brace Jovanovich, 1968); Alberto Moravia, "Congo on My Mind," *New York Times Magazine,* 7 Oct. 1984, pp. 34, 63–64, 68–70; Patrick Marnham, *Fantastic Invasion* (New York: Harcourt Brace Jovanovich, 1980); Edward Hoagland, "Africa Brought Home: *Heart of Darkness* and Its Journey Downriver," *Harpers,* May 1985, pp. 71–72; Nadine Gordimer, "The Congo River," in *The Essential Gesture* (1961, rpt. New York: Penguin, 1989), pp. 157–85; Paul Hyland, *The Black Heart: A Voyage in Central Africa* (New York: Paragon, 1990); Joseph Hone, *Africa of the Heart* (New York: William Morrow, 1986).

7. Naipaul, "Conrad's Darkness," p. 236.

8. Ibid., p. 233. Naipaul reflects further on his relation to Conrad in Bharati Mukherjee and Robert Boyers, "A Conversation with V. S. Naipaul," *Salmagundi,* 54 (Fall 1981), 9–10. Chris Searle stages a brief but suggestive contrast between Naipaul and Conrad in "Naipaulacity: A Form of Cultural Imperialism," *Race and Class,* 26 (1984), 61.

9. Graham Greene, "Congo Journal," in *In Search of a Character: Two African Journals* (London: Bodley Head, 1961).

10. Greene, *Journey Without Maps,* p. 248.

11. Joseph Conrad, *Heart of Darkness* (1902; rpt. Harmondsworth, England: Penguin, 1982), p. 51.

12. Cf. Hayden White, *Tropics of Discourse: Essays in Cultural Criticism* (1978; Baltimore: Johns Hopkins University Press, 1985), p. 179.

13. Greene, *Journey Without Maps,* p. 20. This sentiment is similarly formulated on pp. 97 and 158.

14. M. M. Mahood, *The Colonial Encounter: A Reading of Six Novels* (London: Rex Collings, 1977), p. 127.

15. Paul Fussell mistakenly asserts: "Somewhat like Conrad's *Heart of Darkness,* [Greene] uses the action of the jungle trip as an immense metaphor of a return through adulthood back to adolescence and finally to the inland of early childhood." *Abroad: British Literary Traveling Between the Wars* (Oxford: Oxford University Press, 1980), p. 67.

16. Greene, *Journey Without Maps,* p. 20.

17. Ibid., p. 249,

18. Arendt, *Imperialism,* p. 65.

19. Ibid., p. 65.

20. Ibid., p. 69.

21. Ibid., p. 71.

22. Benita Parry, *Conrad and Imperialism: Ideological Boundaries and Visionary Frontiers* (London: Macmillan, 1983).

23. Greil Marcus, "Journey up the River: An Interview with Francis Coppola," *Rolling Stone,* 1 Nov. 1979, p. 53.

24. Coppola is quite precise about his intentions here. Brando's suggestion that he play Kurtz as someone who had changed sides and dressed in V.C. clothes made Coppola nauseous: "That almost made me vomit. I said, "Hey Marlon, I may not know everything about this movie—but one thing I know it's not about our guilt." Ibid., p. 54.

25. Ibid., pp. 53, 56. Coppola reaffirms this sentiment when he remarks: "I chose to go with a stylized treatment, up the river into primitive times."

26. Johannes Fabian, *Time and the Other: How Anthropology Makes Its Object* (New York: Columbia University Press, 1983), p. 17.

27. The scenario wherein Americans are dragged down by a hybrid of the Vietnamese jungle and Conrad's wilderness is again dramatized by the Vietnam veteran Philip Caputo in his nonfictional memoir, *A Rumor of War.* Even more striking that Caputo's generic and geographical mélange is his decision to leave his debt to *Heart of Darkness* perfectly unattributed. Neither Conrad nor the title of his novella is mentioned anywhere. This despite a prologue to Caputo's book that closes as follows: "There was nothing familiar out where we were, no churches, no police, no laws, no newspapers, or any of the restraining influences without which the earth's population of virtuous people would be reduced by ninety-five percent. It was the dawn of creation in the Indochina bush, an ethical as well as a geographical wilderness. Out there, lacking restraints, sanctioned to kill, confronted by a hostile country and a relentless enemy, we sank into a brutish state. The descent could be checked only by the net of a man's inner values, the attribute that is called character. There were a few—and I suspect Lieutenant Calley was one—who had no net and plunged all the way down, discovering in their bottommost depths a capacity for malice they probably never suspected was there." This mixture of allusion, citation and synopsis verges on plagiarism. But plagiarism of a stalwart classic like *Heart of Darkness* differs from plagiarism of a more obscure text. For here Caputo takes advantage of an assumed knowledge that has broken loose from the novella and is already circulating in an essentialized form. In a sense it is Western discourse about Third World societies that has plagiarized Conrad, extracting and reshuffling a set of familiar images of strangeness that lie handy for any author faced with the trauma of bringing the "indescribable" tropics home. Hence, as recently as 1978, it was still possible for an American anthropologist, Hoyt Anderson, to produce

an ethnography entitled *Mind in the Heart of Darkness: Value and Self-Identity Among the Tswana of Southern Africa* (New Haven: Yale University Press, 1978).

The impact of *Heart of Darkness* on a wider discourse about Africa has been sustained through its mobilization by the fashion world to serve the eighties and nineties vogue for imperial nostalgia. A little predictably, the novella is quoted in the mail order catalogues for Banana Republic, the highly successful chain of what would once have been called tropical outfitters that has become empire's sartorial revival house. *Heart of Darkness'* capacity to serve as a magnet for all the bric-a-brac of African chic fantasized by Western imaginations was strikingly dramatized by a full-page Bergdorf Goodman ad in *The New York Times,* 9 March 1986, entitled "The Congo Line." The text of the ad read: "Nearly everyone, it seems, is doing the Congo. There are enough camouflage colors, tribal prints and safari motifs around to mount your own production of 'Heart of Darkness.' You'll find the selection we've made does rather splendidly for real urban life as well. Think of how cosmopolitan the zebra skins in El Morocco always looked. Consider, for example, our African accents on one: shell-bordered leather belts from Jill Stuart banded in pony skin that's printed with the sort of primitive narrative drawings you'd expect to find on the wall of a cave. Or, from Donatella Pellini, graphic, neo-savage jewelry, from beads to nose-ring earrings. . . . Another felicitous exercise in primtive-modern double talk: Michael Katz's native-for-night white silk evening separates, printed in witch-doctor-ish masks accented by very un-African pastel jewels."

Sometimes the annexation of Conrad by those who market Africa in travel and fashion is more subtle, if no less insidious. One can share, for example, Ngugi wa Thiong'o's unease when he observes of a neocolonial theater in Nairobi: "One of their favourite advertisements in tourist brochures is the supposedly dramatic slogan: A Professional Theatre in the Heart of Africa. They just about avoided advertising a professional theatre in the *Heart of Darkness.*" "Kenyan Culture: The National Struggle for Survival," in *Writers in Politics* (London: Heinemann, 1981), p. 44.

28. See Rob Nixon, "Preparations for Travel: The Naipaul Brothers' Conradian Atavism," *Research in African Literatures,* 22 (1991), 177–90.

29. Veronica Geng, "Mistah Kurtz. He Dead," *The New Yorker,* 3 Sept. 1979, p. 71.

30. All Naipaul's engagements with *Heart of Darkness* are stripped clean of any romantic questing after the unconscious and are devoid of the ancestral-utopian dimensions that Greene drew from it. In part, this change is a measure of the distance between the 1930s and the 1970s. Since the early 1950s, the African independence struggles have caused the political character of the continent's relations to the West to be writ so large that it has become more difficult for travel writers in the postcolonial era to abstract Africa into any version of Arcady.

31. For convenience, I use the name Zaire throughout to refer to the former

Belgian Congo after its independence in 1960. The country was, however, only officially christened Zaire in 1971.

32. Naipaul, "A New King for the Congo," p. 210.

33. Naipaul, *A Congo Diary,* pp. 11, 13.

34. Michael Crowder, ed., *The Cambridge History of Africa,* vol. 8 (Cambridge: Cambridge University Press, 1984), p. 729.

35. Renee C. Fox, Willy de Craemer, and Jean-marie Ribeaucourt, "The Second Independence: A Case Study of the Kwilu Rebellion in the Congo," *Comparative Studies in Society and History,* 8 (1965–66), 103.

36. Cf. Shiva Naipaul's remark, in a passage where he stresses *Heart of Darkness*'s continued relevance: "Civilized man, it seems, can no more cope with prolonged exposure to the primitive than the primitive can cope with prolonged exposure to him." *North of South,* p. 347.

37. Naipaul, "A New King for the Congo," pp. 208, 210.

38. Ibid., p. 207. See also Naipaul's remark in *A Congo Diary:* "The Intercontinentals of Africa—the outposts of progress" (p. 36). Naipaul has expressed a special fondness for "An Outpost of Progress" (a story that was, in a sense, a trial run for *Heart of Darkness*), declaring it to be "the finest thing Conrad wrote." "Conrad's Darkness," p. 232. This affection is further reflected on by M. Banning Eyre, in "Naipaul at Wesleyan," *South Carolina Review,* 14 (1982), 35–36.

39. The quoted phrase is Naipaul's capsule description of "An Oupost of Progress." See "Michael X and the Black Power Killings in Trinidad," p. 75.

40. Naipaul, "A New King for the Congo," p. 214.

41. Ibid., p. 218.

42. Ibid.

43. Crowder, *The Cambridge History of Africa,* p. 718.

44. Ali Mazrui, *Political Values and the Educated Class in Africa* (Berkeley and Los Angeles: University of California Press, 1978), p. 53.

45. Crowder, *The Cambridge History of Africa,* p. 722. See also Ellen Ray, ed., *Dirty Work 2: The CIA in Africa* (Secaucus, N.J.: Lyle Stuart, 1979); Nzongola-Ntalaja, ed., *The Crisis in Zaire: Myths and Realities* (London: Zed, 1986).

46. Katangese Foreign Minister Evariste Kimba, quoted in Richard D. Mahoney, *JFK: Ordeal in Africa* (Oxford: Oxford University Press, 1983), p. 70.

47. The only period when the United States withheld its support from Zaire was during Mobutu's brief, abortive attempt to nationalize industry, between 1974 and 1975.

48. Guy Gran, ed., *Zaire: The Political Economy of Underdevelopment* (New York: Praeger, 1979), p. 310.

49. Naipaul, "A New King for the Congo," p. 188. See Frantz Fanon, *The Wretched of the Earth,* trans. Constance Farrington (1963; rpt. New York: Grove Press, 1968), p. 221.

50. Kwame Anthony Appiah, "Out of Africa: Topologies of Nativism," *The Yale Journal of Criticism,* 2 (Fall 1988), 164.

51. Naipaul, "A New King for the Congo," p. 219.

52. Naipaul, *A Congo Diary,* p. 41.

53. Ibid., p. 13.

54. *Sunday Times (London),* 20 Jan. 1985, p. 11.

55. Chinua Achebe, "An Image of Africa," *Massachusetts Review,* 18 (1977), 790. Achebe reflects further on some of these sentiments in "Viewpoint," *The Times Literary Supplement,* 1 Feb. 1980, p. 113. For another African challenge to the Conradian legacy, see Peter Nazareth, "Out of Darkness: Conrad and Other Third World Writers," *Conradiana,* 14 (1982), 173–88.

56. Achebe, "An Image of Africa," p. 793.

57. Cedric Watts, "A Bloody Racist: About Achebe's View of Conrad," *The Yearbook of English Studies,* 13 (1983), 203.

58. Derek Walcott, *The Fortunate Traveller* (New York: Farrar, Straus, Giroux, 1981), pp. 93–94.

59. I have discussed the tradition of enlisting *The Tempest* counterhegemonically in "African and Caribbean Appropriations of *The Tempest,*" *Critical Inquiry,* 14 (1987), 557–78. Among the writers who have mobilized Shakespeare's play in this manner are the Barbadians George Lamming and Edward Kamu Braithwaite, the Martinican Aimé Césaire, the Cuban Roberto Fernandez Retamar, the Kenyan Ngugi wa Thiong'o, and the Nigerian John Pepper Clark.

60. Kwame Anthony Appiah, "Strictures on Structures: The Prospects for a Structuralist Poetics of African Fiction," in *Black Literature and Literary Theory,* ed. Henry Louis Gates, Jr. (New York: Methuen, 1984), p. 146.

61. Moravia, "Congo on Mind," and *Which Tribe Do You Belong To?* (New York: Farrar, Strauss and Giroux, 1974). Here one should also mention Patrick Marnham's African travelogue *Fantastic Invasion* (New York: Harcourt Brace Jovanovich, 1980), which takes both its title and epigraph from Conrad but otherwise skirts the more persistent enticements of the neo-Conradian tradition: the notions of Africa as a heart of darkness and of Africa as Kurtz's turf. The PBS documentary on the River Congo (broadcast 2 Nov. 1985), in its series *River Journey,* makes some of the obligatory bows to Conrad's text. The popular American travel writer Edward Hoagland has reflected glancingly (and uncritically) on the way Conrad's Africa has been appropriated by certain of the later writers.

62. Evelyn Waugh, *Labels: A Mediterranean Journal* (1930; rpt. London: Penguin, 1985), p. 13.

63. Moravia, "Congo on my Mind," p. 34. In an inset accompanying Moravia's essay we can observe Conrad's insistent itinerary passing from the world of literary travelers into the world of tourists: "Some agencies specializing in custom travel will, however, put together a trip for those who wish to follow in the wake of Joseph Conrad. In New York, three such agencies are. . . ." (p. 68).

64. Dean MacCannell, *The Tourist: A New Theory of the Leisure Class* (New York: Schocken Books, 1976), esp. pp. 123–31.

65. Gide, *Travels in the Congo,* p. 48.

66. Naipaul, "Conrad's Darkness," p. 231.

Chapter 5

1. Bharati Mukherjee and Robert Boyers, "A Conversation with V. S. Naipaul," *Salmagundi,* 54 (Fall 1981), 6.

2. Quoted in Joseph Epstein, "A Cottage for Mr. Naipaul," *The New Criterion,* 6 (1987), 10–11.

3. Margaret Thatcher, quoted in Martin Barker, "Racism—the New Inheritors," *Radical Philosophy,* 21 (1984), 2.

4. For a concentrated example of Naipaul's Manichaean division of the world into metropolitan civilization and the barbarism of the periphery, see his essay on Argentina, "The Return of Eva Peron," in *The Return of Eva Peron, with the Killings in Trinidad* (1980; rpt. New York: Vintage, 1981), pp. 170–71. Naipaul uses the violence that engulfed the society in the seventies as an occasion for exposing its pretensions to being civilized, i.e. European. But his analysis of Argentina's barbarism rests on the unexamined premise that Europe serves as a historically dependable yardstick of civilization.

5. "What's Wrong with Being a Snob?" *The Saturday Evening Post,* 3 June, 1967; rpt. Robert D. Hamner, ed., *Critical Perspectives on V. S. Naipaul* (London: Heinemann, 1979), p. 37.

6. In Curt Suplee, "Voyager with the Dark and Comic Vision—Through the World of Islam and Beyond, with V. S. Naipaul," *Washington Post,* 19 Nov. 1981, p. c-17.

7. For first-hand accounts of the forest rituals of anti-colonial resistance that emerged from Gikuyu culture, see W. Itote, '*Mau Mau*' *General* (Nairobi: East African Publishing House, 1967); O. Odinga, *Not Yet Uhuru* (London: Heinemann, 1967); G. Wachira, *Ordeal in the Forest* (Nairobi: East African Publishing House, 1968); C. Waciuma, *Daughter of Mumbi* (Nairobi: East African Publishing House, 1969); and J. Wamweya, *Freedom Fighter* (Nairobi: East African Publishing House, 1971).

8. On this score, see especially Johannes Fabian, *Time and the Other: How Anthropology Makes Its Object* (New York: Columbia University Press, 1983), pp. 1–35.

9. V. S. Naipaul, *The Enigma of Arrival* (New York: Knopf, 1989), p. 163.

10. V. S. Naipaul, *An Area of Darkness* (1964; rpt. New York: Vintage, 1981), p. 171.

11. Scornful of Laraine's mind, Naipaul takes a salacious interest in her body: "Her cheekbones were high; her neck was slender. But her leanness was of the sort which holds fleshy surprises; her breasts were good and full. I did not think it was the body of someone who would be allowed to remain a seeker for long." Ibid., p. 172.

12. V. S. Naipaul, *India: A Wounded Civilization* (1977; rpt. Harmonds-

worth, England: Penguin, 1979), p. 121. Cf. ibid., p. 27, and V. S. Naipaul, *The Overcrowded Barracoon* (1972; rpt. New York: Vintage, 1984), p. 80, for additonal reflections on the hypocrisy of idealistic Western responses to India.

13. Naipaul, "A Second Visit," in *The Overcrowded Barracoon,* p. 86.

14. Naipaul, "Michael X and the Black Power Killings in Trinidad," in *The Return of Eva Peron,* pp. 3–97; "An Island Betrayed," *Harpers,* Mar. 1984, pp. 61–72.

15. Cf. his critique of "the people who keep up with 'revolution' as with the theatre, the revolutionaries who visit centers of revolution, but with return air tickets, the people for whom Malik's kind of Black Power was an exotic but safe brothel." "Michael X and the Black Power Killings in Trinidad," p. 31.

16. See especially William Rubin, ed., *"Primitivism" in 20th Century Art* (New York: Museum of Modern Art, 1984); James Clifford, "Histories of the Tribal and the Modern," *Art in America,* Apr. 1985, pp. 164–77; and Hilton Kramer, "The 'Primitivism' Conundrum," *The New Criterion,* Dec. 1984, pp. 1–7.

17. The efforts to segregate aesthetic from ethnographic discourses were destined to fail. At the entrance to the exhibit I noted the following attempt at clarification: "As our focus is on the modernists' experience of tribal art, and not on ethnological study, we have not included anthropological hypotheses regarding the religious or social purposes that originally surrounded these objects."

18. For an excellent, related analysis of problems of postmodernity, "authenticity," and cultural value, see Kwame Anthony Appiah, "Is the Post- in Postmodernism the Post- in Postcolonial?" *Critical Inquiry,* 17 (Winter 1991), 336–57. Of particular relevance are Appiah's reflections on the 1987 show, "Perspectives on African Art," at the Center for African Art in New York.

19. Kramer, "The 'Primitivism' Conundrum," p. 6.

20. Naipaul suffers from a paradigmatically colonial fear of engulfment. He speaks of "a fear of being swallowed up by the bush, a fear of the people of the bush. . . . They are the enemies of the civilization which I cherish." Michiko Kakutani, "Naipaul Reviews His Past from Afar," *New York Times,* 1 Dec. 1980, p. C15.

21. Epstein, "A Cottage for Mr. Naipaul," p. 9.

22. Naipaul reiterates this point in his *Newsweek, Transition, Salmagundi,* and *Listener* interviews.

23. Naipaul, *India: A Wounded Civilization,* p. 43. In selecting the Congo as the nadir of primitivism, Naipaul reaffirms his connection to the *Heart of Darkness* tradition, as discussed in the previous chapter. Naipaul completed his essay on Zaire, where he focuses on the absence of history and the nation's delusions about its past, just a few months before beginning *India: A Wounded Civilization.*

24. Ibid., p. 174.

25. Ibid., p. 119.

26. V. S. Naipaul, *The Middle Passage: Impressions of Five Societies—British, French and Dutch—in the West Indies and South America* (1962; rpt. London: Andre Deutsch, 1981), p. 90.

27. Naipaul, "The Return of Eva Peron," p. 153. On this score, Naipaul remarks further: "In Argentina, unmade, flawed from its conception, without a history, still only with annals, there can be no feeling for a past, for a heritage, for shared ideals, for a community of all Argentines." Ibid., p. 160.

28. V. S. Naipaul, "Epilogue, from a Journal: The Circus of Luxor," in *In a Free State* (1971; rpt. London: Penguin, 1973), p. 246.

29. Benedict Anderson, *Imagined Communities: Reflections on the Origin and Spread of Nationalism* (London: Verso and New Left Books, 1983).

30. Eric Hobsbawm and Terence Ranger, eds., *The Invention of Tradition* (Cambridge: Cambridge University Press, 1983).

31. *India: A Wounded Civilization,* pp. 129–30. When Mukherjee later questioned the validity of this statement, Naipaul reiterated both his conviction that the Indian past cannot be shaped historically and the assumption that this impossibility stems from an underlying lack of achievement. See Mukherjee and Boyers, "A Conversation with V. S. Naipaul," pp. 19–21.

32. Cf. V. Y. Mudimbe's critique of the "commonly accepted valorization principle that transmutes historical genres into human history and claims to explain, from the truth of the Western enunciative space of models, the articulation of history as an absolute order of both universal power and knowledge." *The Invention of Africa: Gnosis, Philosophy, and the Order of Knowledge* (Bloomington: Indiana University Press, 1988), p. 192.

33. Naipaul, *The Middle Passage,* p. 29.

34. V. S. Naipaul, *The Loss of El Dorado: A History* (1969; rpt. Harmondsworth, England: Penguin, 1981).

35. Naipaul discusses the genesis and personal significance of the El Dorado project in *The Enigma of Arrival,* pp. 154–60.

36. Ibid., p. 159.

37. In its tone and its denial of historical or human substance to Trinidad, Naipaul's antihistory connects cleanly with the passage from Froude that serves as the epigraph to *The Middle Passage:* "There has been no saint in the West Indies since las Casas, no hero unless philonegro enthusiasm can make one out of Toussaint. There are no people there in the true sense of the word, with a character and purpose of their own." *The Middle Passage,* p. 7.

38. Naipaul, *The Loss of El Dorado,* p. 18.

39. Ibid., p. 18.

40. Ibid., p. 14.

41. Ibid.

42. A. C. Wade, "The Novelist as Historian," *The Literary Half-Yearly,* 11 (July 1970), 183. Jesse A. Noel, another West Indian historian, is similarly perturbed by Naipaul's short-shrifting of black history in Trinidad. Noel charges, moreover, that Naipaul neglects "the positive contributions of Chacon, Roume, and Bolivar." See Jesse A. Noel, "Historicity and Homelessness in V. S. Naipaul," *Caribbean Studies,* 11, 3 (1972), 83–87.

43. C. L. R. James, *The Black Jacobins* (1938; rpt. New York: Vintage, 1963).

44. "C. L. R. James," in Marho (Radical Historians Organizations), ed., *Visions of History: Interviews* (Manchester: Manchester University Press, 1983), p. 275.

45. Naipaul, *The Loss of El Dorado,* p. 32.

46. John Updike, "Fool's Gold," *The New Yorker,* 8 Aug. 1970; rpt. Hamner, *Critical Perspectives on V. S. Naipaul,* p. 154.

47. Naipaul, *The Loss of El Dorado,* p. 14.

48. Eric Williams, *History of the People of Trinidad and Tobago* (1962; rpt. London: Andre Deutsch, 1964), p. 11.

49. Naipaul's argument for historical stasis does a particular disservice to Trinidad's labor movement. Organized around the oil and sugar industries, it has enjoyed periods of significant social impact since the mid-1930s. "Buzz" Butler, perhaps the Caribbean's most celebrated trade unionist and leader of the British Empire Workers' and Citizens' Home Rule Party, was anything but an El Dorado–style fantasist.

50. Bridget Brereton, *A History of Modern Trinidad: 1783–1962* (London: Heinemann, 1981).

51. Updike, "Fool's Gold," p. 154.

52. Naipaul, *The Enigma of Arrival,* pp. 158–59.

53. Ibid., p. 159.

54. Georg Wilhelm Frederick Hegel, *The Philosophy of History,* trans. J. Sibree. (New York: Dover, 1956), p. 99; Hugh Trevor-Roper, quoted in Stanley Diamond, *In Search of the Primitive: A Critique of Civilization.* (New Brunswick: Transaction, 1974), pp. 2–3.

55. Mudimbe, *The Invention of Africa,* p. 189.

Chapter 6

1. V. S. Naipaul, "Jasmine," in *The Overcrowded Barracoon* (1972; rpt. New York: Vintage, 1984), pp. 23–29.

2. V. S. Naipaul, *The Mimic Men* (1967; Harmondsworth, England: Penguin, 1969). A concern with mimicry is especially prominent in *The Middle Passage, The Overcrowded Barracoon, India: A Wounded Civilization, The Return of Eva Peron,* and his uncollected essay on Grenada, "An Island Betrayed." Naipaul makes a rhetorical variant of mimicry, technological parasitism, central to his representation of Islamic societies in *Among the Believers.*

3. Curt Suplee, "Voyager with the Dark and Comic Vision—Through the World of Islam and Beyond, with V. S. Naipaul," *Washington Post,* 19 Nov. 1981, p. C-17.

4. Paul Theroux, "V. S. Naipaul," *Modern Fiction Studies,* 30 (Autumn 1984), 454. Naipaul has reiterated this point on other occasions. See, for example, the interviews with Mukherjee and Boyers and with Rowe-Evans.

5. Quoted in ibid., p. 448.

6. Of course, if one pressed Naipaul's theory to its logical conclusion, the

United States, itself a postcolonial society, should also suffer from the taint of mimicry.

7. If Naipaul uses "colonial" as a synonym for both *colonial* and *postcolonial,* Bill Ashcroft, Gareth Griffiths, and Helen Tiffin, do precisely the opposite in their otherwise useful book, *The Empire Writes Back: Theory and Practice in Post-colonial Literatures* (London: Routledge, 1989). "We use the term 'post-colonial' to cover all the culture affected by the imperial process from the moment of colonization to the present day." (p. 2).

8. V. S. Naipaul, *The Middle Passage: Impressions of Five Societies—British, French and Dutch—in the West Indies and South America* (1962; rpt. London: Andre Deutsch, 1981), p. 7.

9. Introduction to *East Indians in the Caribbean: Colonialism and the Struggle for Identity,* Proceedings of a Symposium on East Indians in the Caribbean, The University of the West Indies, June 1975. Millwood, N.Y.: Krause International, 1982), p. 9. "The Return of Eva Peron" is studded with similar pronouncements.

10. V. S. Naipaul, *The Loss of El Dorado: A History* (1969; rpt. Harmondsworth, England: Penguin, 1981), p. 332.

11. Ibid., pp. 332–33.

12. Ian Hamilton, "Without a Place," *The Times Literary Supplement,* 30 July 1971, p. 897.

13. On a separate occasion he remarked that he had decolonized himself through the process of writing. See Raoul Pantin, "Portrait of an Artist: What Makes Naipaul Run," *Caribbean Contact,* 1 (1973), 18.

14. Adrian Rowe-Evans, "Interview with V. S. Naipaul," *Transition,* 40 (1971), 57–58.

15. Quoted in Mihir Bose, "A Tour of Naipauland," *Literary Review,* 57 (1983), 19.

16. Here I would join with the Guyanese-born writer, Angus Richmond, in lamenting that Naipaul has not taken advantage of his prestige in Britain to help defuse racism by interpreting the cultures of the black arrivals to that nation's white majority. See Richmond, "Naipaul: The Mimic Man," *Race and Class,* 24, 2 (1982), 130. See Peter Fryer, *Staying Power: The History of Black People in Britain* (London: Pluto Press, 1984) for an impressive account of the colonial backdrop to post–World War II immigration in the United Kingdom.

17. See, respectively, Naipaul, "Without a Place," p. 40; *The Middle Passage,* p. 78; and "East Indian," in *the Overcrowded Barracoon,* p. 32.

18. M. B. Angrosino, "V. S. Naipaul and the Colonial Image," *Caribbean Quarterly,* 21 (1975), pp. 1–11.

19. Naipaul, *An Area of Darkness,* p. 273.

20. Naipaul, "In the Middle of the Journey," in *The Overcrowded Barracoon,* p. 44.

21. Frantz Fanon, *The Wretched of the Earth,* trans. Constance Farrington (1963; rpt. New York: Grove Press, 1968), p. 251. The book was first published in French in 1961. I would doubt whether Naipaul was influenced by Fanon's use

of the term, given that *The Middle Passage* predates the English edition of Fanon's text. Moreover, the novels that Naipaul wrote in the 1950s contain intimations of his theory of mimicry.

22. Ibid., p. 175.

23. Ibid., pp. 173, 178.

24. The bibliography of Caribbean popular culture is formidable. For some prominent accounts, see the introduction to Roger D. Abrahams and John F. Szwed, eds., *After Africa: Extracts from British Travel Accounts and Journals of the Seventeenth, Eighteenth, and Nineteenth Centuries Concerning the Slaves, Their Manners, and Customs in the British West Indies* (New Haven: Yale University Press, 1983); Chris Searle, *Words Unchained: Language and Revolution in Grenada* (London: Zed, 1984); and Edward Kamu Braithwaite, "Timehri," *Savacou,* 2 (Sept. 1970), 35–44.

25. Cf. Wolfgang J. Mommsen's account of the role of the "bridgehead class" in metropolitan–periphery relations. *Theories of Imperialism,* trans. P. S. Falla (Chicago: University of Chicago Press, 1980), p. 138.

26. Salman Rushdie alludes to the phenomenon of the *chamcha* in "The Empire Strikes back with a Vengeance," *The Times* (London) (3 July 1982), p. 7. On the box-wallahs, see *An Area of Darkness,* p. 61.

27. Amilcar Cabral, Fanon's contemporary and fellow theorist of neocolonialism, refused even to grace Third World middle classes with the title "national bourgeoisies." See "The Weapon of Theory," in *Revolution in Guinea,* trans. Richard Handyside (New York: Monthly Review Press, 1969), p. 101.

28. Naipaul, "In the Middle of the Journey," in *The Overcrowded Barracoon,* p. 45. See, for instance, "Jashmed into Jimmy," in *The Overcrowded Barracoon,* pp. 47–54.

29. V. S. Naipaul, "The Crocodiles of Yamoussoukro," in *Finding the Centre: Two Narratives* (New York: Knopf, 1984), pp. 149, 166–68, 184.

30. Kwame Nkrumah, *Neo-colonialism, the Last Stage of Capitalism* (1965; rpt. New York: International, 1984), p. ix. Cf. Nyerere's assertion: "Our countries are effectively being governed by people who have only the most marginal interest in our affairs—if any—and even that only in so far as it affects their own well-being. That, in fact, is the meaning—and the practise—of neo-colonialism." Address to the Convocation of the University of Ibadan, 17 Nov. 1976, in Harry Goulbourne, ed., *Politics and State in the Third World* (London: Macmillan, 1979), p. 253.

31. Ibid., p. xi.

32. For a recent account of the politics of aid, see Marcus Linear, *Zapping the Third World: The Disaster of Development Aid* (London: Pluto Press, 1985). Linear is skeptical of aid either as an unambiguously philanthropic gesture or as a serious measure for redressing the imbalance in economic power between North and South.

33. For instance, 60 percent of the international sugar market is controlled by four transnationals. Certain West Indian prime ministers—notably Guyana's

Cheddi Jagan, Jamaica's Michael Manley, and Grenada's Maurice Bishop—have protested such circumstances and made a commitment to act against them. All three were socialists, advocates of a new international economic order, and outspoken supporters of the Non-Aligned Movement as a forum for seeking to temper foreign control. And all three had their initiatives subverted largely by powerful American (and in Jagan's case British) interventions.

34. Naipaul, *The Middle Passage,* p. 6. The amendment has been retained in every subsequent edition of the book.

35. Vicky Randall and Robin Theobald, *Political Change and Underdevelopment: A Critical Introduction to Third World Politics* (London: Macmillan, 1985), pp. 50–64.

36. Quoted in Daniel A. Offiong, *Imperialism and Dependency: Obstacles to African Development.* Washington, D.C.: Howard University Press, 1982), p. 122. On the issue of clientship, see also Noam Chomsky and Edward S. Herman, *The Washington Connection and Third World Fascism* (Boston: South End Pres,, 1979).

37. Harry Magdoff, "Imperialism Without Colonies," in *Studies in the Theory of Imperialism,* ed. Roger Owen and Bob Sutcliffe (New York: Longman, 1972), pp. 144–70.

38. Influential dependency theorists include André Gunder Frank, *Capitalism and Underdevelopment in Latin America* (New York: Monthly Review Press, 1967) and *Latin America: Underdevelopment or Revolution: Essays in the Development of Underdevelopment and the Immediate Enemy* (New York: Monthly Review Press, 1969). Immanuel Wallerstein, *The Modern World System* (New York: Academic Press, 1976) and *The Capitalist World Economy* (Cambridge: Cambridge University Press, 1979); Samir Amin, *Accumulation on a World Scale: A Critique of the Theory of Underdevelopment* (New York: Monthly Review Press, 1974); Walter Rodney, *How Europe Underdeveloped Africa* (1972; rpt. Washington, D.C.: Howard University Press, 1981). Fernandez Henrique Cardoso's "Dependency and Development in Latin America," *New Left Review,* 74 (1972), 83–95, with its notion of dependent capitalist development, stands as a prominent example of the reformist, nationalist strand of dependency theory.

39. For persuasive critique of some of the more grandiose dimensions of dependency theory, see Peter Worsley, *The Three Worlds: Culture and World Development* (Chicago: University of Chicago Press, 1984), p. 22; Neil Lazarus, *Resistance in Postcolonial African Fiction* (New Haven: Yale University Press, 1990), pp. 196–99; and V. Y. Mudimbe, *The Invention of Africa: Gnosis, Philosophy, and the Order of Knowledge* (Bloomington: Indiana University Press, 1988), pp. 3–5.

40. Albert Memmi, *The Colonizer and the Colonized,* trans. Howard Greenfeld (Boston: Beacon Press, 1967) and *Dependence: A Sketch for a Portrait of the Dependent,* trans. Philip A. Facey (Boston: Beacon Press, 1984); O. Dominique Mannoni, *Prospero and Caliban: The Psychology of Colonization,* trans. Pamela Powesland (New York: Praeger, 1964).

41. Mannoni, *Prospero and Caliban,* p. 86.

42. See Frantz Fanon, *Black Skins, White Masks,* trans. Charles Lam Markmann (New York: Grove Press, 1967), pp. 83–108; Aimé Césaire, *Discourse on Colonialism,* trans. Joan Pinkham (New York: Monthly Review Press, 1972), pp. 39–43.

43. Suplee, "Voyager with a Dark and Comic Vision," p. C-17. Naipaul's choice of phrase carries similar implications when he observes, regarding India, that "No other country was more fitted to welcome a conqueror" and, again, that it "invited conquest." See *An Area of Darkness,* pp. 222, 213.

44. Naipaul, *The Return of Eva Peron,* p. 41.

45. See, for example, Naipaul, *The Overcrowded Barracoon,* p. 285; *The Middle Passage,* p. 111; *The Return of Eva Peron,* pp. 59, 123, 147, 177.

46. Naipaul, *The Return of Eva Peron,* p. 147.

47. Naipaul, *The Middle Passage,* pp. 110–11.

48. Marlow's projection onto the Congolese in *Heart of Darkness* is the most familiar literary instance of this.

49. Naipaul's reliance on English renders him dependent on a narrow, unrepresentative class—the intellectuals—for his information and impressions. His interviews are preponderantly with the university-educated elite, journalists, and students. A disproportionate number of his informants have either studied in the United States or are planning to study there.

50. Naipaul, *Among the Believers,* p. 111.

51. Naipaul, *An Area of Darkness,* p. 47.

52. See Sudhai Rai, *V. S. Naipaul: A Study in Expatriate Sensibility* (New Delhi: Arnold–Heinemann, 1982), p. 16.

53. Naipaul, *Among the Believers,* p. 3.

54. Charles Michener, "The Dark Visions of V. S. Naipaul," *Newsweek,* 16 Nov. 1981, p. 110.

55. Naipaul, *Among the Believers,* pp. 12–13.

56. Ibid., p. 168. For related assertions, see ibid., pp. 15, 82, 121, 167, 234.

57. The dream of the perfect return to Islam is not, of course, integral to all forms of Islam, but it was frequently expressed by the revivalists interviewed on his travels.

58. Naipaul, "A New King for the Congo," in *The Return of Eva Peron,* p. 218.

59. Naipaul, *Among the Believers,* p. 375.

60. Hugh Trevor-Roper, "Born Again," *New York Review of Books,* 5 Nov. 1981, p. 11.

61. Eugene Goodheart, "Naipaul's Mandarin Sensibility," *Partisan Review,* 50 (1983), p. 254. Naipaul's remark appears in *Among the Believers,* p. 289.

62. Naipaul, *Among the Believers,* p. 33.

63. Ibid., p. 81. The image is used similarly on p. 38.

64. Reza Baraheni, *The Crowned Cannibals: Writing on Repression in Iran* (New York: Vintage, 1977), p. 5.

65. The estimates of political prisoners are for 1975. For further discussion, see also Chomsky and Herman, *The Washington Connection and Third World Fascism.*

66. Naipaul, *Among the Believers,* pp. 32, 9–10.

67. "Resurgent—one might also say insurgent—Islam has provided us with another contemporary evolution of behaviour that seems to repudiate conventional interpretations of rationality. . . . Now there was nothing intrinsically wrong with the Shah's ambitions for his country. One might argue with the details—the use of torture and so on—but not with the overall intention. . . . Up to a point, with Persepolis providing the background, one could even sympathise with the Shah's Napoleonic vision of himself. National saviours do tend to have their little ways. . . . The Shah was—finally a comprehensible figure. . . . Not so the adversaries with whom he had to contend." Shiva Naipaul, "The Illusion of the Third World," in *An Unfinished Journey* (New York: Viking, 1987), pp. 36–37.

68. Baraheni, *The Crowned Cannibals,* p. 4.

69. Ibid., p. 429.

70. Eqbal Ahmed, "Islam and Politics," in *Islam, Politics and the State: The Pakistan Experience,* ed. Mohammed Asghar Khan (London: Zed, 1985), p. 19.

71. Ibid., p. 19.

72. V. S. Naipaul, "Our Universal Civilization," *New York Times,* 5 Nov. 1990, p. A21.

73. Fanon, *The Wretched of the Earth,* p. 47.

74. V. S. Naipaul, "An Island Betrayed," *Harpers,* Mar. 1984, pp. 61–72.

75. The quoted phrase is Fred Halliday's. See "Cold War in the Caribbean," *New Left Review,* 141 (1983), 8.

76. Naipaul, "An Island Betrayed," p. 63.

77. Chris Searle, "Naipaulacity: A Form of Cultural Imperialism," *Race and Class,* 26 (1984), 45–62.

78. Naipaul, "An Island Betrayed," p. 63. For a contrary view to Naipaul's of Grenadian socialism, see Fitzroy Ambursley and James Dunkerley, *Grenada: Whose Freedom?* (London: Latin American Bureau, 1984).

79. Naipaul, "An Island Betrayed," p. 63.

80. On the New Jewel Movement's economic successes, see Ambursley and Dunkerley, *Grenada: Whose Freedom?,* pp. 40–45. On advances in literacy and education, see Chris Searle, *Words Unchained: Language and Revolution in Grenada* (London: Zed, 1984).

81. Naipaul, "An Island Betrayed," p. 73.

82. Cf. Searle's comment about the revolution at large: "It mimicked nothing, although it strove to learn from the strengths and mistakes of other processes." "Naipaulacity," p. 57.

83. Homi K. Bhabha, "Of Mimicry and Man: The Ambivalence of Colonial Discourse," *October,* 28 (1984), 126.

84. Naipaul, *The Overcrowded Barracoon,* p. 229.

85. Jack Beatty, "The Return of Eva Peron," *The New Republic,* 11 Apr. 1980, p. 36.

86. Naipaul, "The Intellectual in the Post-Colonial World," p. 78.

87. Homi K. Bhabha, "The Commitment to Theory," *New Formations,* 5 (Summer 1988), 131.

88. Audre Lorde, *Zami: A New Spelling of My Name* (New York: Crossing Press, 1982), p. 226.

89. Salman Rushdie, "In Good Faith," in *Imaginary Homelands* (London: Granta Books, 1991), p. 398.

90. Suplee, "Voyager with the Dark and Comic Vision," p. C-1.

Conclusion

1. His early English essay "London" (1958) was principally about his difficulties in setting out as a writer, while his scant American essays were confined to public personalities—Norman Mailer and John Steinbeck. These are included in *The Overcrowded Barracoon* (1972; rpt. New York: Vintage, 1984). Naipaul's only recent uncollected American essay is "Among the Republicans," *New York Review of Books,* 25 Oct. 1984, pp. 5, 8, 10, 12, 14–17.

2. V. S. Naipaul, *The Enigma of Arrival* (New York: Knopf, 1987), p. 52.

3. Ibid., p. 53.

4. Ibid., p. 66.

5. V. S. Naipaul, *A Turn in the South* (1989; rpt. New York: Vintage, 1989), p. 221.

6. Ibid., p. 77.

7. Thomas D'Evelyn, "Where Timeless Themes Hang Like Spanish Moss," *Christian Science Monitor,* 6 Mar. 1989, p. 13.

8. Arnold Rampersad, "V. S. Naipaul: Turning in the South," *Raritan,* 10 (Summer 1990), 34.

9. Naipaul, *The Overcrowded Barracoon,* p. 247.

10. Naipaul, *A Turn in the South,* p. 306.

11. Ibid., p. 296.

12. Ibid., p. 304.

13. James Applewhite, "A Trip with V. S. Naipaul," *Raritan,* 10 (Summer 1990), 54.

14. Naipaul, *A Turn in the South,* p. 164

15. "Andrew Robinson Meets V. S. Naipaul," *The Literary Review,* October 1990, p. 21.

16. Ibid.

17. Ibid., p. 22.

18. V. S. Naipaul, *India: A Million Mutinies Now* (Calcutta: Rupa, 1990), p. 351.

19. Ibid., p. 518.

20. See, for example, Firdaus Kanga, "Seeing and Looking Away," *Times*

Literary Supplement, 5–11 Oct. 1990, p. 1059; James Buchan, "Outsider Not Quite at Home," *The Spectator,* 29 Sept. 1990, p. 34.

21. Naipaul: *India: A Million Mutinies Now,* pp. 517–18.

22. Amitav Ghosh, "In India, Death and Democracy," *New York Times,* 26 Nov. 1990, p. A19.

23. Naipaul, *India: A Million Mutinies Now,* p. 387.

24. Ibid., p. 178.

25. Some of these I have quoted in the introduction. Cf. also his remark: "Unhappy in his extended family, he was distrustful of larger, communal groupings." *The Enigma of Arrival,* p. 111.

26. V. S. Naipaul, *The Return of Eva Peron, with the Killings in Trinidad* (1980; rpt. New York: Vintage, 1981), pp. 71, 74; *The Middle Passage: Impressions of Five Societies—British, French and Dutch—in the West Indies and South America* (1962; rpt. London: Andre Deutsch, 1981), p. 6.

27. Hamish Keith, "V. S. Naipaul Discusses How Writing Changes the Writer," *Ndaanan,* 4, 1–11 (1974), 62.

28. Eugene Goodheart, "V. S. Naipaul's Mandarin Sensibility," *Partisan Review,* 50 (1983), 251.

29. See, for instance, Naipaul's remark: "I do have a great distrust of *causes,* simply because they *are* causes and they have to simplify, to ignore so much. As a man of action one would be continually weakened by harking after the truth. . . ." Adrian Rowe-Evans, "Interview with V. S. Naipaul," *Transition,* 40 (1971), 58. In *An Area of Darkness* (1964; rpt. New York: Vintage, 1981), p. 188, he writes of his determination to shield himself from "the corruption of causes," and he expresses a similar sentiment in his *Newsweek* interview (Charles Michener, "The Dark Visions of V. S. Naipaul," *Newsweek,* 16 Nov. 1981, p. 105).

30. Naipaul, *The Enigma of Arrival,* p. 52.

31. Naipaul, *The Return of Eva Peron,* p. 233.

32. Derek Walcott, "Interview with V. S. Naipaul," *Sunday Guardian* (Trinidad), 17 Mar. 1965, p. 13.

33. *The Enigma of Arrival,* p. 53.

34. Quoted in Michael Neill, "Guerillas and Gangs: Frantz Fanon and V. S. Naipaul," *Ariel,* 13 (1982), 62.

BIBLIOGRAPHY

Primary Texts

Naipaul, V. S. *The Middle Passage: Impressions of Five Societies—British, French and Dutch—in the West Indies and South America.* 1962; rpt. London: Andre Deutsch, 1981.

———. *An Area of Darkness.* 1964; rpt. New York: Vintage, 1981.

———. *The Loss of El Dorado: A History.* 1969; rpt. Harmondsworth, England: Penguin, 1981.

———. *In a Free State.* 1971; rpt. London: Penguin, 1973.

———. *The Overcrowded Barracoon.* 1972; rpt. New York: Vintage, 1984.

———. Foreword to Seepersad Naipaul, *The Adventures of Gurudeva and Other Stories.* London: Andre Deutsch, 1976.

———. *India: A Wounded Civilization.* 1977; rpt. Harmondsworth, England: Penguin, 1979.

———. *The Return of Eva Peron, with The Killings in Trinidad.* New York: Alfred A. Knopf, 1980.

———. *A Congo Diary.* Los Angeles: Sylvester and Orphanos, 1980.

———. *Among the Believers: An Islamic Journey.* 1981; rpt. New York: Vintage, 1982.

———. *Finding the Centre: Two Narratives.* New York: Alfred A. Knopf, 1984.

———. "An Island Betrayed." *Harpers,* Mar. 1984, pp. 61–72.

———. *The Enigma of Arrival.* New York: Alfred A. Knopf, 1987.

———. *A Turn in the South.* 1989; rpt. New York: Vintage, 1990.

———. *India: A Million Mutinies Now.* Calcutta: Rupa, 1990.

Secondary Texts

Abrahams, Roger, and John Szwed. *After Africa: Extracts from British Travel Accounts and Journals of the Seventeenth, Eighteenth, and Nineteenth Centuries Concerning the Slaves, Their Manners, and Customs in the British West Indies.* New Haven: Yale University Press, 1983.

Abu-Lughod. *Arab Rediscovery of Europe: A Study in Cultural Encounters.* Princeton: Princeton University Press, 1963.

Achebe, Chinua. "An Image of Africa." *Massachusetts Review,* 18 (1977), 782–93.

Achebe, Chinua. *"Viewpoint." Times Literary Supplement,* 1 Feb. 1980, p. 113.

Ahmad, Aijaz. "Jameson's Rhetoric of Otherness and the National Allegory." *Social Text,* 17 (1987), 3–25.

Ahmed, Eqbal. "Islam and Politics." In *Islam, Politics and the State: The Paki-*

stan Experience. Ed. Mohammed Asghar Khan. London: Zed, 1985, pp. 1–30.

Ajami, Fouad. "In Search of Islam." *New York Times Book Review*, 25 Oct. 1981, pp. 7, 30, 32.

Adorno, Theodor. *Minima Moralia. Reflections from Damaged Life*. Trans. E. F. N. Jephcott. 1951; rpt. London: Verso, 1984.

Alverson, Hoyt. *Mind in the Heart of Darkness: Value and Self-Identity Among the Tswana of Southern Africa*. New Haven: Yale University Press, 1978.

Ambursley, Fitzroy, and James Dunkerley. *Grenada: Whose Freedom?* London: Latin American Bureau, 1984.

Amin, Samir. *Accumulation on a World Scale: A Critique of the Theory of Underdevelopment*. New York: Monthly Review Press, 1974.

Amis, Martin. "Books of the Year." *The Observer Review*, 6 Dec. 1981, p. 25.

Anderson, Benedict. *Imagined Communities. Reflections on the Origin and Spread of Nationalism*. London: Verso and New Left Books, 1983.

———. "James Fenton's Slideshow." *New Left Review*, 158 (1986), 81–90.

Anderson, Hoyt. *Mind in the Heart of Darkness: Value and Self-Identity Among the Tswana of Southern Africa*. New Haven: Yale University Press, 1978.

Anderson, Perry. "Components of the National Culture." *New Left Review*, 50 (1968), 3–56.

Robinson, Andrew. "Andrew Robinson Meets V. S. Naipaul." *Literary Review*, Oct. 1990, 21–24.

Angrosino, M. B. "V. S. Naipaul and the Colonial Image." *Caribbean Quarterly*, 21 (1975), 1–11.

Anon. "V. S. Naipaul." *Sunday Times* (London), 20 Jan. 1985, p. 11.

———. "The Congo Line." *New York Times*, 9 Mar. 1986, p. 5.

———. "An Area of Brilliance." *Trinidad Guardian*, 5 Dec. 1971, p. 8.

———. "Nowhere to Go." *Times Literary Supplement*, 8 Oct. 1971, p. 1199.

———. "Naipaul Gets Eliot Award." *New York Times*, 16 Sept. 1986, p. C20.

———. "Angry Young Indian." *Newsweek*, 19 Apr. 1965, p. 103.

Appiah, Kwame Anthony. "Strictures on Structures: The Prospects for a Structuralist Poetics of African Fiction." In *Black Literature and Literary Theory*. Ed. Henry Louis Gates, Jr. New York: Methuen, 1984, pp. 127–50.

———. "Out of Africa: Topologies of Nativism," *Yale Journal of Criticism*, 2 (Fall 1988), 153–78.

———. "Is the Post- in Postmodernism the Post- in Postcolonial?" *Critical Inquiry*, 17 (Winter 1991), 336–57.

Arendt, Hannah. *The Origins of Totalitariansim*. Part 2: *Imperialism*. 1951; rpt. New York: Harcourt Brace Jovanovich, 1968.

Applewhite, James. "A Trip with V. S. Naipaul," *Raritan*, 10 (Summer 1990), 48–54.

Asad, Talal. *Anthropology and the Colonial Encounter*. London: Ithaca Press, 1973.

————. "A Comment on the Idea of Non-Western Anthropology." In *Indigenous Anthropology in Non-Western Countries*. Ed. Hussein Fahim. Durham, N.C.: Carolina Academic Press, 1982, pp. 283–87.

Ashcroft, Bill, Gareth Griffiths, and Helen Tiffin. *The Empire Writes Back: Theory and Practice in Post-colonial Literatures*. New York: Routledge & Kegan Paul, 1989.

Baraheni, Reza. *The Crowned Cannibals: Writing on Repression in Iran*. New York: Vintage, 1977.

Bhabha, Homi K. "Of Mimicry and Man: The Ambivalence of Colonial Discourse." *October,* 28 (1984), 125–33.

————. "The Commitment to Theory." *New Formations,* 5 (Summer 1988), 111–32.

————. "Novel Metropolis." *New Statesman and Society,* 16 Feb. 1990, pp. 16–18.

Beatty, Jack. "The Return of Eva Peron." *New Republic,* 11 Apr. 1980, p. 36.

Benjamin, Walter. *Illuminations*. New York: Schocken, 1969.

Bingham, Nigel. "The Novelist V. S. Naipaul Talks to Nigel Bingham About His Childhood in Trinidad." *The Listener,* 7 Sept. 1972, pp. 20–21.

Birbalsingh, Frank. *Passion & Exile: Essays in Caribbean Literature*. London: Hansib, 1988.

Bordwich, Fergus. "Anti-Political Man: V. S. Naipaul Reconsidered," *Working Papers* 9 (Sept./Oct. 1982), 36–41.

Bose, Mihir. "A Tour of Naipauland." *Literary Review,* 57 (1983).

Bowen, Elenore Smith. *Return to Laughter*. New York: Harper & Row, 1954.

Braithwaite, Edward Kamu. "Timehri." *Savacou,* 2 (Sept. 1970), 35–44.

Brantlinger, Patrick. "Victorians and Africans: The Genealogy of the Myth of the Dark Continent." *Critical Inquiry,* 12 (1985), 166–203.

Brennan, Timothy. *Salman Rushdie and the Third World: Myths of the Nation*. London: MacMillan, 1989.

Brereton, Bridget. *A History of Modern Trinidad 1783–1962*. London: Heinemann, 1981.

Bruckner, Pascal. *The Tears of the White Man*. Trans. William R. Beer. 1983; rpt. New York: Free Press, 1986.

Bryden, Ronald. "The Novelist V. S. Naipaul." *The Listener,* 22 Mar. 1973, p. 367.

Brown, Wayne. "On Exile and the Dialect of the Tribe." *Guardian* (Trinidad), 8 Nov. 1971, p. 19.

Buchner, James. "Outsider Not Quite at Home." *The Spectator,* 29 Sept. 1990.

Bulmer, Ralph, and Ian Majnep. *Birds of My Kalam Country*. Aukland: Aukland Univ. Press, 1977.

Cabral, Amilcar. *Revolution in Guinea*. Trans. Richard Handyside. New York: Monthly Review Press, 1969.

Caputo, Philip. *A Rumor of War*. New York: Rinehart and Winston, 1977.

Carby, Hazel and Hall, Stuart, ed. *The Empire Strikes Back: Race and Racism in 70s Britain*. London: Hutchinson, 1982.

Cardoso, Fernandez Henrique. "Dependency and Development in Latin America." *New Left Review,* 74 (1972), 83–95.

Césaire, Aimé. *Discourse on Colonialism.* Trans. Joan Pinkham. New York: Monthly Review Press, 1972.

———. *The Collected Poetry.* Trans. Clayton Eshleman and Annette Smith. Berkeley: University of California Press, 1983.

Cesara, Manda. [Karla Powe, pseud.] *Reflections of a Woman Anthropologist: No Hiding Place.* New York: Academic Press, 1982.

Chomsky, Noam, and Edward S. Herman. *The Washington Connection and Third World Fascism.* Boston: South End Press, 1979.

Clark, John Pepper. *America. Their America.* 1964; rpt. New York: Africana, 1971.

Clifford, James. "Histories of the Tribal and the Modern." *Art in America,* Apr. 1985, pp. 164–77.

———. *The Predicament of Culture: Twentieth-Century Ethnography, Literature, and Art.* Cambridge, Mass.: Harvard University Press, 1988.

———and George Marcus, eds. *Writing Culture: the Poetics and Politics of Ethnography.* Berkeley: University of California Press, 1986.

Conrad, Joseph. *Heart of Darkness.* 1902; rpt. Harmondsworth, England: Penguin, 1982.

Coombes, Orde, ed. *Is Massa Day Dead?* New York: Doubleday, 1974.

Crapanzano, Vincent. *Tuhami: Portrait of a Moroccan.* Chicago: University of Chicago Press, 1980.

Crawford-Young, M. "Zaire, Rwanda and Burundi." In *The Cambridge History of Africa.* Vol. 8. Ed. Michael Crowder. Cambridge: Cambridge University Press, 1984, pp. 698–751.

Cudjoe, Selwyn R. *Resistance and Caribbean Literature.* Athens: Ohio University Press, 1980.

———. "V. S. Naipaul and the Question of Identity." In *Voices from Under; Black Narrative in Latin America and the Caribbean.* Ed. Selwyn R. Cudjoe. Westport, Conn.: Greenwood Press, 1984, pp. 89–99.

———. *V. S. Naipaul: A Materialist Reading.* Amherst: University of Massachusetts Press, 1988.

Dahlie, Halvard, and Ian Adam. "Editorial." *Ariel: A Review of International English Literature,* 13, 4 (1982), 3–6.

D'Evelyn, Thomas. "Where Timeless Themes Hang Like Spanish Moss." *Christian Science Monitor,* 6 Mar. 1989, p. 13.

Diamond, Stanley. *In Search of the Primitive: Critique of Civilization.* New Brunswick: Transaction, 1974.

Didion, Joan. *Salvador.* New York: Simon and Schuster, 1983.

Dumont, Jean-Paul. *The Headman and I.* Austin: University of Texas Press, 1978.

———. "A Matter of Touristic 'indifference'." *American Ethnologist,* 11 (1984), 139–51.

Dzik, Eileen. "Words of Revolt." [Interview with Breyten Breytenbach.] *Passion*, June–July 1986, p. 11.

Elliott, Michael. "Naipaulia." *New Republic*, 16 Nov. 1987, pp. 13–14.

Enright, D. J. "Who Is India? *Encounter*, Dec. 1984, p. 60.

Enzensberger, Hans Magnus. "Tourists of the Revolution." In *Critical Essays*. Ed. Reinhold Grimm and Bruce Armstrong. New York: Continuum, 1982, pp. 159–85.

Epstein, Joseph. "A Cottage for Mr. Naipaul." *New Criterion*, Oct. 1987, pp. 6–15.

Eyre, M. Banning. "Naipaul at Wesleyan." *South Carolina Review*, 14 (1982), 34–47.

Ezekiel, Nissim. "Naipaul's India and Mine." In *New Writing in India*. Ed. Adil Jussawalla. Baltimore: Penguin, 1974.

Fabian, Johannes. *Time and the Other: How Anthropology Makes Its Object*. New York: Columbia University Press, 1983.

Fahim, Hussein, ed. *Indigenous Anthropology in Non-Western Countries*. Durham, N.C.: Carolina Academic Press, 1982.

Fanon, Frantz. *The Wretched of the Earth*. Trans. Constance Farrington. 1963; rpt. New York: Grove Press, 1968.

———. *Black Skins, White Masks*. Trans. Charles Lam Markmann. New York: Grove Press, 1967.

Fox, Renee C., Willy de Craemer, and Jean-marie Ribeaucourt. "The Second Independence: A Case Study of the Kwilu Rebellion in the Congo." *Comparative Studies in Society and History*, 8 (1965–66), 78–110.

Frank, Andre Gunder. *Capitalism and Underdevelopment in Latin America*. New York: Monthly Review Press, 1967.

———. *Latin America: Underdevelopment or Revolution: Essays on the Development of Underdevelopment and the Immediate Enemy*. New York: Monthly Review Press, 1969.

Fryer, Peter. *Staying Power: The History of Black People in Britain*. London: Pluto Press, 1984.

Fussell, Paul. *Abroad: Literary Traveling Between the Wars*. New York: Oxford University Press, 1980.

Garebian, Keith. "V. S. Naipaul's Negative Sense of Place." *Journal of Commonwealth Literature*, 10 (1975), 23–35.

Gates, Henry Louis, Jr. "Critical Fanonism." *Critical Inquiry* 17 (Spring 1991), 457–70.

Geng, Veronica. "Mistah Kurtz. He Dead." *New Yorker*, 3 Sept. 1979, p. 71.

Genovese, Eugene. "They'll Take Their Stand," *New Republic*, 13 Feb. 1989, pp. 30–34.

Ghosh, Amitav. "In India, Death and Democracy." *New York Times*, 26 Nov. 1990, p. A19.

Gide, André. *Travels in the Congo*. Trans. Dorothy Bussy. 1929; rpt. New York: Modern Age, 1937.

Gilroy, Paul. *There Ain't No Black in the Union Jack.* London: Hutchinson, 1987.

Goodheart, Eugene. "V. S. Naipaul's Mandarin Sensibility." *Partisan Review,* 50 (1983), 244–56.

Gordimer, Nadine. *The Essential Gesture.* 1961; rpt. New York: Penguin, 1989.

Gottfried, Leon. "A Skeptical Pilgrimage." *Modern Fiction Studies,* 30 (1984), 567–72.

———. "Preface: The Face of V. S. Naipaul." *Modern Fiction Studies,* 30 (1984), 439–44.

Goulbourne, Harry, ed. *Politics and State in the Third World.* London: Macmillan, 1979.

Gowda, H. H. Anniah. "Naipaul in India." *The Literary Half-Yearly,* 2 (1970), 163–70.

Gran, Guy, ed. *Zaire: The Political Economy of Underdevelopment.* New York: Praeger, 1979.

Greene, Graham. *In Search of a Character: Two African Journals.* London: Bodley Head, 1961.

———. *Collected Essays.* London: Bodley Head, 1969.

———. *Journey Without Maps.* 1936; rpt. Harmondsworth, England: Penguin, 1978.

Greene, Martin. *Dreams of Adventure, Deeds of Empire.* New York: Basic Books, 1979.

Gurr, Andrew. *Writers in Exile: The Creative Use of Home in Modern Literature.* Atlantic Highlands, N.J.: Humanities Press, 1981.

Gussow, Mel. "The Enigma of V. S. Naipaul's Search for Himself in Writing." *New York Times,* 25 Apr. 1987, p. 16.

———. "Writer Without Roots." *New York Times Magazine,* 26 Dec. 1976, pp. 8, 9, 18, 19, 22.

Halliday, Fred. "Cold War in the Caribbean." *New Left Review,* 141 (1983), 5–22.

Hamilton, Alex. "Living a Life on Approval: Interview with V. S. Naipaul." *Guardian* (London), 4 Oct. 1971, p. 8.

Hamilton, Ian. "Without a Place." *The Times Literary Supplement,* 30 July 1971, pp. 897–98.

Hamner, Robert D. "Conversation with Derek Walcott." *World Literature Written in English,* 16 (1977), 409–20.

———, ed. *Critical Perspectives on V. S. Naipaul.* London: Heinemann, 1979.

———. *V. S. Naipaul.* New York: Twayne, 1973.

Hardwick, Elizabeth. "Meeting V. S. Naipaul." *New York Times Book Review,* 13 May 1979, p. 1.

Hare, David. *A Map of the World.* London: Faber and Faber, 1982.

Harris, Wilson. "In the Name of Liberty." *Third Text* 11 (Sum. 1990), 7–15.

Hayman, Ronald. "V. S. Naipaul in Interview." *Books and Bookmen,* 24 (1979), pp. 23–26.

Hegel, Georg Wilhelm Frederick. *The Philosophy of History.* Trans. J. Sibree. New York: Dover, 1956.

Heilbut, Anthony. *Exiled in Paradise. German Refugee Artists and Intellectuals in America from the 1930s to the Present.* New York: Viking, 1983.

Henry, Jim Douglas. "Unfurnished Entrails—the Novelist V. S. Naipaul." *The Listener,* 25 Nov. 1971, p. 721.

Hoagland, Edward. "Africa Brought Home: *Heart of Darkness* and Its Journey Downriver." *Harpers,* May 1985, pp. 71–74.

Hobsbawn, Eric, and Terrence Ranger, eds. *The Invention of Tradition.* Cambridge: Cambridge University Press, 1983.

Hone, Joseph. *Africa of the Heart.* New York: William Morrow, 1986.

Howe, Irving. "A Dark Vision." *New York Times Book Review,* 13 May 1979, p. 1.

Hyland, Paul. *The Black Heart: A Voyage in Central Africa.* New York: Paragon, 1990.

Itote, W. *'Mau Mau' General.* Nairobi: East African Publishing House, 1961.

Hughes, Peter. *V. S. Naipaul.* New York: Routledge & Kegan Paul, 1988.

Hynes, Samuel. *The Auden Generation: Literature and Politics in England in the 1930s.* London: Bodley Head, 1976.

James, C. L. R. *The Black Jacobins.* 1938; rpt. New York: Vintage, 1963.

Kabbani, Rana. *Europe's Myths of Orient.* Bloomington: Indiana University Press, 1986.

Kakutani, Michiko. "Naipaul Reviews His Past from Afar." *New York Times,* 1 Dec. 1980, p. C15.

Kanga, Firdaus. "Seeing and Looking Away." *Times Literary Supplement,* 5–11 Oct. 1990.

Kazin, Alfred. "V. S. Naipaul, Novelist as Thinker." *New York Times Book Review,* 1 May 1977, p. 7.

Keith, Hamish. "V. S. Naipaul Discusses How Writing Changes the Writer." *Ndaanan,* 4, 1–11 (1974), 61–63.

Kelly, Richard. *V. S. Naipaul.* New York: Continuum, 1989.

Kermode, Frank. "In the Garden of the Oppressor," *New York Times Book Review,* Mar. 22, 1987, pp. 11–12.

King, John. " 'A Curiously Colonial Performance': The Eccentric Vision of V. S. Naipaul and J. L. Borges." *The Yearbook of English Studies,* 13 (1983), 228–43.

Kramer, Hilton. "The 'Primitive' Conundrum." *The New Criterion,* Dec. 1984, pp. 1–7.

Kramer, Jane. "From the Third World." *New Times Book Review,* 13 Apr. 1980, p. 1.

Lamming, George. *The Pleasures of Exile.* 1960; rpt. London: Allison & Busby, 1984.

Lazarus, Neil. *Resistance in Postcolonial African Fiction.* New Haven: Yale University Press, 1990.

Leach, Edmund. *Claude Lévi-Strauss*. New York: Viking, 1970.

Leiris, Michel. *L'Afrique fântome*. 1934; rpt. Paris: Gallimard, 1950.

Lennox, Grant. "Naipaul Joins the Chorus." *Tapia,* 6 July 1975, pp. 6–7.

Lévi-Strauss, Claude. *Tristes Tropiques*. Trans. John Russell. 1955; rpt. New York: Atheneum, 1970.

Lindfors, Bernth. "The West Indian Conference on Commonwealth Literature." *World Literature Written in English,* 19 (1971), 10.

Linear, Marcus. *Zapping the Third World: The Disaster of Development Aid.* London: Pluto Press, 1985.

Lorde, Audre. *Zami: A New Spelling of My Name.* New York: Crossing Press, 1982.

Lovelace, Earl. "Poor Naipaul! He Has Become His Biggest Joke." *Express* (Trinidad), 26 Oct. 1970, p. 10.

McCarthy, Mary. "Exiles, Expatriates and Internal Emigrés." *The Listener,* 25 Nov. 1971, 705.

MacCannell, Dean. *The Tourist: A New Theory of the Leisure Class.* New York: Schocken Books, 1976.

Magdoff, Harry. "Imperialism Without Colonies." In *Studies in the Theory of Imperialism*. Ed. Roger Owen and Bob Sutcliffe. New York: Longman, 1972, pp. 144–70.

Mahoney, Richard D. *JFK: Ordeal in Africa*. Oxford: Oxford University Press, 1983.

Mahood, M. M. *The Colonial Encounter: A Reading of Six Novels.* London: Rex Collings, 1977.

Maja-Pearce, Adewale. "The Naipauls on Africa: An African View." *Journal of Commonwealth Literature,* 20 (1985), 111–17.

Malak, Amin. "V. S. Naipaul and the Believers." *Modern Fiction Studies,* 30 (1984), 561–66.

Manganaro, Marc, ed. *Modernist Anthropology: From Fieldwork to Text.* Princeton: Princeton University Press, 1990.

Mann, Harveen Sachdeva. "Variations on the Theme of Mimicry: Naipaul's *The Mystic Masseur* and *The Suffrage of Elvira*." *Modern Fiction Studies,* 30 (1984), 467–85.

Mannoni, O. Dominique. *Prospero and Caliban: The Psychology of Colonization*. Trans. Pamela Powesland. New York: Praeger, 1964.

Marcus, Bruce, and Michael Taber. *Maurice Bishop Speaks: The Grenada Revolution 1979–83*. New York: Pathfinder Press, 1983.

Marcus, George E., and Dick Cushman. "Ethnographies as Texts." *Annual Review of Anthropology,* 2 (1982), 25–69.

Marcus, Greil. "Journey up the River: An Interview with Francis Coppola." *Rolling Stone,* 1 Nov. 1979, pp. 51–57.

Marcus, George E. and Michael M. J. Fischer. *Anthropology as Cultural Critique. An Experimental Moment in the Human Sciences.* Chicago: University of Chicago Press, 1986.

Marho (Radical Historians Organization), ed. *Visions of History: Interviews.* Manchester: Manchester University Press, 1983.

Marnham, Patrick. *Fantastic Invasion.* New York: Harcourt Brace Jovanovich, 1980.

Mazrui, Ali. *Political Values and the Educated Class in Africa.* Berkeley and Los Angeles: University of California Press, 1978.

McWatt, Mark, ed. *West Indian Literature and Its Social Context: Proceedings of the Fourth Annual Conference on West Indian Literature.* Barbados: University of West Indies Press, 1985.

Memmi, Albert. *The Colonizer and the Colonized,* trans. Howard Greenfeld. Boston: Beacon Press, 1967.

———. *Dependence: A Sketch for a Portrait of the Dependent.* Trans. Philip A. Facey. Boston: Beacon Press, 1984.

Michener, Charles. "The Dark Visions of V. S. Naipaul." *Newsweek,* 16 Nov. 1981, pp. 104–115.

Miller, Christopher L. *Blank Darkness: Africanist Discourse in French.* Chicago and London: University of Chicago Press, 1985.

Miller, Karl. "V. S. Naipaul and the New Order." In *Critical Perspectives on V. S. Naipaul.* Ed. Robert D. Hamner. London: Heinemann, 1977, pp. 111–26.

Mishra, Vijay. "Mythic Fabulation: Naipaul's India." *New Literature Review,* 4 (1978), 59–65.

Mommsen, Wolfgang J. *Theories of Imperialism.* Trans. P. S. Falla. Chicago: University of Chicago Press, 1980.

Moravia, Alberto. *Which Tribe Do You Belong To?* Trans. Angus Davidson. New York: Farrar, Straus and Giroux, 1974.

———. "Congo on My Mind," *New York Times Magazine,* 7 Oct. 1984, pp. 34, 63–64, 68–70.

Mudimbe, V. Y. *The Invention of Africa: Gnosis, Philosophy, and the Order of Knowledge.* Bloomington: Indiana University Press, 1988.

Mukasa, Ham. *Sir Apolo Kagwa Discovers Britain.* 1904; rpt. London: Heinemann, 1975.

Mukherjee, Bharati, and Robert Boyers. "A Conversation with V. S. Naipaul." *Salmagundi,* 54 (Fall 1981), 4–22.

Nachman, Larry David. "The Worlds of V. S. Naipaul." *Salmagundi,* 54 (Fall 1981), 59–76.

Naipaul, Shiva. *Beyond the Dragon's Mouth: Stories and Pieces.* 1984; rpt. New York: Viking, 1985.

———. *Journey to Nowhere: A New World Tragedy.* 1980; rpt. New York: Penguin, 1982.

———. *North of South: An African Journey.* 1978; rpt. Harmondsworth, England: Penguin, 1980.

———. *An Unfinished Journey.* New York: Viking, 1987.

Naipaul, V. S. "Liza of Lambeth." *Queens Royal College Chronicle,* 23 (1948), 42–43.

———. *The Mystic Masseur.* 1957; rpt. Harmondsworth, England: Penguin, 1964.

———. *The Suffrage of Elvira.* 1958; rpt. Harmondsworth, England: Penguin, 1971.

———. "Letter to Maria." *New Statesman,* 5 July 1958, p. 14.

———. "Where the Rum Comes From." *New Statesman,* 4 (1958), p. 21.

———. *Miguel Street.* 1959; rpt. Harmondsworth, England: Penguin, 1969.

———. "Caribbean Medley." *Vogue,* 15 Nov. 1959, pp. 90, 92–93.

———. "The Little More." *The Times* (London), 13 July 1961, p. 13.

———. "Dark Places." *New Statesman,* 18 Aug. 1961, p. 222.

———. *A House for Mr. Biswas.* 1961; rpt. Harmondsworth, England: Penguin, 1969; New York: Vintage, 1984.

———. "Did You Hear That?" *The Listener,* 15 Mar. 1962, p. 197.

———. "Tea with an Author." *Bim,* 9 (1962), 79–81.

———. "Trollope in the West Indies." *The Listener,* 15 Mar. 1962, p. 461.

———. "Cricket." *Encounter,* Sept. 1963, 73–75; rpt. in *The Overcrowded Barracoon* 1972; rpt. New York: Vintage, 1984.

———. *Mr. Stone and the Knights Companion.* 1963; rpt. Harmondsworth, England: Penguin, 1973.

———. "Trinidad." *Mademoiselle,* (May 1964), 187–88.

———. "Speaking of Writing." *The Times* (London). 2 Jan. 1964, p. 11.

———. "The Documentary Heresy." *Twentieth Century,* 173 (1964), 107–8.

———. "Critics and Criticism." *Bim,* 10 (1964), 74–77.

———. "Night Watchman's Occurrence Book." *The Spectator,* 27 Nov. 1964, pp. 719, 721–22.

———. "They Are Staring at Me." *Saturday Evening Post,* 10 Apr. 1965, pp. 82–84.

———. "Interview." *Sunday Guardian* (Trinidad), 7 Mar. 1965, pp. 5, 7.

———. *A Flag on the Island,* 1967; rpt. Harmondsworth, England: Penguin, 1969.

———. "What's Wrong with Being a Snob?" *Saturday Evening Post,* 3 June 1967, pp. 12, 18.

———. *The Mimic Men.* 1967; Harmondsworth, England: Penguin, 1969.

———. "Graham Greene," *The Daily Telegraph Magazine.* 8 Mar. 1968, pp. 28–32.

———. "I Don't Consider Myself a West Indian." *Guyana Graphic,* 30 Nov. 1968, p. 3.

———. "Et in America Ego!" *The Listener,* 4 Sept. 1969, pp. 302–4.

———. "Without a Dog's Chance." *New York Review of Books,* 18 May 1972, pp. 9–11.

———. *In a Free State.* Harmondsworth, England: Penguin, 1973.

———. *Guerillas.* New York: Knopf, 1975.

———. Introduction to *East Indians in the Caribbean: Colonialism and the Struggle for Identity.* Proceedings of a Symposium on East Indians in the

Caribbean, The University of the West Indies, June 1975. Millwood, N.Y.: Krause International, 1982.

————. *A Bend in the River.* 1979; rpt. New York: Vintage, 1980.

————. "A Note on a Borrowing from Conrad." *New York Review of Books,* 16 Dec. 1982, pp. 37–38.

————. "Writing 'A House for Mr. Biswas.' " *New York Review of Books,* 16 Nov. 1983, pp. 22–23.

————. "Among the Republicans." *New York Review of Books,* 25 Oct. 1984, pp. 5, 8, 10, 12, 14–17.

————. "Our Universal Civilization." *New York Times,* 5 Nov. 1990, p. A21.

Nair, Rukmini Bhaya and Bhattacharya, Rimli. "Salman Rushdie: The Migrant in the Metropolis." *Third Text* 11 (Sum. 1990).

Nandakumar, Prema. *The Glory and the Good.* New York: Asia Publishing House, 1965.

Nazareth, Peter. "Out of Darkness: Conrad and Other Third World Writers." *Conradiana,* 14 (1982), 173–88.

————. "The Mimic Men as a Study of Corruption." In *Critical Perspectives on V. S. Naipaul.* Ed. Robert D. Hamner. London: Heinemann, 1977, pp. 137–52.

Narasimhaiah, C. D. "Somewhere Something Has Snapped." *The Literary Criterion,* Summer 1965, pp. 32–44.

Neill, Michael. "Guerillas and Gangs: Frantz Fanon and V. S. Naipaul." *Ariel,* 13 (1982), 21–62.

Nightingale, Margaret. "V. S. Naipaul as Historian Combatting Chaos." *Southern Review* (Australia), 13 (1980), 239–50.

Nixon, Rob. "African and Caribbean Appropriations of *The Tempest.*" *Critical Inquiry,* 14 (1987), 557–78.

————. "Preparations for Travel: The Naipaul Brothers' Conradian Atavism." *Research in African Literatures,* 22 (1991), 177–90.

Nzongola-Ntalaja, ed. *The Crisis in Zaire: Myths and Realities.* London: Zed, 1986.

Nkrumah, Kwame. *Neo-colonialism, the Last Stage of Capitalism.* 1965; rpt. New York: International, 1984.

Noel, Jesse. "Historicity and Homelessness in V. S. Naipaul." *Caribbean Studies* 11, 3 (1972), 83–87.

O'Brien, Conor Cruise, Edward Said, and John Lukacs. "The Intellectual in the Post-Colonial World: A Discussion with Conor Cruise O'Brien, Edward Said and John Lukacs." *Salmagundi,* 70–71 (Spring–Summer 1986), 65–81.

Odinga, O. *Not Yet Uhuru.* London: Heinemann, 1967.

Offiong, Daniel A. *Imperialism and Dependency: Obstacles to African Development.* Washington D.C.: Howard University Press, 1982.

Pantin, Raoul. "Portrait of an Artist: What Makes Naipaul Run." *Caribbean Contact,* 1 (1973), 15, 18–19.

———. "The Ultimate Transient." *Caribbean Contact* 2 (1973), 4, 23.

Parry, Benita. *Conrad and Imperialism: Ideological Boundaries and Visionary Frontiers.* London: Macmillan, 1983.

Patnaik, Prabhat. "Imperialism and the Growth of Indian Capitalism." In *Studies in the Theory of Imperialism.* Ed. Roger Owen and Bob Sutcliffe. Harlow, England: Longman, 1972, pp. 210–29.

Patterson, John. "Challenging C. L. R. James and the Naipauls." *Sunday Guardian* (Trinidad), 18 Oct. 1970, pp. 7, 10.

———. "The Naipaul Bogey." *Sunday Guardian* (Trinidad), 15 Nov. 1970, p. 8.

Pearce, Jenny. *Under the Eagle: U.S. Intervention in Central America and the Caribbean.* New York: Monthly Review Press, 1984.

Porter, Denis. "Reinventing Travel: Stendahl's Roman Journey." *Genre,* 16 (1983), 467–76.

Pratt, Mary Louise. "Scratches on the Face of the Country: or, What Mr. Barrow Saw in the Land of the Bushmen." *Critical Inquiry* 12, 1 (1985), 119–43.

———. "Field Work in Common Places." In *Writing Culture: The Poetics and Politics of Ethnography.* Ed. James Clifford and George E. Marcus. Berkeley: University of California Press, 1986, pp. 27–50.

Prescott, Lynda. "Past and Present Darkness: Sources for V. S. Naipaul's *A Bend in the River.*" *Modern Fiction Studies* 30 (1984), 547–60.

Rabinow, Paul. *Reflections on Fieldwork in Morocco.* Berkeley: University of California Press, 1977.

Rai, Sudha. *V. S. Naipaul: A Study in Expatriate Sensibility.* New Delhi: Arnold–Heinemann, 1982.

Ramchand, Kenneth. *The West Indian Novel and Its Background.* London: Faber & Faber, 1970.

Rampersad, Arnold. "V. S. Naipaul in the South." *Raritan,* 10 (Summer 1990), 24–47.

Randall, Vicky, and Robin Theobald. *Political Change and Underdevelopment: A Critical Introduction to Third World Politics.* London: Macmillan, 1985.

Rao, Raja. "Out of Step with Shiva." *Book Week* 29 Aug. 1965, p. 4.

Ray, Ellen, ed. *Dirty Work 2: The CIA in Africa.* Secaucus, N.J.: Lyle Stuart, 1979.

Richmond, Angus. "Naipaul: The Mimic Man." *Race and Class,* 24, 2 (1982), 125–36.

Roach, Eric. "V. S. Naipaul." *Trinidad Guardian,* 17 May 1967, p. 5.

Robbins, Bruce. "Homelessness and Worldliness." *Diacritics,* 13 (Fall 1983), 69–77.

Rodney, Walter. *How Europe Underdeveloped Africa.* 1972; rpt. Washington D.C.: Howard University Press, 1981.

Rohlehr, Gordon. "The Ironic Approach: The Novels of V. S. Naipaul." In *Critical Perspectives on V. S. Naipaul,* ed. Robert D. Hamner. London: Heinemann, 1979, 178–93.

Rowe-Evans, Adrian. "V. S. Naipaul [interview]." *Transition,* 40 (1971), 56–62.

Rubin, William, ed. *"Primitivism" in 20th Century Art*. New York: Museum of Modern Art, 1984.

Rushdie, Salman. "The Empire Strikes back with a Vengeance." *The Times* (London), 3 July 1982, p. 7.

———. "Imaginary Homelands." *London Review of Books,* Oct. 1982, p. 18.

———. *Imaginary Homelands.* London: Granta Books, 1991.

Saakana, Amon Saba. *The Colonial Legacy in Caribbean Literature.* Trenton, N.J.: Africa World Press, 1987.

Said, Edward. *Orientalism.* 1978; rpt. New York: Vintage, 1979.

———. "Bitter Dispatches from the Third World." *The Nation,* 3 May 1980, pp. 23–25.

———. "Expectations of Inferiority." *New Statesman,* 16 Oct. 1981, pp. 21–22.

———. *The World, the Text, and the Critic.* Cambridge, Mass.: Harvard University Press, 1983.

———. "Reflections on Exile." *Granta,* 13 (1984), 157–72.

———. "Orientalism Reconsidered." *Cultural Critique,* 1 (1985), 89–107.

———. "Intellectuals in the Post-Colonial World." *Salmagundi,* 70–71 (Spring–Summer 1986), 44–64.

———. "Representing the Colonized: Anthropology's Interlocutors." *Critical Inquiry,* 15 (Winter 1989), 205–25.

Sangari, Kumkum, "The Politics of the Possible." *Cultural Critique* (Fall 1987), 157–86.

Sass, Louis A. "Anthropology's Native Problems: Revisionism in the Field." *Harpers,* May 1986, pp. 49–57.

Seabrook, Jeremy, and Trevor Blackwell. "Mrs. Thatcher's Religious Pilgrimage." *Granta,* 6 (1983), 39–52.

Searle, Chris. "Naipaulacity: A Form of Cultural Imperialism." *Race and Class,* 26 (1984), 45–62.

———. *Words Unchained: Language and Revolution in Grenada.* London: Zed, 1984.

Seehadri, Vijay. "Naipaul from the Other Side." *Threepenny Review,* 22 (Summer 1985), 5–6.

Seymour-Smith, Martin. "Exile's Story." *The Spectator,* 5 May 1967, p. 528.

Shenker, Israel. "V. S. Naipaul, Man Without a Society." *New York Times Book Review,* 17 Oct. 1971, pp. 4, 22–24.

Singh, H. B. "V. S. Naipaul: A Spokesman for Neo-Colonialism." *Literature and Ideology* 2 (1969), 71–85.

Sivanandan, A. "The Enigma of the Colonized: Reflections on Naipaul's Arrival." *Race and Class,* 32, 1 (1990), 33–43.

Spivak, Grayatri Chakravorty. *The Post-Colonial Critic: Interviews, Strategies, Dialogues.* New York: Routledge & Kegan Paul, 1990.

Steiner, George. *Extraterritorial: Papers on Literature and the Language Revolution.* Harmondsworth, England: Penguin, 1972.

Suleri, Sara. "Naipaul's Arrival." *Yale Journal of Criticism,* 2 (Fall 1988), 25–50.

Sunshine, Catherine A. *The Caribbean: Survival, Struggle and Sovereignty.* Boston: Epica, 1985.

Suplee, Curt. "Voyager with the Dark and Comic Vision—Through the World of Islam and Beyond, with V. S. Naipaul." *Washington Post,* 19 Nov. 1981, pp. C–1, C–17.

Tagoe, Nana Wilson. "No Place: V. S. Naipaul's Vision of Home in the Caribbean." *Caribbean Review,* 10 (1980), 37–41.

Thelwell, Michael. *Duties, Pleasures, and Conflicts: Essays in Struggle.* Amherst: University of Massachusetts Press, 1987.

Theroux, Paul. *V. S. Naipaul: An Introduction to His Work.* New York: Africana, 1972.

———. "V. S. Naipaul." *Modern Fiction Studies,* 30 (Autumn 1984), 445–55.

Thieme, John. "V. S. Naipaul and the Hindu Killer." *Journal of Indian Writing in English,* 9 (1981), 70–86.

———. "A Hindu Castaway: Ralph Singh's Journey in The Mimic Men." *Modern Fiction Studies,* 30 (1984), 505–18.

———. *The Web of Tradition: Uses of Allusion in V. S. Naipaul's Fiction.* Hertfordshire, England: Dangaroo, 1987.

Thomas, Clive Y. *The Poor and the Powerless: Economic Policy and Change in the Caribbean.* London: Latin American Bureau, 1988.

Thomas, J. J. *Froudacity.* 1889; rpt. London: New Beacon, 1969.

Torgovnick, Marianna. *Gone Primitive: Savage Intellects, Modern Lives.* Chicago: University of Chicago Press, 1990.

Trinh T. Minh-ha. *Woman, Native, Other: Writing Postcoloniality and Feminism.* Bloomington: Indiana University Press, 1989.

Trevor-Roper, Hugh. "Born Again." *New York Review of Books,* 5 Nov. 1981, p. 11.

Updike, John. "Fool's Gold." *New Yorker,* 8 Aug. 1970, 72–76. Rpt. in *Critical Perspectives on V. S. Naipaul.* Ed. Robert D. Hamner. London: Heinemann, 1977, pp. 153–58.

———. *Hugging the Shore: Essays and Criticism.* New York: Alfred A. Knopf, 1983.

Van Den Abbeele, Georges. "Sightseers: The Tourist as Theorist." *Diacritics,* 10 (Dec. 1980), 3–14.

Wachira, G. *Ordeal in the Forest.* Nairobi: East African Publishing House, 1968.

Wachiuma, C. *Daughter of Mumbi.* Nairobi: East African Publishing House, 1969.

Wade, A. C. "The Novelist as Historian." *The Literary Half-Yearly,* 11 (1970), 179–84.

Walcott, Derek. "Interview with V. S. Naipaul." *Sunday Guardian* (Trinidad), 17 Mar. 1965, 5, 7.

———. *Dream on Monkey Mountain and Other Plays.* New York: Farrar, Straus and Giroux, 1970.

———. *The Fortunate Traveller.* New York: Farrar, Straus, and Giroux, 1981.

————. "The Garden Path." *New Republic,* 13 Apr. 1987, pp. 27–31.

Wallerstein, Immanuel. *The Modern World System.* New York: Academic Press, 1976.

————. *The Capitalist World Economy.* Cambridge: Cambridge University Press, 1979.

Walsh, William. *V. S. Naipaul.* Edinburgh: Oliver & Boyd, 1973.

Walt, Vivienne. "Elbow Room in Hell." *Village Voice,* 2 Apr. 1985, p. 30.

Wamweya, J. *Freedom Fighter.* Nairobi: East African Publishing House, 1971.

————. *Writers in Politics.* London: Heinemann, 1981.

Watts, Cedric. "A Bloody Racist: About Achebe's View of Conrad." *The Yearbook of English Studies,* 13 (1983), 196–209.

Waugh, Evelyn. *Labels: A Mediterranean Journal.* 1930; rpt. London: Penguin, 1985.

————. *When the Going Was Good.* 1946; rpt. Boston: Little, Brown, 1984.

Webb, Peter. "The Master of the Novel." *Newsweek,* 18 Aug. 1980, pp. 34–38.

Webster, Steven. "Realism and Reification in the Ethnographic Genre." *Critique of Anthropology,* 6 (1986), 39–62.

————. "The Historical Materialist Critique of Surrealism and Postmodernist Ethnography." In *Modernist Anthropology: From Fieldwork to Text.* Ed. Marc Manganaro. Princeton: Princeton University Press, 1990, 266–99.

White, Hayden. *Tropics of Discourse: Essays in Cultural Criticism.* 1978; rpt. Baltimore: Johns Hopkins University Press, 1985.

Williams, Eric. *History of the People of Trinidad and Tobago.* 1962; rpt. London: Andre Deutsch, 1964.

————. *British Historians and the West Indies.* New York: Scribners, 1967.

Williams, Raymond. *The Country and the City.* New York: Oxford University Press, 1973.

————. *Writing in Society.* London: Verso, 1983.

Winokur, Scott. "The Unsparing Vision of V. S. Naipaul," *Image,* 5 May 1991, pp. 8–15.

Worsley, Peter. *The Three Worlds: Culture and World Development.* Chicago: University of Chicago Press, 1984.

Yapp, M. E. "With the Revivalists." *The Times Literary Supplement,* 11 Dec. 1981, p. 1433.

INDEX

Abrahams, Roger, 48
Abu-Lughod, Ibrahim, 57
Achebe, Chinua, 104–6, 132
Africa, 102–8, 112–13, 167–68, 188–89 *n*.
    33. *See also* Naipaul, Vidiadhar
    Surajprasad, works: "The Crocodiles
    of Yamoussoukro"; "A New King for
    the Congo"
Africa, invention of, 102–3, 129
Afrikaners, 95, 98
Ahmad, Aijaz, 79, 175 *n*. 175
Ahmed, Eqbal, 152
Ajami, Fouad, 83
America. *See* United States of America
American South, 163–68
Amin, Idi, 102
Amin, Samir, 142
Amis, Martin, 44
Anderson, Benedict, 72, 121
Anderson, Perry, 43
Angrosino, M. B., 136
Anthropology, 66–72, 98, 141. *See also*
    Ethnography
Antitourism, 61–65
Appiah, Kwame Anthony, 102–3, 106
Applewhite, James, 164, 167, 172
Arendt, Hannah, 91, 95–96, 98
Argentina, 50, 120, 134, 168, 198 *n*. 27
Asad, Talal, 79
Atlantic Monthly, 7
Auerbach, Erich, 24
Autobiography
    and ethnography, 66–72
    and travel writing, 66–72, 80–81

BBC, 8, 38
Bakhtin, Mikhail, 69
Banana Republic, 193, *n*. 27
Baraheni, Reza, 150–51
Barbarism, 42, 57, 83, 93, 109, 111–12,
    122, 146, 152, 196 *n*. 4
Basso, Hamilton, 61–62
Beatty, Jack, 157
Berrio, Fernando, 124
Bhabha, Homi K., 156–58
Bishop, Maurice, 156
Blixen, Karen, 22, 44

Blues, 165
Bowen Elenore Smith, 71, 74
Boyers, Robert, 63
Braithwaite, Edward Kamu, 20, 132
Brecht, Bertolt, 82
Brennan, Timothy, 175 *n*. 2
Brereton, Bridget, 127
Breytenbach, Breyten, 24–25
British Guiana, 130, 144–45. *See also*
    Guyana
Byron, Robert, 52, 56

Cabrera Infante, Guillermo, 17
Caputo, Philip, 91, 192 *n*. 27
Caribbean. *See also* Trinidad
    American hegemony in, 140–41
    Amerindians, 125, 144
    colonization of, 19–20, 121–28
    connection to Africa, 120
    tourism, 60–65, 157
    Victorian attitudes to, 45–53
Caribbean Voices, 8
Caribbean writers
    migration to England, 19–21, 40, 43
    triregional affiliations, 20
Cary, Joyce, 133
Caste, 8, 67–68, 112
Césaire, Aimé, 64, 106, 143
Chatwin, Bruce, 57
Chaudhuri, Nirad, 41
Christian Science Monitor, 165
CIA, 150
Civilization, 42, 58–59, 109, 147–48, 151–
    52, 197 *n*. 20
Clark, John Pepper, 57
Class
    middle classes in "Third World," 132,
        137–41, 201 *n*. 27
    in Naipaul, 21, 35–36, 137–39, 163, 182
        n. 4
Client states, 102, 141–42, 150–51
Clifford, James, 66, 69, 117
Cold War, 101–2
Colonialism, 11, 33, 109, 116, 132–33,
    135, 143–45, 152, 173. *See also*
    Imperialism

223